INTERNATIONAL LAW AND THE USE OF ARMED FORCE

Since the UN Charter came into effect in 1945, there have been numerous incidents in which one or more of the five major powers (at least arguably) violated the Charter's Article 2(4) prohibition of force. Such incidents notwithstanding, this book demonstrates how the Charter restrains the major powers' military actions. As an instrument of international order, the Charter provides a framework of legal rules restricting the use of armed force. Although these rules are subject to auto-interpretation by the major powers (as a consequence of their veto), they create an expectation of compliance that subjects the major powers' military actions to international scrutiny. To reduce the likelihood of resistance from states threatened by such actions, major powers exercise prudential restraint, altering the manner and timing of their military actions in accordance with the legal arguments offered to justify those actions as consistent with the Charter and therefore not threatening to the existing international order.

The book evaluates the efficacy of the Charter using large-N methods and five case studies: US intervention in the Caribbean, 1953–61; Anglo-French intervention in Egypt, 1956; Soviet intervention in Hungary, 1956; US–British intervention in Iraq, 1990–98; and US–British intervention in Iraq, 1999–2003. The book's extensive focus on the two Iraq cases provides a basis for timely evaluation of the continuing salience and possible reforms of the UN Charter system.

This book will be of much interest to students of security studies, the UN, international law, and international relations.

Joel H. Westra is an Assistant Professor in the Department of Political Science at Calvin College in Grand Rapids, Michigan. He holds a PhD in Political Science from the University of Chicago.

CONTEMPORARY SECURITY STUDIES

NATO'S SECRET ARMIES
Operation Gladio and terrorism in Western Europe
Daniele Ganser

THE US, NATO AND MILITARY BURDEN-SHARING
Peter Kent Forster and Stephen J. Cimbala

RUSSIAN GOVERNANCE IN THE TWENTY-FIRST CENTURY
Geo-strategy, geopolitics and new governance
Irina Isakova

THE FOREIGN OFFICE AND FINLAND 1938–1940
Diplomatic sideshow
Craig Gerrard

RETHINKING THE NATURE OF WAR
Edited by Isabelle Duyvesteyn and Jan Angstrom

PERCEPTION AND REALITY IN THE MODERN YUGOSLAV CONFLICT
Myth, falsehood and deceit 1991–1995
Brendan O'Shea

THE POLITICAL ECONOMY OF PEACEBUILDING IN POST-DAYTON BOSNIA
Tim Donais

THE DISTRACTED EAGLE
The rift between America and Old Europe
Peter H. Merkl

THE IRAQ WAR
European perspectives on politics, strategy, and operations
Edited by Jan Hallenberg and Håkan Karlsson

STRATEGIC CONTEST
Weapons proliferation and war in the greater Middle East
Richard L. Russell

PROPAGANDA, THE PRESS AND CONFLICT
The Gulf War and Kosovo
David R. Willcox

MISSILE DEFENCE
International, regional and national implications
Edited by Bertel Heurlin and Sten Rynning

GLOBALISING JUSTICE FOR MASS ATROCITIES
A revolution in accountability
Chandra Lekha Sriram

ETHNIC CONFLICT AND TERRORISM
The origins and dynamics of civil wars
Joseph L. Soeters

GLOBALISATION AND THE FUTURE OF TERRORISM
Patterns and predictions
Brynjar Lia

NUCLEAR WEAPONS AND STRATEGY
The evolution of American nuclear policy
Stephen J. Cimbala

NASSER AND THE MISSILE AGE IN THE MIDDLE EAST
Owen L. Sirrs

WAR AS RISK MANAGEMENT
Strategy and conflict in an age of globalised risks
Yee-Kuang Heng

MILITARY NANOTECHNOLOGY
Potential applications and preventive arms control
Jurgen Altmann

NATO AND WEAPONS OF MASS DESTRUCTION
Regional alliance, global threats
Eric R. Terzuolo

EUROPEANISATION OF NATIONAL SECURITY IDENTITY
The EU and the changing security identities of the Nordic states
Pernille Rieker

INTERNATIONAL CONFLICT PREVENTION AND PEACE-BUILDING
Sustaining the peace in post conflict societies
Edited by T. David Mason and James D. Meernik

CONTROLLING THE WEAPONS OF WAR
Politics, persuasion, and the prohibition of inhumanity
Brian Rappert

CHANGING TRANSATLANTIC SECURITY RELATIONS
Do the U.S., the EU and Russia form a new strategic triangle?
Edited by Jan Hallenberg and Håkan Karlsson

THEORETICAL ROOTS OF US FOREIGN POLICY
Machiavelli and American unilateralism
Thomas M. Kane

CORPORATE SOLDIERS AND INTERNATIONAL SECURITY
The rise of private military companies
Christopher Kinsey

TRANSFORMING EUROPEAN MILITARIES
Coalition operations and the technology gap
Gordon Adams and Guy Ben-Ari

GLOBALIZATION AND CONFLICT
National security in a 'new' strategic era
Edited by Robert G. Patman

MILITARY FORCES IN 21ST CENTURY PEACE OPERATIONS
No job for a soldier?
James V. Arbuckle

THE POLITICAL ROAD TO WAR WITH IRAQ
Bush, 9/11 and the drive to overthrow Saddam
Nick Ritchie and Paul Rogers

BOSNIAN SECURITY AFTER DAYTON
New perspectives
Edited by Michael A. Innes

KENNEDY, JOHNSON AND NATO
Britain, America and the dynamics of alliance, 1962–68
Andrew Priest

SMALL ARMS AND SECURITY
New emerging international norms
Denise Garcia

THE UNITED STATES AND EUROPE
Beyond the neo-conservative divide?
Edited by John Baylis and Jon Roper

RUSSIA, NATO AND COOPERATIVE SECURITY
Bridging the gap
Lionel Ponsard

INTERNATIONAL LAW AND INTERNATIONAL RELATIONS
Bridging theory and practice
Edited by Tom Bierstecker, Peter Spiro, Chandra Lekha Sriram and Veronica Raffo

DETERRING INTERNATIONAL TERRORISM AND ROGUE STATES
US national security policy after 9/11
James H. Lebovic

VIETNAM IN IRAQ
Tactics, lessons, legacies and ghosts
Edited by John Dumbrell and David Ryan

UNDERSTANDING VICTORY AND DEFEAT IN CONTEMPORARY WAR
Edited by Jan Angstrom and Isabelle Duyvesteyn

PROPAGANDA AND INFORMATION WARFARE IN THE TWENTY-FIRST CENTURY
Altered images and deception operations
Scot Macdonald

GOVERNANCE IN POST-CONFLICT SOCIETIES
Rebuilding fragile states
Edited by Derick W. Brinkerhoff

EUROPEAN SECURITY IN THE TWENTY-FIRST CENTURY
The challenge of multipolarity
Adrian Hyde-Price

ETHICS, TECHNOLOGY AND THE AMERICAN WAY OF WAR
Cruise missiles and US security policy
Reuben E. Brigety II

INTERNATIONAL LAW AND THE USE OF ARMED FORCE
The UN Charter and the major powers
Joel H. Westra

INTERNATIONAL LAW AND THE USE OF ARMED FORCE

The UN Charter and the major powers

Joel H. Westra

Routledge
Taylor & Francis Group
LONDON AND NEW YORK

First published 2007
by Routledge
2 Park Square, Milton Park, Abingdon, Oxon OX14 4RN

Simultaneously published in the USA and Canada
by Routledge
270 Madison Ave, New York, NY 10016

Routledge is an imprint of the Taylor & Francis Group, an informa business

Transferred to Digital Printing 2009

Typeset in Sabon by Wearset Ltd, Boldon, Tyne and Wear

British Library Cataloguing in Publication Data
A catalogue record for this book is available from the British Library

Library of Congress Cataloging in Publication Data
Westra, Joel H.
International law and the use of armed force : the UN charter and the major powers / Joel H. Westra.
p. cm.
Includes bibliographical references
1. Intervention (International law) 2. Aggression (International law) 3. Self-defense (International law) 4. Pacific settlement of international disputes. I. Title.
KZ6376.W48 2007
341.5′84—dc22
2006034190

ISBN10: 0–415–77098–X (hbk)
ISBN10: 0–415–49515–6 (pbk)
ISBN10: 0–203–08891–3 (ebk)

ISBN13: 978–0–415–77098–9 (hbk)
ISBN13: 978–0–415–49515–8 (pbk)
ISBN13: 978–0–203–08891–3 (ebk)

Dedicated to the memory of my friend and mentor

Professor Ross M. Lence
1943–2006

GUADEAMUS

CONTENTS

ILLUSTRATIONS

Figures

Tables

ACKNOWLEDGMENTS

This book has benefited from the assistance of numerous individuals and organizations. Duncan Snidal provided useful advice and direction from the project's beginning as a dissertation proposal at the University of Chicago. Jack Goldsmith, Ian Hurd, Seth Jones, Dong Sun Lee, John Mearsheimer, Michelle Murray, Jennifer Mitzen, Don Moon, Takayuki Nishi, Robert Pape, Rita Parhad, Eric Posner, Susan Pratt, Chad Rector, Sebastian Rosato, John Schuessler, Milan Svolik, Lora Viola, Erik Voeten, and others provided useful comments along the way. Participants at the Autumn 2002 and Winter 2004 Program on International Politics, Economics and Security (PIPES), the 2003 Annual Meeting of the International Studies Association (ISA), the 2003 and 2004 Annual Meetings of the Midwest Political Science Association (MPSA), the Winter 2004 Program on International Security Policy (PISP), and the 2006 CISS Millennium Conference helped me to refine and clarify my arguments and to bolster the evidence used to support them. Noëlle McAlpine provided timely and accurate translation of French primary source material. The Andrew W. Mellon Foundation, the Program on International Security Policy (PISP), and the John G. Tower Center for Political Studies provided financial support for research and writing. My family and friends provided needed encouragement, while my wife Julie provided helpful suggestions, endless patience, and untiring devotion.

1

THE FUNCTIONING OF THE UN CHARTER AS A RESTRAINT ON MILITARY ACTION

Article 2(4) of the UN Charter prohibits "the threat or use of force against the territorial integrity or political independence of any State." Nevertheless, since the Charter came into effect on 24 October 1945, there have been numerous incidents in which the major powers (at least arguably) violated this prohibition, although they offered arguments to the contrary and the Security Council either failed to approve a resolution addressing the legality of the actions taken or was prevented from doing so because of the veto that the major powers wield in their capacity as the five permanent members of the Security Council. Given the frequency of these arguably illegal uses of armed force, how (if at all) does the Charter function as a restraint upon the major powers' military actions?

This is a question that intersects fundamental theoretical debates concerning the varying roles of power, interests, and ideas in international relations, and its significance extends to ongoing policy debates concerning Security Council reforms and the future of the United Nations system. Yet, there has been surprisingly little effort devoted to answering it. The recent war in Iraq and other incidents have demonstrated the willingness of the major powers to engage in arguably illegal uses of armed force, but the effects that the Charter has had in such incidents have not been examined thoroughly, and the mechanisms by which it functions have not been specified clearly.

This book undertakes these tasks, conceptualizing the Charter as a legal instrument designed to instantiate and sustain the existing, post-World War II international order. The prohibition of force contained within the Charter is, in effect, a contractual agreement between the major powers and less powerful states not to use armed force to alter or overturn that order. The Charter provides a general framework of obligatory rules, which provides a written record of states' legal obligations, thereby creating an expectation of compliance that subjects their actions to scrutiny. The willingness of less powerful states to accept the continuation of the existing order (and their own relative power positions within that order) depends on the ability of the major powers to demonstrate their commitment to upholding their legal obligations in sustaining that order. Doing so requires that the major powers exercise prudential restraint, altering the manner and timing of their military actions in accordance with the legal arguments they have offered (or intend to offer) to justify those actions as consistent with the Charter and therefore not threatening to the existing order. Failure to demonstrate such commitment increases the likelihood of resistance from states that perceive the major powers' actions as threatening to the existing order and to their own relative power positions within that order. The Charter, then, functions indirectly, eliciting prudential restraint through the increased likelihood of resistance against unrestrained actions.

Existing explanations

Because the Charter functions indirectly, its impact is not always apparent. The Charter's preamble expresses the determination of UN member states "to save succeeding generations from the scourge of war." However, with the Security Council often stymied by veto or threat of veto, it might appear to the casual observer that the Charter functions only to restrain the actions of less powerful states, whose lack of veto subjects them to the coercive threat of UN-authorized enforcement action.[1]

This is the answer given by realists, based on a conceptualization of the Charter and other international law as expressions of state dominance (see Spinoza 1670 [1951], 1677 [1951]; Austin 1832 [2000]). According to the realist model, the Charter operates via the arguments and actions of major powers to elicit coercive restraint from less powerful states. A major power's legal arguments transmit information regarding its preferred outcome in a disagreement or crisis, and an accompanying material restraint elicits that outcome (Hasenclever *et al.* 1997: 104–9). These arguments appeal to the "optimism" and "moralism" of domestic audiences, and therefore leaders use them also to generate domestic support for actions they have taken (Krasner 1999: 6; Mearsheimer 2001: 23).

Although superficially compelling, there are two problems with the realist model. Firstly, although realists recognize that noncompliance is frequent when international law affects the core security concerns of states (Mearsheimer 1994/95: 39–43), they fail to recognize that states comply with the Charter even when coercion is absent (Henkin 1979: 39), and that coercion often is absent because of the costs that its exercise entails. Secondly, realists fail to recognize that, while domestic audiences seem to be motivated more by concerns of national security than by standards of international legality (Reiter and Stam 2002: 144–63), states routinely offer arguments to assert the legality of their actions under the Charter (Schachter 1984c: 1623; Gray 2000: 22–3). It would seem, then, that states (including the major powers) must have some interest in complying with the Charter – or at least in maintaining the appearance of compliance.

This interest in compliance is the focus of regime theorists, whose work is based on a conceptualization of the Charter and other international law as rationally designed sets of rules that provide a more efficient means of pursuing gains (see Vattel 1758 [1863]; Bentham 1789 [1843]). According to the regimes model, the Charter operates via the "shadow of the future" (Axelrod 1984: 174–5) to produce reciprocal restraints on state action. Assured of repeated interactions, states restrain their own actions in order to cooperate with other states that do likewise (Oye 1985: 12–18; Keohane 1986: 13). As a legalized agreement, the Charter helps to facilitate reciprocity among states by constraining self-serving autointerpretation of rules and increasing the costs of reneging (Abbott and Snidal 2000: 427). In response to violations of the Charter, states reciprocate by refusing to cooperate with those states that have violated it (Aceves 1997: 243–56). Regime theorists argue, then, that major powers are unlikely to choose policies that violate the Charter (or that violate it more clearly than other policies would), because by violating the Charter they would forfeit the benefits derived from stable interaction with other states (Simmons 2000: 582–5; Guzman 2002: 1844–51).

Because the regimes model is more directly applicable to issues of peacetime international law, its application to the Charter suffers three shortcomings. Firstly, as regime theorists admit, there is significant potential for miscalculation in making decisions regarding the use of armed force, because the payoffs from strict compliance with the Charter may be difficult to measure in relation to the large, short-term payoffs possible from *fait accompli* situations common in the security realm and are, in fact, likely to be outweighed by them (Henkin 1971: 549, 1979: 69; Guzman 2002: 1883–4). Moreover, even if long-term payoffs are not outweighed by short-term payoffs, military crises may make it difficult for policymakers to make such calculations, because there may not be sufficient opportunity for deliberation (Sheikh 1974: 2). Secondly, ambiguity of language may lead to uncertainty as to whether or not some actions violate the Charter. The Charter text does not clearly specify which uses of armed force are "consistent with the Purposes of the United Nations" (Art. 2.4), or used in the exercise of "the inherent right of individual or collective self-defense" (Art. 51), or otherwise not directed against "the territorial integrity or political independence of any state" (Art. 2.4), making determinations of legality uncertain. Thirdly, and most problematically, reciprocity via a tit-for-tat strategy, which involves punishing defection in one period by defecting in a subsequent period and then resuming cooperation (Axelrod 1984: 31–54), is unsuited to decentralized enforcement of the Charter, because there is no incentive for a state to defect from the rules of the Charter by retaliating against a major power with direct military force. The high costs associated with such action provide an incentive for states to "free ride" (Olson 1971) rather than joining in retaliation, and the costs associated with economic and diplomatic sanctions provide a similar incentive.[2]

Liberal theorists have attempted to overcome these shortcomings by conceptualizing the Charter and other international law as expressions of shared social purpose. According to the liberal model, the Charter operates via transnational interaction to produce domestic-level restraints on state action. Domestic political processes constitute states' social identities and social purposes (Moravcsik 1997: 525–8, 541–7), and interaction among states having a shared social purpose produces a system of rules that defines relationships among them and supports the realization of their shared goals (McDougal 1960: 339–40; Andrews 1975: 524–5). Transnational actors introduce these rules into other states' domestic policy debates and pressure them to adopt these rules as part of their domestic social structures (Cortell and Davis 1996: 451–8; Price 1998: 628). International law "frames" these rules in a way that "resonates" with domestic audiences because of "ideational affinity" to other, already-accepted frameworks, thereby enhancing and mobilizing the promotion of compliance (Nadelmann 1990: 479–86; Keck and Sikkink 1998: 204; Payne 2001: 38–9). Liberal theorists argue that, as international law becomes "entrenched" in domestic processes, domestic decision-making becomes "enmeshed" with it (Koh 1997: 2646–54). Domestic law then reflects it, individuals gradually absorb it, and "[w]ith acceptance comes observance, then the habit and inertia of continued observance" (Henkin 1979: 315). This process is most effective in liberal states, because they have a domestic political culture that is premised upon the rule of law (Henkin 1979: 63; Slaughter 1995: 513–20).

There are problems with the liberal model as well – two in particular. First, critics have noted that major powers in general are more likely to violate international law than less powerful states are (Jackson and Sykes 1997; Jacobson and Weiss 2001), regardless of whether or not they are liberal (Alvarez 2001). Second, because the liberal model does not distinguish among issue areas, it offers little insight into the relative frequency of the major powers' apparent noncompliance with the Charter as compared with most other international obligations – an important distinction that should not be ignored.

Drawing upon the insights of discourse theory and constructivism, other scholars have attempted to remedy these defects by conceptualizing the Charter and other international law as sets of obligatory rules that define membership within an international community (see Grotius 1625 [1901]). According to this communal obligation model, the Charter operates via social learning (Checkel 2001: 557–9) and argumentation (Risse 2000: 8–9, 20–3) within the Security Council to produce collective restraint on state action. As a product of consensus among states, the Charter provides a standard for assessing the legitimacy of state actions (Falk 1969: 33–54). It creates pressure for major powers to demonstrate that they are responsible members of the international community by adapting their behavior to the legitimate standards of the community (Franck 1990: 196–204; Hurd 2000: 44–6, 63–8). The major powers respond to this pressure by choosing "legally correct" courses of action and offering legal arguments to justify their actions (Scott 1994: 324). They use the Charter text as a basis for deliberation and argumentation, offering arguments to suggest that they have considered the interests of other states before taking action (Johnstone 2003b: 454; Mitzen 2005: 411). As this practice of deliberation within the Security Council is internalized, the major powers come to see their actions from the perspective of the international community (Arend 1998: 124–5). They develop a capacity and inclination for approaching problems collectively, become increasingly unlikely to use armed force without seeking prior authorization from the Security Council, and seek to gain the approval of other members of the international community through arguments propounding shared understandings of law (Johnstone 2003b: 443–61; Mitzen 2005: 411). Collectively, the Security Council confers legitimacy on these shared understandings (Caron 1993: 556–62).

This model has its own shortcomings, the most important of which is its narrow focus. By considering only communal aspects of international law, the communal obligation model excludes cases in which major powers repeatedly attempt to justify their actions with arguments not derived from a shared understanding of law nor aimed at achieving consensus. Excluding such cases (for example, cases in which the Security Council is not involved or in which the Security Council takes no action), the communal obligation model provides, at best, a limited explanation of how the Charter functions as a restraint upon the major powers' military actions.

In addition to their individual shortcomings, all of these models rely, at least implicitly, on a strict positivist view of international law, in which actions are categorized dichotomously and there is no gray area (see Figure 1.1). From this viewpoint, uses of armed force – even in self defense – are subject to the control of the Security Council (Brownlie 1963 [1981]: 273), and the Charter is an effective restraint only to the extent that it "push[es]

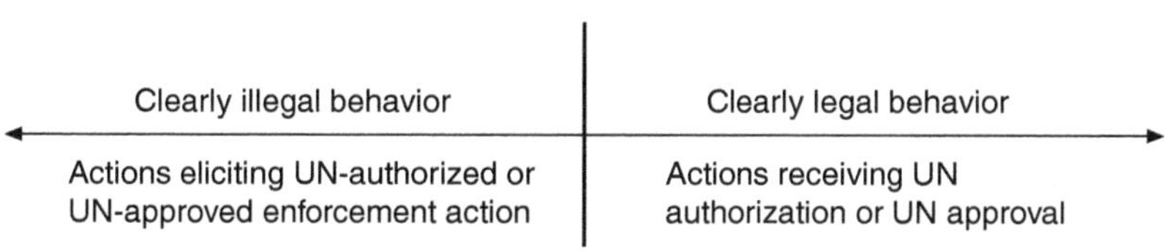

Figure 1.1 A strict positivist view of international law and the UN Charter.

states away from war and promotes peace" (Mearsheimer 1994/95: 7; see also Glennon 2001: 2–3; Mitzen 2005: 412). Assessing the efficacy of the Charter in this manner, however, misconstrues both its underlying purpose and its institutional form.

The UN Charter as a system of prudential restraint

As elaborated in Article 1(1), the Charter's underlying purpose is "[t]o maintain international peace and security." The consistent coupling of these two concepts throughout the Charter text is not accidental (Wolfrum 1994: 50), insofar as the Charter's purpose is not simply to achieve peaceful outcomes to international disputes, but rather to provide greater clarity, stability, and predictability of state interactions. It is an instrument of international order that alters the costs and risks associated with using armed force. The prohibition of force contained within it is, in effect, a contractual agreement between the major powers and less powerful states not to use armed force to alter or to overturn the existing, post-World War II international order – the basic patterns of activity and expectations that characterize interaction among states within the balance of power that emerged following World War II (Gilpin 1981: 42–3; Bull 1995: 3–19).

The Charter takes the form of an incomplete contract that lacks a centralized means of interpretation. It provides a general framework of legal rules, but these rules are subject to autointerpretation by the major powers as a consequence of the veto. Thus, while the strict positivist view of international law categorizes uses of armed force dichotomously, as either legal or illegal behavior, such actions are more appropriately categorized incrementally,[3] along a range from clearly legal behavior to clearly illegal behavior (see Figure 1.2). A use of armed force is clearly legal if it receives explicit authorization or approval from the Security Council. It is clearly illegal if it elicits enforcement action authorized or approved by the Security Council.[4] Most actions, then, belong in a category of arguably legal or illegal behavior.

This incremental view of law is normally associated with customary international law, rather than treaty law, but it is useful for the purposes of this analysis because the parameters that delimit the Charter's prohibition of force[5] are defined in such manner that they can be understood to

Clearly illegal behavior	Arguably legal or illegal behavior	Clearly legal behavior
Actions eliciting UN-authorized or UN-approved enforcement action	All other actions	Actions receiving UN authorization or UN approval

Figure 1.2 An incremental view of international law and the UN Charter.

encompass a range of meaning. As Stein (1985: 464) notes, for treaties in which these parameters are imprecise, although "ambiguity of language has replaced the ambiguity of nature or of events [in customary law] as the central problem of international law analysis," the actual pattern of legal argumentation among states remains much the same; states offer arguments that contain competing definitions of the treaty parameters. Nevertheless, because the Charter provides a written record of the major powers' legal obligations, it creates an expectation of compliance that subjects their military actions to the scrutiny of other states (Morrow 2000: 63) – irrespective of the veto. Accordingly, when a major power uses armed force, it offers arguments to account (Scott and Lyman 1968) for the discrepancy between its actions and other states' expectations of compliance with its legal obligations under the Charter. Through its arguments, a major power propounds a particular understanding of the Charter's prohibition of force and the imprecisely defined parameters that delimit it. In doing so, a major power attempts to persuade other states (both major powers and less-powerful states) that its actions are reasonably justified and to signal to them that it remains committed to the existing international order. Legal arguments are uniquely suited to this purpose because they correspond to other states' background expectations under the Charter (Abbott and Snidal 2000: 401), link past actions to future intentions (Goldsmith and Posner 2002: S137; 2005: 183), and contain claims derived explicitly from a codified framework of law that inherently sustains the existing order.

If states are persuaded that a major power's actions are in accord with the Charter's underlying purpose and thus reasonably justified, then they may respond with acceptance and thereby confer legitimacy on those actions. However, if states are not persuaded that a major power's actions are in accord with the Charter's underlying purpose and thus are not reasonably justified, then they are likely to respond with resistance to that major power because its actions appear threatening to the existing order and to their relative power positions within that order. Thus, to maintain the persuasiveness of the accounts they provide for their actions, the major powers must exercise prudential restraint, altering the manner and timing of their actions in accordance with the arguments they have offered (or intend to offer), or else engage in strategies of denial and/or rhetorical evasion (Shannon 2000: 295). Such restraint may have significant impact on both the conduct and the outcome of a major power's military operations, as subsequent chapters demonstrate.

This prudential restraint model is inherent in the writings of Hobbes (1650 [1999], 1651 [1994]) and is articulated in the work of various classical realists, including Carr (1946 [1964]), Schwarzenberger (1939, 1941), and Morgenthau (1940; Morgenthau and Thompson 1993). These theorists argue that international law evokes prudential restraint within powerful states, which use it to legitimate the exercise of their power.

However, they fail to specify a clear mechanism by which international law actually functions, and lacking such a mechanism, they fall back to the realist model outlined above. This book develops the mechanism that these theories have lacked, and in doing so, demonstrates the impact of the Charter on the major powers' military actions and the arguments that they offer for those actions.

Focusing on uses of armed force by the major powers is not to suggest that less powerful states have not engaged in arguably illegal uses of armed force as well. It is the major powers, however, that are the "hard" cases. While less powerful states are subject to UN-authorized or UN-approved enforcement action, there lacks an explicit enforcement mechanism against the major powers (because of the veto). One of this book's key contributions to existing theory is to outline an implicit enforcement mechanism (Robinson 1999), namely the anticipated likelihood of resistance by less powerful states (withholding basing rights, transit rights, etc.) against a major power that has used armed force in a manner to suggest that it is no longer committed to the existing international order. Examining the functioning of this mechanism does not require consideration of less powerful states, because it is the anticipated likelihood of resistance from these states that motivates the major powers and not the actual resistance itself. Moreover, any bias that might be introduced into the study by focusing only on the major powers (i.e., the "hard" cases) serves to strengthen the proposed model. If the Charter can restrain the actions of the major powers in the absence of an explicit enforcement mechanism, surely it can restrain the actions of less powerful states as well.

Overview of the book

In developing and testing this model, the remainder of the book proceeds as follows. Chapter 2 focuses on the Charter's Article 2(4) prohibition of force, conceptualizing the Charter as a contractual agreement among states having a shared interest in sustaining the existing, post-World War II international order. The chapter examines the content, form, and persuasiveness of arguments offered by major powers to account for their military actions and thereby signal their commitment to sustaining the existing international order. It includes large-n tests that assess the types of claims comprising these arguments and the extent to which coordination may be emerging among the major powers regarding the precise meaning of the Charter's prohibition of force.

Chapter 3 further develops the prudential restraint model by examining the role of the Charter in legitimating the exercise of power and creating a likelihood of resistance that serves as an implicit enforcement mechanism against major powers that violate the Charter. The chapter includes large-n tests that assess the level of dissent within the Security Council and the responses of other states following a major power's use of armed force. It also introduces the case studies, contained in subsequent chapters, which focus on the particular legal arguments offered by the major powers for their military actions and the manner and extent to which those arguments and other factors affected decision-making processes and outcomes.

Chapters 4 through 8 examine legal arguments and their relation to decision-making processes and outcomes in five historical cases: United States intervention in the Caribbean from 1953 through 1961; Anglo-French intervention in Egypt in 1956; Soviet intervention in Hungary in 1956; US–British intervention in Iraq from 1990 through 1998; and US–British intervention in Iraq from 1999 through 2003. The chapters demonstrate in each of these cases how the major powers courted a real and considerable risk of failure in an attempt to maintain the persuasiveness of their legal arguments and thereby signal their continuing commitment to the existing international order.

Chapter 9 concludes by examining the implications of the prudential restraint model for the continued salience of the UN Charter system. It considers the challenges posed by the emergence of US military pre-eminence, including recent military interventions in Kosovo, Afghanistan, and Iraq, and assesses possible UN reform.

2

THE UN CHARTER AND LEGAL ARGUMENTATION

Because of the prohibition of force codified in Article 2(4) of the UN Charter, when a major power uses armed force, it offers arguments to account for the discrepancy between its actions and other states' expectations of strict compliance with its legal obligations under the Charter. Such arguments serve as signals, because they transmit information used by other states to assess the major powers' continuing commitment to the existing order. This chapter demonstrates how the major powers' attempts to provide persuasive accounts for their military actions affect the content and form of the arguments they offer. Subsequent chapters demonstrate how such attempts affect the manner and timing of those actions.

The Charter's purpose and its historical context

To comprehend the impact of the Charter on the major powers' military actions and the arguments that accompany those actions, it is necessary to begin with a clear understanding of the relationship between the Charter's form and purpose, as well as its historical context. The Charter expresses the "determination" of UN member states "to save succeeding generations from the scourge of war" by "uniting [their] strength to maintain international peace and security" (UN Charter, Preamble). To this end, member states have conferred upon the Security Council "primary responsibility for the maintenance of international peace and security" and have agreed "to join in affording mutual assistance in carrying out the measures decided upon by the Security Council" (UN Charter, Art. 24, 49).

In consideration of these provisions, legal scholars have characterized the Charter as an instrument of international peace (see Waldock 1952: 492; Dinstein 1988: 82; Brownlie 2003: 699). By characterizing the Charter in this way, they have emphasized parts of the Preamble referencing the aim of UN member states to "live together in peace," parts of Article 1 referencing the purposes of the United Nations in taking "effective measures for the prevention and removal of threats to the peace" and "appropriate measures to strengthen universal peace," and parts of Article

2 juxtaposing the prohibition of "the threat or use of force against the territorial integrity or political independence of any state" with the injunction to "settle ... international disputes by peaceful means." Such emphasis, for example, forms the basis of Brownlie's (1963 [1981]: 113) authoritative study of the Charter as the "essential juridical basis ... of world peace."

Nevertheless, such emphasis is misplaced. Although the "prevention and removal of threats to the peace" and the promotion of peaceful settlement of international disputes figure prominently among the Charter's stated purposes, these purposes are subsumed into the Charter's larger, overarching goal of establishing and maintaining a stable international order (Hoffmann 1961: 206–11). As Wolfrum (1994: 50) suggests, references to "international peace" throughout the Charter text consistently are embedded in the phrase "international peace and security" to signify a "comprehensive and co-operative" approach to achieving states' "overall interest of international security." This signification was consistent throughout all stages of Charter negotiations, beginning with the Four-Power Draft of July 1943, which called for the establishment of a "system of general security." Following the conferences in Moscow and Teheran, planners from the United States, the United Kingdom, and the Soviet Union agreed that the primary function of the proposed post-war organization would be "to establish and maintain peace and security, by force if necessary" (Hoopes and Brinkley 1997: 76, 111). Indeed, under the initial US proposal for the 1944 Dumbarton Oaks conference, security was to be the sole purpose of the organization, and the Soviet proposal suggested that the organization be called the "International Security Organization" (Hilderbrand 1990: 105–8). Planners at Dumbarton Oaks considered peaceful settlement and peacekeeping provisions only during the latter stages of the conference, and delegates to the 1945 San Francisco conference accorded these provisions similarly desultory treatment (Russell 1958: 227–8).

Major power delegates at San Francisco acquiesced to demands for a preamble containing aspirational references to "international peace and justice" only because they believed its inclusion would allow the remainder of the document to be written in more general terms (Russell 1958: 898). The British delegation believed it would appeal to emotions and to "posterity" (Wheeler-Bennett and Nicholls 1972: 544), while the US delegation believed it would be "relatively innocuous" to the Charter's larger purpose of maintaining international order (Schlesinger 2003: 161–7). These references were a natural outgrowth of the public relations campaign that US President Franklin Roosevelt had used to generate support for the war among an isolationist domestic constituency by expanding the stated aims of the war to include the establishment of a just and lasting peace (Campbell 1973: 27; Hilderbrand 1990: 5; Hoopes and Brinkley 1997: 206).

As adopted at the San Francisco conference, the Charter defines the conditions and rules of the international system to ensure the basic patterns of activity and expectations that characterize interactions among states, in accordance with the underlying distribution of power (Gilpin 1981: 42–3; Bull 1995: 3–19). The Charter helps to sustain the existing order by limiting states' recourse to armed force and by establishing rules of exclusion (Beetham 1991: 65) to distinguish the five major powers from less powerful states through their permanent membership in the Security Council. It is an agreement under which both major powers and less powerful states have contracted not to use armed force to alter or to overturn the existing international order (Hilderbrand 1990: 34). Peace is preserved only insofar as the existing order is not threatened. The Charter, then, does not prohibit all uses of armed force (Bowett 1958: 152; Stone 1958: 43) – only aggression, that is, uses of armed force that threaten the existing international order insofar as they are directed "against the territorial integrity or political independence" of other states or are otherwise "inconsistent with the Purposes of the United Nations" (UN Charter, Art. 2.4).

Delegates in San Francisco settled on the phrases "threats to the peace" and "breaches of the peace" so as to avoid using the term "war" within the body of the Charter text, hoping thereby to avoid problems of interpretation regarding actions short of war as had been widespread under the League of Nations Covenant (Russell 1958: 234; McCoubrey and White 1992: 22–5). They coupled these concepts with the term "aggression" in Article 39 to clarify that that the Charter was to be an instrument of international order and not simply an instrument of peace, although they did not explicitly define "aggression" because they believed that its meaning was generally understood (Russell 1958: 464–6) and that any attempt to define it more precisely would limit the Security Council's "primary responsibility for the maintenance of international peace and security" (UN Charter, Art. 24). Soviet planners had already insisted at Dumbarton Oaks that the term "aggression" be included within the Charter text to demonstrate the Charter's fundamental purpose (Wheeler-Bennett and Nicholls 1972: 206–7). Hilderbrand (1990: 44–5) goes so far as to suggest that Soviet Premier Josef Stalin's remark to British Foreign Secretary Anthony Eden in December 1941, regarding the establishment of a post-war international organization, was based on the calculation that such an organization would allow the major powers (including the Soviet Union) to maintain their privileged status within the post-war international order, while also helping to contain aggression – particularly German aggression.

The existing, post-World War II international order is an historically unique product of the outcome of the war and the end of colonialism. Throughout the inter-war years, there were revisionist powers (such as Germany, Japan, and the Soviet Union) that withdrew from the League of Nations or were expelled from it, leading to the collapse of the League and the failure of the Covenant that established it. By contrast, throughout the postwar era the five major powers have acted as status quo powers, and thus it is assumed herein that they were and have remained generally satisfied with their relative power positions within the international system (Jervis 1976: 101–7; Gaddis 1986: 120–3).[1]

As Glennon (2001: 136–7) notes, because the major powers were generally satisfied with their relative power positions following World War II, "the legalist model that emerged from the postwar conferences embodied that disposition." In framing the Charter, the major powers agreed not to use armed force to alter or overturn the existing, post-World War II international order, while at the same time preserving for themselves a special position within that order through permanent membership within the Security Council. Planners at Dumbarton Oaks discussed this position explicitly (Hilderbrand 1990: 194), and delegates at San Francisco deemed it to be commensurate with the major powers' relative power advantage (Russell 1958: 96, 241; Schlesinger 2003: 193–4).

In contrast to the major powers, however, less powerful states have not necessarily remained satisfied with their own relative power positions – even if they were at the time of the San Francisco conference – because they remain at a significant disadvantage in comparison to the major powers (Kennan 1951: 96–7). Following their emergence from colonialism, many of these states have become increasingly important due to their control of strategic resources (such as oil) and their potential as military bases and transit routes (David 1989: 61–80; Desch 1989: 108–20). Both the planners at Dumbarton Oaks and the delegates at San Francisco recognized that creating a workable solution to the problem of international order would require accommodating the increasing importance of these states, while at the same time acknowledging the relative power advantage of the five major powers (Russell 1958: 228; Hilderbrand 1990: 49; Hoopes and Brinkley 1997: 146; Ryan 2000: 18).

As Ikenberry (2001: 258–9) suggests, to bind less powerful states to an emerging, post-war international order, it was necessary that the major powers offer them a more favorable bargain than they otherwise would have been able to negotiate, based on their relative power positions at the time. In the case of the Charter, less powerful states gained a commitment from the major powers not to use armed force against them, except when taken in self-defense (UN Charter, Art. 51) or otherwise "consistent with the Purposes of the United Nations" (UN Charter, Art. 2.4). In return, the major powers gained a commitment from less powerful states not to use armed force to change the existing balance of power and acceptance from them of the major powers' relative power advantage and their veto within the Security Council (Russell 1958: 245–8, 445–6; Schlesinger 2003: 172). As a consequence of these tradeoffs, both the major powers and less powerful states have a shared interest in the existing, post-World War II international order. The prohibition of force contained within the Charter is, in effect, a contractual agreement among them not to use armed force to alter or to overturn that order, because they have a shared interest in it. As US Secretary of State Cordell Hull suggested in the summer of 1944, the Charter system is a "mutual affair" reflecting the interests of all states (Hilderbrand 1990: 65).

The Charter's purpose and its institutional form

Although the tradeoffs contained within the Charter correspond to Ikenberry's basic logic, Ikenberry excludes the Charter from his analysis of the post-World War II settlement, presumably because the Charter's institutional form is inconsistent with the larger theoretical framework he proposes. According to Ikenberry's (2001: 63) definition, the Charter is not a "binding institutional order," in part because there lacks an entity with the authority to establish its meaning and application. The Charter's parameters are not defined precisely, and in interpreting these parameters, the Security Council functions as a quasi-judicial body (Schachter 1964) that lacks an effective system of precedent and an effective system of delegation beyond the major powers themselves. Nevertheless, this institutional form is consistent with the Charter's underlying purpose.

As codified in the Charter text, the prohibition of force has three basic parameters delimiting it. First, the prohibition applies to threats or uses of armed force against "the territorial integrity or political independence of any state" (UN Charter, Art. 2.4). Second, the prohibition applies to threats or uses of armed force exercised "in a manner inconsistent with the Purposes of the United Nations" (UN Charter, Art 2.4), that is, used in a manner inconsistent with "maintain[ing] international peace and security, . . . tak[ing] effective collective measures for the prevention and removal of threats to the peace, and . . . the suppression of acts of aggression or other breaches of the peace" (UN Charter, Art. 2.1), or "develop[ing] friendly relations among nations based on respect for the principle of equal rights and self-determination of peoples" (UN Charter, Art. 2.2). Third, the prohibition does not apply to threats or uses of armed force in exercise of "the inherent right of individual or collective self-defense if an armed attack occurs . . . until the Security Council has taken measures necessary to maintain international peace and security" (UN Charter, Art. 51). Any use of armed force outside of these parameters is an illegal "threat to the peace, breach of the peace, or act of aggression" (UN Charter, Art. 39).

Determining which uses of armed force constitute aggression is of central importance, because such actions would threaten the existing order. Insofar as the major powers were and have remained generally satisfied with the existing order, it is not necessary that the Charter restrain them from undertaking uses of armed force intended to alter or to overturn that order.

What is necessary is that the Charter restrain them from undertaking uses of armed force that, although not intended to alter or to overturn the existing order, do in fact threaten that order. The Charter text, however, does not explicitly define the parameters that delimit its prohibition of force (Ferencz 1972: 492). There is ambiguity as to which threats or uses of armed force are directed against "the territorial integrity or political independence of any state" (UN Charter, Art. 2.4) and/or undertaken in a manner consistent with "the inherent right of individual or collective self-defense" (UN Charter, Art. 51) or "the Purposes of the United Nations" (UN Charter, Art. 2.4). Such ambiguity renders the Charter imprecise, giving rise to competing arguments among states regarding the proper definition of these parameters and the legality of most uses of armed force.

As "principal judicial organ of the United Nations" (UN Charter, Art. 92), the International Court of Justice (ICJ) has jurisdiction over disagreements that arise among states regarding the Charter's prohibition of force. However, a proposal to assign to the ICJ primary competence to decide questions of Charter interpretation was explicitly rejected during Charter negotiations (Russell 1958: 877–90), and thus the ICJ has jurisdiction only in cases that both sides have agreed to refer to it – unless a state has accepted its compulsory jurisdiction under Article 36(2) of the ICJ Statute. Because most states have not accepted the compulsory jurisdiction of the ICJ,[2] few cases regarding the Charter's Article 2(4) prohibition of force come before it. The task of deciding such disagreements, then, is in effect delegated to the Security Council by Article 39 of the Charter, which holds that the Security Council shall determine "the existence of any threat to the peace, breach of the peace, or act of aggression."

The Security Council functions more like a political body than a legal body (Schachter 1964), a distinction that has two important implications for the manner in which the Charter functions. First, the Security Council lacks an effective system of precedent. Any member of the United Nations may bring a matter to the attention of the Security Council by communicating it to the UN Secretary-General. When the Security Council acts on such matters, it lacks the authority to make binding legal interpretations (Higgins 1970: 5–6) and its decisions are not intended to establish precedent, although its decisions inevitably become part of what Schachter (1964: 964) refers to as a "stream of decisions that will normally be looked to as a source of law." Because matters arise before the Security Council outside of the direct control of its members, precedents that arise from Security Council decisions can have unforeseen consequences. As Schachter and others (Schwebel 1972: 433; Graefrath 1998: 242–3; Gray 2000: 14–16) note, in an attempt avoid these consequences, the Security Council generally renders decisions that avoid explicit judgments, and hence precedent generated through Security Council decisions contributes minimal "specificity" to imprecise Charter parameters.

Second, in matters involving uses of armed force by major powers, there is in effect no delegation beyond the major powers themselves. Whether cast singly or in combination with other states, the negative vote of a major power can veto any proposed Security Council resolution, except in decisions pertaining to the peaceful settlement of disputes (UN Charter, Art. 27.3). Such decisions are infrequent (Higgins 1970: 2), however, because the major powers can deny that they are parties to a dispute, claim that a matter is a "situation" and not a "dispute" (UN Charter, Art. 33–5), or claim that a matter does not pertain to "peaceful settlement" because it is a "threat to the peace, breach of the peace, or act of aggression" (UN Charter, Art. 39). Although procedural decisions are not subject to veto, the determination of whether a decision is procedural or substantive is (UN Charter, Art. 27). There is, then, no final arbiter to decide among competing understandings of law propounded by the major powers and thereby to determine the legality of their uses of armed force.

This institutional form derives from two key difficulties associated with legally restricting states' uses of armed force. First, legally restricting the use of armed force entails high uncertainty. Due to the complexity of events, states cannot predict with certainty all possible future actions (Williamson 1985: 3), and more importantly, the long-term effects that those actions might have on the stability of the existing order. However, placing more precise restrictions on the use of force might be counterproductive because, as Sir Austen Chamberlain argued famously, it might render the prohibition of force nothing more than "a trap to the innocent and a signpost to the guilty," while failing to solve the problems that result from the complexity of events (Schwebel 1972: 424–5; see also Russell 1958: 465, 898). Second, restricting the use of armed force entails high sovereignty costs (Abbott and Snidal 2000: 435–7). It places external authority over some of the most significant decisions that states make, thus constraining what Krasner (1999: 14–25) calls Westphalian sovereignty, "the exclusion of external actors from the authority structure of a given state." Applying Krasner's definitions, the Charter is in effect a tradeoff between Westphalian sovereignty and international legal sovereignty, which Krasner defines as "the practices associated with mutual recognition ... between territorial entities that have formal juridical independence." It preserves international legal sovereignty at the expense of one of the most fundamental aspects of Westphalian sovereignty – the resort to war – which states are most unlikely to relinquish because it pertains directly to the prospects for state survival.

For issues in which there is much uncertainty and in which legalization poses high costs to state sovereignty, states often choose "softer" forms of legalization, combining high obligation with moderate precision and moderate delegation (Abbott and Snidal 2000: 422–3). International agreements of this sort can be thought of as incomplete contracts that lack a centralized means of interpretation. Specifying an agreed framework of rules in the form of written law clarifies the extent to which states have shared interests and provides a record of their legal obligations, thereby creating an expectation of compliance that subjects their actions to scrutiny (Morrow 2000: 63–4). Moderate precision and delegation, however, allow states that acknowledge such rules as binding on them under the principle of *pacta sunt servanda* to dispute the content and application of those rules (Arend 1998: 138). Thus, while the Charter specifies rules prohibiting uses of armed force that would threaten the existing order, these rules are defined imprecisely and are subject to autointerpretation by the major powers. This institutional form dampens concerns of uncertainty and mitigates sovereignty costs (Abbott and Snidal 2000: 435) by specifying a basic legal framework to govern states' interactions while allowing the major powers to judge for themselves the extent to which particular actions are in accord with law's underlying purpose. As Reisman (1984: 643; 1991: 38) argues, it is this combination of a "gray area . . . extended between the black letter of the Charter and the bloody reality of world politics" and the "safety valve" provided by the veto that has made the Charter acceptable to the major powers.

Arguments offered under the Charter

The Charter's institutional form affects the content and form of arguments that are offered. Although the major powers are obligated to comply with the terms of the Charter, they may engage in autointerpretation of it (Abbott *et al.* 2000: 409–10; Goldstein *et al.* 2000: 386), offering legal arguments that propound understandings of law distinct from those propounded by other states. States' understandings of law are specifications of their obligations under a legal agreement that takes the form of an incomplete contract; they consist of states' definitions of the parameters that delimit their legal obligations, and are derived from their conceptions of the agreement's fundamental purpose and of which actions are consistent with that purpose (Morgenthau 1940: 282). States' understandings of their obligation to refrain from "the threat or use of armed force against the territorial integrity or political independence of any state" (UN Charter, Art. 2.4) may overlap considerably, because these understandings derive from the Charter text. However, they also may differ considerably, because differences in relative power, geographical position, history, or strategy lead states to prefer different understandings of law and because the complexity of events involving most uses of armed force generates much uncertainty. Because of the ambiguities contained within the Charter text, divergent understandings might all be reasonably consistent with it.[3]

In the absence of a centralized authority to decide among competing understandings of law, one state's understanding cannot bind another state that manifestly refuses to accept it (see *The Lotus Case*, (1927) 10 PCIJ

Reports, Series A). Under customary international law, this principle is known as the principle of the "persistent objector." However, it is also applicable to codified international law for which there is no centralized means of interpretation (Stein 1985: 464–6). The veto preserves the major powers' ability to advance particular understandings of the Charter in a manner like that of a persistent objector to a norm of customary international law. The major powers must offer arguments within a range of meaning delimited by the Charter's parameters, but they need not accept parameter definitions shared by other states, and the arguments they offer need not necessarily be intended to produce consensus on those definitions (Weil 1983: 438–40).

Arguments as signals[4]

Although codifying legal rules narrows their range of meaning, ambiguities remain, varying according to the precision with which a treaty's parameters are defined. The parameters of the Charter limit states to three affirmative defenses[5] for their uses of force. As shown in Table 2.1, these affirmative defenses may take ten different forms.

Table 2.1 Affirmative defenses for arguably illegal uses of armed force

The actions taken were part of "the inherent right of individual or collective self-defense."	The actions were taken in response to direct aggression in the form of an "armed attack."
	The actions were taken in response to indirect aggression tantamount to an "armed attack."
	The actions were taken in anticipation of an "armed attack" to which a state has clearly committed itself and as such can be said already to have "occurred."
	The actions were taken to protect citizens abroad against an imminent or ongoing "armed attack."
The actions taken were not directed against "the territorial integrity or political independence of any state."	The actions were taken in response to the invitation of a lawful government or with its consent.
	The actions were taken as a lawful vindication of legal rights.
	The actions were taken to recover lawful territory.
The actions taken were "consistent with the purposes of the United Nations."	The actions were taken as part of a lawful humanitarian intervention.
	The actions were taken in accordance with a Security Council resolution.
	The actions were taken as part of a regional arrangement for the "maintenance of international peace and security."

States most frequently claim that their uses of armed force were part of their "inherent right of individual or collective self-defense if an armed attack occurs" (UN Charter, Art. 51). This affirmative defense takes four basic forms. First, a state may claim that it acted in response to direct aggression in the form of an "armed attack," as the Soviet Union did to justify its actions against China in 1969. Second, a state may claim that it acted in response to indirect aggression tantamount to an "armed attack," as the United States did to justify its actions against Nicaragua in 1984. Third, a state may claim that it acted in anticipation of an "armed attack" to which a state has clearly committed itself and as such can be said already to have "occurred," as the United States did to justify its actions against Sudan and Afghanistan in 1998. Finally, a state may claim that it acted in self-defense to protect its citizens abroad against an imminent or ongoing "armed attack," as France did to justify its intervention in Ivory Coast in 2002.

Alternatively, states may claim that their uses of armed force were not directed against "the territorial integrity or political independence of any state" (UN Charter, Art. 2.4). This affirmative defense takes three basic forms. First, a state may claim that it acted in response to the invitation of a lawful foreign government or with its consent, as the Soviet Union did to justify its intervention in Afghanistan in 1979. Second, a state may claim that its actions were a lawful vindication of its legal rights, as the United Kingdom did to justify its actions against Albania in 1949. Third, a state may claim that its actions were taken to recover its lawful territory, as the United Kingdom did to justify its actions against Argentina in 1982.

States also may claim that their uses of armed force were "consistent with the Purposes of the United Nations" (UN Charter, Art. 2.4). This affirmative defense takes three basic forms as well. First, a state may claim that its actions were taken as part of a lawful humanitarian intervention, as the United Kingdom and France did to justify their actions in Iraq in 1992. Second, a state may claim that its actions were taken in accordance with an existing Security Council resolution, as the United States and the United Kingdom did to justify their invasion of Iraq in 2003. Third, a state may claim that its actions were taken under Article 52 of the Charter as part of a regional action for the maintenance of international peace and security, as the United States did to justify its naval quarantine of Cuba in 1962.

In offering arguments such as these, a major power provides an account for its military actions – a set of claims that addresses the discrepancy between its actions and the expectation of compliance created by the legal obligations codified within the Charter (Scott and Lyman 1968: 46). These obligations provide guidelines regarding which actions are aggressive, insofar as they are likely to threaten the existing order. Based on these guidelines, other states assess the major powers' actions and the arguments that accompany those actions (Cohen 1980: 131). Thus, whether intended or not, accounts serve as signals, because they transmit information used by other states to assess the major powers' commitment to the existing order (Franck and Weisband 1971: 6–7; Kratochwil 1989: 42; Bull 1995: 136).

Information unaccompanied by actions or threats of actions that would alter the cost–benefit calculations of other states can have no direct effect on those states' actions, although such information can have an indirect effect as a signal (Crawford 1990: 216; Gibbons 1992: 212). A state may choose to make this signal more credible by accompanying the arguments it offers with actions that have costs exceeding the benefits that would accrue to it from transmitting false information. Communication of this sort serves as a "costly" signal (Fearon 1995: 390–401), providing credible information regarding commitments or intentions that separates one type of state from another.

Alternatively, states may choose to send "weak" signals, which transmit information unaccompanied by actions having such costs. Communication of this sort provides less credible information regarding commitments or intentions than communication accompanied by costly actions does, because transmitting such information is, in itself, virtually costless and hence all types of states may attempt to signal the same way (Spence 1973: 358–61; Weinberger 2003: 93). Weak signals, then, are less credible than costly signals for separating one type of state from another, and states are unlikely to upgrade their prior beliefs regarding a state simply because that state sends a weak signal. Nevertheless, as Goldsmith and Posner (2005: 167–84) argue, because states are likely to downgrade their prior beliefs regarding a state that acts like an aggressor, unreliable partner, or cheater but fails to send even a weak signal of its commitment to upholding its legal obligations, sending even a weak signal might prevent other states from downgrading their prior beliefs regarding the state that sends it.

Legal arguments offered under the Charter serve a similar function. As a contractual agreement among states not to use armed force to alter or to overturn the existing international order, the Charter subjects the major powers' actions to the scrutiny of other states. Because a major power's use of armed force may suggest that it is no longer committed to the existing order, major powers offer arguments to demonstrate that their actions are in accordance with their particular understandings of the Charter and not intended to alter or to overturn the existing order. By transmitting information regarding the major powers' particular understandings of the Charter, these arguments serve as signals. States are unlikely to adjust their beliefs regarding a major power simply because it offered an argument to account for its use of armed force (Jervis 1970: 17). However, they would be likely to downgrade their beliefs regarding that major power if it failed to offer such an argument. Its failure to do so would signal to them that it is no longer committed to the existing order and that it might intend to alter or to overturn that order. Conversely, by providing an account for its actions, a major power signals its continuing commitment to the existing order and attempts thereby to prevent other states from downgrading their prior beliefs regarding its commitment to that order (Goldsmith and Posner 2005: 172–4). The credibility of these signals ultimately depends on the costs associated with them, even though other states might not be able to observe such costs, a point that we will take up again later.

The significance of legal arguments

States are legally obligated to report actions involving the use of armed force to the Security Council (UN Charter, Art. 51, 53). However, the Security Council does not address every incident reported to it, and thus in addition to or instead of offering arguments in the Security Council, major powers may offer arguments in the General Assembly or in public speeches and letters. They offer such arguments because there is an expectation of compliance with the Charter that subjects all military actions to the scrutiny of other states – not because there is an expectation of argumentation or deliberation within the Security Council or elsewhere. Indeed, many such arguments are not offered in the Security Council nor deliberated there.

Although states have offered arguments for their uses of armed force throughout history, those offered within a legal framework are distinctive, composed in a style of language that is specific to legal professionals across the globe (Falk 1969: 62–4; Higgins 1970: 10–11; Schachter 1977: 217–18, 1991: 25–32). These arguments have three characteristics that make them uniquely suited for sending signals of commitment to the existing order.

First, legal arguments correspond to other states' background expectations (Scott and Lyman 1968) under the Charter. As a legal instrument, the Charter subjects states' actions to a specific type of scrutiny, according to "the general rules, procedures, and discourse of international law" (Abbott *et al.* 2000: 401). Consequently, states' background expectations are that the arguments used to account for uses of armed force should be legal in form. These expectations are reinforced over time as states learn to use established procedures and to offer legal arguments to account for their actions (Schachter 1964: 960–1; Higgins 1970: 17). Although the particular form of argument itself does not send a signal of a major power's commitment to the existing order, because of states' background expectations if a major power fails to offer a legal argument, then other states are likely to infer from the argument it does offer that the major power is not committed to the existing order and that it may have aggressive intentions. Thus, whether offered in the Security Council or elsewhere, legal arguments are situationally appropriate, that is, "anchored to the background expectations of the situation" (Scott and Lyman 1968: 53).

Second, legal arguments link past actions to future intentions. As Goldsmith and Posner (2002: S137, 2005: 183) note, "[a]ppeal to law is a way of saying that past actions provide evidence of future intentions." By offering legal arguments to account for its actions, a major power makes explicit the "obligatory content" of those actions.

Third, and most importantly, legal arguments contain claims derived explicitly from the Charter, a codified framework of law that is inherently sustaining of the existing international order. They are limited to particular types of claims, while excluding others. Legal arguments offered under the Charter are limited to:

(1) claims regarding the inclusivity of legal rules;
(2) claims regarding priority among legal rules;
(3) claims regarding the proper interpretation of legal rules;
(4) claims regarding the application of legal rules to facts;
(5) claims regarding the determination of relevant facts.

They exclude other types of claims, specifically claims regarding the proper reference for rules.[6]

Claims regarding the inclusivity of legal rules address whether or not a particular rule is appropriately included among those rules agreed to be pertinent to the situation. Claims regarding priority among legal rules address whether or not certain rules have priority over other rules pertinent to the situation. Claims regarding the proper interpretation of legal rules address the extent to which a particular understanding of law accords with the law's underlying purpose. Claims regarding the application of legal rules to facts address whether or not these rules apply to a particular set of facts. Claims regarding the determination of relevant facts address whether or not certain events transpired or the particular manner or sequence in which they transpired (Boyle 1985: 108–12). All of these claims reflect areas of dispute regarding accepted rules for state interaction.

By contrast, claims regarding the proper reference for rules address the proper locus from which to derive rules to govern state interaction (Boyle 1985: 112). These claims reference alternative bases for assessing state conduct, such as principles of morality, justice, fairness, or efficiency. Unlike legal arguments, arguments that contain claims regarding the proper reference for rules derive from principles that might threaten the existing order, and for this reason purposefully were excluded from the Charter text. Such arguments are less credible as signals of commitment than legal arguments are, because they are likely to be perceived as "camouflaged attempts to impose a new international order" (Koskenniemi 1989: 3; see also Schachter 1984b: 649).

Because international law often seems "fair and right," domestic audiences are inclined to accept legal claims as justifications for actions taken by states (Abbott and Snidal 2002: 142), even when those claims are directed primarily at other state actors. Domestic audiences, however, do not necessarily accept international law and its contribution to the existing international order as the only standard by which to judge the rightness of their national policy. As Bull (1995: 74) notes, international order "is not the only value in relation to which international conduct can be shaped, nor is it necessarily an overriding one." Consequently, a major power might reference principles of morality, justice, and fairness when offering arguments for its actions, but when it does so, it will give legal claims priority over other types of claims and will distinguish between the two, as a signal to other states of its continuing commitment to the existing order. Explanatory hypothesis H_1 follows:

> H_1: If there is a binding legal obligation to sustain the existing international order by refraining from the use of armed force, then major powers will offer legal arguments to account for their actions and thereby signal to other states that they remain committed to the existing order.

The persuasiveness of legal arguments

The more persuasive an account, the more credible the signal it sends. An account's persuasiveness is a function of the perceived likelihood that the argument containing it was offered in good faith and the extent to which the claims comprising it provide a basis for inferring future restraint.

An argument offered in good faith is an argument that contains only veridical claims, that is, claims that represent a major power's actual understanding of the Charter and its actions in a particular incident. Conversely, an argument offered in bad faith is an argument that contains one or more averidical claims, that is, claims that misrepresent either a major power's understanding of the Charter or its actions. When a major power offers an argument in good faith, it is transmitting information that reflects its particular understanding of the Charter and is intended to persuade other states that its actions are reasonably justified under the Charter (Schwarzenberger 1955: 312–14). The major power is not attempting to conceal the unlawfulness of its actions by misrepresenting those actions or its understanding of the Charter. In certain instances, especially in instances of humanitarian intervention, a major power may have ulterior motives for its actions, which its legal arguments do not reveal. These motives, however, are not important, so long as the major power's actions can be reasonably justified under the Charter and the major power remains committed to sustaining the existing order (Kritsiotis

1998: 1035–7). What is important is that a major power's actions are restrained by its understanding of rules intended to sustain the existing order, whether or not its underlying motives reflect common values or common ideology.

By contrast, a major power that is not committed to sustaining the existing order or only weakly committed to it may offer an argument in bad faith, in an attempt to justify actions that threaten the existing order. Such an argument misrepresents the major power's actions and/or its understanding of the Charter. It is an attempt to portray the actions taken as reasonably justified under the Charter, despite the major power's intention to alter or to overturn the existing order. As Hoffmann (1961: 9–10) suggests, through such arguments, "gaps and ambiguities [in law] become wedges for destruction or subversion of the international order."

If states did not misrepresent their understandings of the Charter, and if those understandings were sufficiently similar, then coordination regarding its precise meaning might emerge among them, with a process of learning helping states to overcome uncertainty (Morrow 1994: 387–8; Abbott and Snidal 2000: 442–4). However, states' understandings are not always similar. As noted above, the complexity of events makes it difficult for states to predict with certainty which actions might threaten the existing order, and differences in relative power, geographic position, history, and strategy lead states to prefer different understandings of the Charter.

Differences in understanding, however, might also reflect disagreements on the relative importance of the various purposes underlying the Charter. As we have seen, the Charter is most fundamentally a legal instrument designed to instantiate and sustain the existing international order. Although planners at Dumbarton Oaks discussed provisions for economic and social cooperation, they made these provisions secondary because of British and Soviet concerns (Hilderbrand 1990: 86–92). Consequently, most states' understandings of the Charter are based primarily on their conceptions of which actions, as a category, would threaten the existing order. They define the Charter's parameters generally to proscribe such actions while allowing for the use of armed force under circumstances in which it would not threaten the existing order. Nevertheless, some states (especially post-colonial states) have emphasized the importance of "promoting and encouraging respect for human rights and for fundamental freedoms of all," as laid out in Article 1(3) of the Charter. These states argued successfully for inclusion within the General Assembly's 1970 *Declaration on Friendly Relations* (UN Doc. A/Res/2625) of a right of "peoples under colonial or racist regimes or other forms of alien domination" to use armed force for just ends, even if doing so would alter the existing order. Because these states' understandings of law derive from their conceptions of which actions respect "fundamental freedoms of all" in addition to which actions might threaten the existing order, they often disagree with states having understandings of law based more directly on conceptions of which actions might threaten the existing order.

A similar disagreement occurred in 1999 among the major powers, when NATO forces launched air strikes in response to Yugoslav President Slobodan Milosevic's refusal to accept the Rambouillet Agreement and to abide by agreed limits on Serb Army and Special Police Forces in the province of Kosovo. The United Kingdom claimed that the use of armed force against Yugoslavia was justified "on the grounds of overwhelming humanitarian necessity" (Roberts 1999: 106), while France claimed that the "humanitarian situation" in Kosovo constituted "a ground that can justify an exception to a rule" of Security Council authorization for the use of armed force.[7] Russia and China, however, condemned the actions as "open aggression" (Paecht 1999: para. 20, 23).

Efforts to define the Charter's parameters more precisely suggest that such differences among states are not insurmountable. Indeed, in 1974 the General Assembly adopted a *Consensus Definition of Aggression* that represented a compromise on the issue of "peoples under colonial and racist regimes or other forms of alien domination" (UN Doc. A/Res/3314), and the Security Council has shown increased willingness to identify situations as "threats to international peace and security" and therefore actionable under Chapter VII of the Charter. Nevertheless, there remains the problem of states deliberately obscuring and/or misrepresenting their particular understandings of the Charter, as evidenced by the "deftly obscured clauses" that Ferencz (1995: 6) argues "were deemed necessary in a process of reaching a consensus" on the definition of aggression. Such misrepresentation and deliberate obscurity make it difficult to ascertain just how similar states' understandings of the Charter might be.

Major powers may misrepresent their understandings of the Charter for various reasons, but the strongest incentive stems from the magnitude and uncertainty of the distributional problems that arise when the use of armed force is possible (Lipson 1984: 13–14). Even a major power that is satisfied with the existing order may misrepresent its particular understanding of the Charter to account for actions that would threaten the existing order if all states were to engage in them but seem necessary to preserve its relative power position. Although the actions lack a reasonable justification, insofar as they are outside of the Charter's parameters, the major power perceives them to be insignificant because they are unlikely to be repeated or because there is a tacit understanding among the major powers that the actions occurred within an area in which the major power has preponderant interest (Fawcett 1982: 119; Vertzberger 1994: 145–51; Bull 1995: 207–18). Nevertheless, because the Charter text does not allow for such exceptions, there is an incentive for major powers to offer arguments in bad faith, misrepresenting their actual understandings of the Charter and thereby disaffirming the unlawfulness of such actions if they were to occur. Explanatory hypothesis H_2 follows:

> H_2: If there is a binding legal obligation to sustain the existing international order by refraining from the use of armed force, then the major powers will have incentive to misrepresent their actual understandings of law in an attempt to disaffirm the unlawfulness of actions that might threaten the existing order.

Distinguishing between arguments offered in good faith and arguments offered in bad faith is difficult, because states have different understandings of the Charter and it may be difficult to establish what events actually transpired in a specific incident. If the version of events described by a major power differs from that described by another state, it does not necessarily mean that either state has offered an argument in bad faith. The version of events described by both states might reflect the information that each has concerning the incident in question. In the same manner, if the understanding of law propounded by a major power differs from that propounded by another state, it does not necessarily mean that either state has offered an argument in bad faith. The argument might reflect a major power's particular understanding of the Charter, despite its divergence from other states' understandings of it (Gray 2000: 23). Accordingly, states are unlikely a priori to assign a high value to the probability that an argument was offered in good faith or in bad faith, but they are likely to be at least somewhat skeptical of any argument offered by a major power because they recognize the incentives that major powers have to offer arguments in bad faith and thereby misrepresent their particular understandings of the Charter. For the account provided by an argument to be persuasive, then, the argument must satisfy what Schachter (1991: 50) calls "the test of legal credibility." States must conclude that the argument is at least as likely to have been offered in good faith as it is to have been offered in bad faith. In other words, the argument is at least as likely to represent the major power's actual understanding of the Charter and its actions as it is to misrepresent them.

Because it is impossible to observe a major power's understanding of the Charter directly, it is impossible to conclude with certainty that an argument has been offered in good faith. States, then, assess the likelihood that an argument was offered in good faith based on two indicators: the coherence of the claims contained within the argument and the plausibility of those claims (Schachter 1984c: 1645). Implausible or incoherent claims indicate that an argument was offered in bad faith, although coherent and plausible claims do not necessarily indicate that an argument was offered in good faith.

Claims are coherent to the extent that they derive from relevant law and apply uniformly to similar cases across time (Dworkin 1986: 176–224; Franck 1988: 741–3). Coherent claims regarding the use of armed force derive explicitly from the Charter, which outlines the accepted legal framework governing decisions regarding the use of armed force. These claims examine the inclusivity, priority, interpretation, and application of the Charter text, while excluding claims derived from alternative bases of conduct. They advance a particular understanding of the Charter's prohibition of force that applies uniformly to similar cases across time and is based on a conception of which actions, as a category, would threaten the existing order. By contrast, claims regarding the use of armed force are incoherent if they derive from a basis other than the Charter text, even if the major power making the claims asserts otherwise. Claims regarding the use of armed force are also incoherent if they provide an account for actions taken under circumstances that, according to claims made previously, comprise a category of behavior that is proscribed as threatening to the existing order, even if the major power making the claims asserts that the circumstances are unique (Henkin 1979: 333). By making such claims, a major power is, in effect, seeking exceptions from the rules necessary to sustain the existing order, and its argument signals to other states that it has only a moderate commitment to the existing order and therefore might act in a manner that poses a threat to that order.

Claims are plausible to the extent that existing evidence confirms the version of events they describe, or at least does not contradict that version of events. Despite the absence of accepted standards of evidence in international law and the ubiquity of plausible denial, a claim can be dismissed as implausible if it describes a version of events for which the existing evidence is either contradictory or nonexistent (Watts 2000: 8). A major power that communicates its actual understanding of the Charter to account for its actions makes plausible and coherent claims, while a major power that makes implausible and incoherent claims misrepresents its understanding of the Charter or its actions in an attempt to disaffirm the unlawfulness of those actions (Schachter 1983: 779). Accordingly, if other states decide that a major power offered an argument containing incoherent or implausible claims, then they are likely to conclude that those claims are averidical and that the major power offered the argument in bad faith.

For an account provided by an argument to be persuasive, however, it is not sufficient merely that states perceive the argument as more likely to have been offered in good faith than in bad faith. In addition, the claims comprising the argument must be sufficiently restrictive to provide a basis for inferring future restraint from the major power that offered it. A major power might offer an argument that represents its actual understanding of the Charter but places no significant restrictions on its actions. The restrictiveness of the claims comprising an argument, then, is the second factor that determines the persuasiveness of the account the argument provides. Together, the perceived likelihood that an argument was offered in good faith and the restrictiveness of the claims that comprise it determine the persuasiveness of the account it provides.

A major power that offers an argument comprising of restrictive claims provides a basis for other states to infer future restraint from it, by transmitting information regarding which actions it believes would threaten the existing order if all states were to engage in them. If states conclude that an argument offered by a major power is likely to have been offered in good faith, they conclude that the argument is likely to represent the major power's actual understanding of the Charter and its actions, and thus that the restrictions it places on actions involving the use of armed force are likely to derive from its conception of which uses of force are not in accord with the Charter. If states also conclude that the claims contained within that argument are sufficiently restrictive, then the account the argument provides will be persuasive to them. The claims comprising it define a limited set of actions as legal, and implicit in that set of actions is an understanding of which types of actors would prefer to place such limits on their own actions (Rabin 1990: 149). The more restrictive the claims made by a major power, the more limited the set of actions that a major power can justify without making claims that are no longer coherent because they no longer apply uniformly to similar cases across time (Henkin 1979: 45). Providing a persuasive account for the use of armed force, then, is not costless, because maintaining its persuasiveness restricts the actions of the major power that provides it. The magnitude and extent of the costs borne by a major power as a result of such restrictions serve to make its signal credible. However, because other states cannot necessarily observe these costs, insofar as restraint is less readily observable than the absence of restraint is, states assess the restrictiveness of the claims contained within an argument according to a minimum threshold of restrictiveness.

Each state may have its own understanding of the Charter's prohibition of force, because the prohibition is not defined precisely in the Charter text and because the complexity of events makes it impossible for states to predict with certainty the long-term effects that particular actions might have on the stability of the existing order. States, then, assess claims against thresholds (Robinson 1999: 218–20) that, although less restrictive than their own understandings of the Charter, define a minimum degree of restrictiveness such that, if a major power offers an argument containing claims that are less restrictive than a state's minimum threshold, then that state will remain unpersuaded by the account the major power provides (Chimni 1993: 57). Thresholds are specific to each state assessing an argument; however, the more restrictive the claims contained within an argument, the greater the likelihood that those claims exceed any individual state's threshold. Explanatory hypothesis H_3 follows:

H_3: If there is a binding legal obligation to sustain the existing international order by refraining from the use of armed force, then major powers will attempt to make their signals of commitment to the existing order credible by including within the arguments they offer claims that are coherent, plausible, and sufficiently restrictive to provide evidence of future restraint.

Empirical analysis

Before developing this model further to address the impact of the Charter on the major powers' military actions, it is necessary to test the hypotheses derived thus far, which pertain to the arguments offered by the major powers for such actions. If the Charter has no impact on the arguments offered by the major powers for their military actions, we would not expect it to have an impact on the actions themselves. For the purposes of testing these hypotheses, the units of observation are incidents (Willard 1988) in which major powers decided to use armed force within or against other states between October 1945 and October 2003.[8] Collecting multiple observations from each incident, we will assess the extent to which such observations are consistent with observable implications derived from the hypotheses laid out above and from existing models. This chapter tests hypotheses H_1 and H_2, while subsequent chapters test hypothesis H_3 and other hypotheses.

Claims comprising the arguments offered by the major powers

The first set of observations used in testing addresses claims comprising the arguments offered by the major powers. According to hypothesis H_1, when a major power engages in arguably illegal military actions, it will offer an argument to account for those actions. The argument will be based on legal claims, which provide a unique means of signaling the major power's commitment to the existing order. Although, for domestic reasons, the argument might also contain nonlegal claims, the major power will distinguish between legal and nonlegal claims by giving legal claims priority, as a signal to other states of its commitment to the existing international order.

The realist model, by contrast, suggests that major powers offer arguments primarily to generate support for their actions from their domestic constituencies (Krasner 1999: 6; Mearsheimer 2001: 23–7). Such arguments need not be strictly legal in form, because they are not intended to serve as signals to other states. Thus, when a major power offers an argument for its use of armed force, the argument will be likely to contain both legal and nonlegal claims and the major power will be unlikely to distinguish between them.

According to the liberal model, international law penetrates into states' domestic legal systems, reconstituting their domestic social identities such that their domestic decision-making becomes enmeshed with it and the arguments they offer reflect its influence (Henkin 1979: 315; Koh 1997: 2646–54). The process is most effective in liberal states, because they are democratic and have a domestic political culture premised upon the rule of law (Henkin 1979: 63; Slaughter 1995: 513–20). Thus, when a liberal major power offers an argument for its use of armed force, the argument will be less likely to contain nonlegal claims than arguments offered by a nonliberal major power.

According to the communal obligation model, through participation in international fora, major powers gradually internalize the practice of using an enduring group framework of shared legal language to justify their actions (Mitzen 2001: 59, 79–83, 91–6, 2005: 411–12; Johnstone 2003b: 445–50). Thus, the arguments offered by a major power for its use of armed force will, over time, become increasingly less likely to contain nonlegal claims.

To evaluate these implications (listed in Table 2.2) in comparison with one another, observations of two variables are coded to represent the claims contained within the arguments offered by the major powers. The first variable, CLAIM_TYPE, represents the types of claims contained within these arguments and is coded as follows, in order of increasing legality of claims. If the arguments offered by a major power for its use of armed force in an incident, *i*, contain only nonlegal claims, then CLAIM_TYPE(*i*) = 0. If a major power offers no arguments for its use of armed force in an incident, *i*, then CLAIM_TYPE(*i*) = 1. If the arguments offered by a major power for its use of armed force in an incident, *i*, contain both legal and nonlegal claims, then CLAIM_TYPE(*i*) = 2. If the arguments offered by a major power for its use of armed force in an incident, *i*, contain only legal claims, then CLAIM_TYPE(*i*) = 3.

Table 2.2 Observable implications regarding the claims contained within the arguments offered by the major powers

Prudential restraint model	Arguments offered by major powers may contain both legal claims and nonlegal claims, but legal claims will have priority over nonlegal claims.
Realist model	Arguments offered by major powers will be likely to contain both legal and nonlegal claims and will be unlikely to distinguish between them.
Liberal model	Arguments offered by liberal major powers will be less likely to contain nonlegal claims than arguments offered by nonliberal major powers.
Communal obligation model	Over time, arguments offered by major powers will become increasingly less likely to contain nonlegal claims.

A second variable, PRIORITY, represents the priority given to the legal claims contained within the major powers' arguments and is coded dichotomously, as follows. If the arguments offered by a major power for its use of armed force in an incident, *i*, contain legal claims only, or if they consistently enumerate legal claims ahead of nonlegal claims or include language that makes the nonlegal claims clearly subordinate to the legal claims, then PRIORITY(*i*) = 1. If the arguments offered by a major power for its use of armed force in an incident, *i*, contain nonlegal claims only or otherwise fail to distinguish between legal claims and nonlegal claims, then PRIORITY(*i*) = 0.

We begin by comparing the prudential restraint model with the realist model. Consistent with the prudential restraint model, legal claims had priority over nonlegal claims in most incidents examined. As shown in Table 2.3, in 106 out of 142 cases (74.6 percent) in which the major powers offered arguments to account for their uses of armed force, legal claims had priority over nonlegal claims in the arguments they offered.[9]

To compare the prudential restraint model with the liberal model and the communal obligation model, however, two additional variables are necessary. These variables test whether regime type and/or the length of time holding a seat as a permanent member of the Security Council affect the types of claims contained within the major powers' arguments. The first variable, REGIME, represents a major power's regime type and political culture. Because the liberal model characterizes a major power as liberal if it is democratically-governed and has a domestic political culture premised upon the rule of law (Henkin 1979: 63; Slaughter 1995: 513–20), observations of REGIME are coded according to the average of the scores given to each major power for political rights and civil liberties by Freedom House (2006) for a particular year.[10] Observations of REGIME are coded as REGIME(*i*) = 7 – FH(*i*), where FH(*i*) denotes the average of the scores for political rights and civil liberties given to a major power by Freedom House during the year in which an incident, *i*, occurred. This transformation reverses the direction of coding to simplify interpretation of the

Table 2.3 Priority of legal claims comprising the arguments offered by major powers (cross tabulation, *n* = 142)

	Only legal claims	*Both types of claims*	*Only nonlegal claims*	*Total*
Priority	76 (53.5%)	30 (21.1%)	0 (0.0%)	106 (74.6%)
No priority	0 (0.0%)	32 (22.5%)	4 (2.8%)	36 (25.4%)

Note
Chi square = 59.6 (df = 2).

data. Hence, while Freedom House scores range from 1 (most liberal) to 7 (least liberal), major powers for which REGIME takes on higher values are more liberal than major powers for which REGIME takes on lower values. A second variable, TIME_ON, represents the length of time that a major power has held a seat as a permanent member of the Security Council. Observations of TIME_ON are coded as TIME_ON(i) = m(i) / 12, where m(i) represents the number of months that a major power has held a seat as a permanent member of the Security Council at the time of an incident, i. This transformation converts the number of months a major power has held a seat as a permanent member of the Security Council to years and fractions of years.

In addition, observations of a control variable, COLD_WAR, are coded to control for changes caused by the end of the Cold War. It has been suggested that the end of the Cold War marked the beginning of a new international order characterized by the end of superpower rivalry and greater emphasis on international law (Caron 1993: 553; Falk 1995: 626–8; Byers 1999: 42; Ku and Diehl 2003: 1). In other words, the types of claims contained within the arguments offered by the major powers may be affected by exogenous changes brought about by the end of the Cold War, rather than by the major powers' regime types, the length of time they have held seats as permanent members of the Security Council, or their attempts to signal to other states their continuing commitment to the existing order. The variable COLD_WAR controls for the possible effects of this exogenous shock and is coded dichotomously, as follows. If an incident, i, occurred in 1990 or later, then COLD_WAR(i) = 0. If an incident, i, occurred in 1989 or earlier, then COLD_WAR(i) = 1. In other words, 1 denotes the presence of the Cold War, and 0 denotes the absence of the Cold War.[11]

The test here will be whether or not the types of claims contained within the major powers' arguments are a function of the regime type of the major power offering the argument, the length of time that major power has held a seat as a permanent member of the Security Council, the end of the Cold War, or some other factor – presumably the major power's attempt to signal its continuing commitment to the existing international order. Because CLAIM_TYPE is an ordinal variable, an ordered probit model is used, with all variables rescaled to the interval [0,1]. The results are shown in Table 2.4.

According to the liberal model, liberal major powers are less likely than nonliberal major powers to include nonlegal claims within the arguments they offer. Thus, the type of claims contained within a major power's arguments should be positively correlated with its regime type, and the coefficient on REGIME should be positive. This implication, however, is not supported by the data. As shown in Table 2.4, the coefficient on REGIME is positive, but with confidence of only 41 percent. Based on the evidence, then, it does not appear that liberal major powers are any less likely than

Table 2.4 Types of claims contained within the arguments offered by major powers as a function of their regime types and time as permanent members of the UN Security Council (ordered probit model, $n = 196$)

Variable name	*Coefficient (standard error)*
Regime	0.171 (0.317)
Time_On	0.001 (0.489)
Cold_War	−0.162 (0.280)

Note
Nagelkerke pseudo R-square = 0.009.

nonliberal major powers to include nonlegal claims within the arguments they offer.

According to the communal obligation model, over time the major powers will become less likely to include nonlegal claims within the arguments they offer. Thus, the type of claims contained within a major power's arguments should be positively correlated with the length of time that the major power has held a seat as a permanent member of the Security Council, and the coefficient on Time_On should be positive. However, this implication is not supported by the data, either. As shown in Table 2.4, the coefficient on Time_On is positive, but with confidence of less than 1 percent. Based on the evidence, then, it does not appear that the length of time a major power has held a seat as a permanent member of the Security Council has any effect on the types of claims contained within the arguments it offers.[12]

These results, combined with the results shown above in Table 2.3, provide support for the prudential restraint model in comparison with the three competing models. Throughout the post-war era, the major powers generally have offered arguments containing legal claims, irrespective of their regime type or the length of time they have held seats as permanent members of the Security Council.

Coordination among the major powers

A second set of observations addresses the extent to which coordination may be emerging among the major powers on the precise meaning of the Charter's prohibition of force. According to hypothesis H_2, because of the magnitude and uncertainty of the distributional problems that arise when the use of armed force is possible, the major powers have incentive to misrepresent their actual understandings of the Charter. By misrepresenting their actual understandings, the major powers disaffirm the unlawfulness of actions that might threaten the existing order but which seem necessary for preserving their relative power positions within that order. Because such misrepresentation impedes the gradual process of learning that might otherwise occur among the major powers, coordination is unlikely to emerge among them.

Here, the implication of the realist model is the same, although the logic differs. According to the realist model, major powers offer arguments for actions they have taken in order to generate support for those actions among their domestic constituencies (Krasner 1999: 6; Mearsheimer 2001: 23–7). Because these arguments are not intended to serve as signals to other states, they do not transmit information regarding the major powers' particular understandings of the Charter, and thus coordination is unlikely to emerge among the major powers.

Disagreements among the major powers serve as indicators of the extent to which coordination may be emerging among them. As Boyle (1985: 108–9) argues, disagreements regarding the inclusivity, priority, or interpretation of legal rules are more fundamental than disagreements regarding the application of legal rules to facts or the determination of facts, because of the greater complexity of the claims they involve. Thus, if the major powers are converging toward a shared understanding of the Charter, the primary disagreements that their legal arguments address are more likely to be over the determination of facts than the application of legal rules to facts or the inclusivity, priority, or interpretation of legal rules. Conversely, if the major powers are not converging toward a shared understanding of the Charter, then the primary disagreements that their arguments address are more likely to be over the inclusivity, priority, or interpretation of legal rules or the application of legal rules to facts than the determination of facts. The implication of both the realist model and the prudential restraint model, then, is that the primary disagreements addressed by a major power's legal arguments are less likely to be over the determination of facts than the application of legal rules to facts or the inclusivity, priority, or interpretation of legal rules, because both theories imply that coordination regarding the precise meaning of the Charter's prohibition of force is unlikely to emerge among the major powers.

Other implications derive from the liberal model and from the communal obligation model. According to the liberal model, as states interact, the arguments they offer transmit information that reflects their domestic social identities (Andrews 1975: 524–5; Moravcsik 1997: 25–8, 41–7). Because liberal major powers have convergent domestic social identities (Slaughter 1995: 528–33), coordination on the precise meaning of the Charter is more likely to emerge among them than among nonliberal major powers. Thus, the primary disagreements addressed by the legal arguments of liberal major powers are more likely to be over the determination of facts than the application of legal rules to facts or the inclusivity, priority, or interpretation of legal rules. Conversely, because their domestic social identities diverge from those of liberal states, the primary disagreements addressed by the legal arguments of nonliberal major powers are more likely to be over the inclusivity, priority, or interpretation of legal rules or the application of legal rules to facts than the determination of facts.

According to the communal obligation model, major powers gradually internalize the practice of using an enduring group framework of shared legal language to justify their actions (Mitzen 2001: 56, 79–83, 91–6, 2005: 411–12). As they do so, their arguments become increasingly likely to contain claims that reflect an understanding of law common to most states (Johnstone 2003a: 446, 2003b: 445–50). Coordination on the precise meaning of the Charter, then, is likely to emerge among them over time, and thus the primary disagreements addressed by the major powers' legal arguments will become increasingly likely to be over the determination of facts rather than the application of legal rules to facts or the inclusivity, priority, or interpretation of legal rules.

To evaluate these implications (listed in Table 2.5) in comparison with one another, observations of an additional variable, COORD, are coded to represent the extent of coordination among the major powers, as indicated by the primary disagreements that their legal arguments address. Observations of COORD are coded as follows, in order of increasing coordination. If a major power offers only nonlegal arguments to account for its uses of

Table 2.5 Observable implications regarding coordination among the major powers on the precise meaning of the Charter's prohibition of force

Prudential restraint model	The primary disagreements addressed by a major power's legal arguments are less likely to be over the determination of facts than over the inclusivity, priority, interpretation, or application of legal rules.
Realist model	The primary disagreements addressed by a major power's legal arguments are less likely to be over the determination of facts than over the inclusivity, priority, interpretation, or application of legal rules.
Liberal model	The primary disagreements addressed by the legal arguments of liberal major powers are likely to be over the determination of facts, while the primary disagreements addressed by the legal arguments of nonliberal major powers are likely to be over the inclusivity, priority, interpretation, or application of legal rules.
Communal obligation model	Over time, the primary disagreements addressed by the major powers' legal arguments will become increasingly likely to be over the determination of facts rather than the inclusivity, priority, interpretation, or application of legal rules.

armed force in an incident, *i*, or if the primary disagreement addressed by the legal arguments it offers is over the inclusivity, priority, or interpretation of legal rules, then COORD(*i*) = 0. If the primary disagreement addressed by a major power's legal arguments in an incident, *i*, is over the application of legal rules to facts, then COORD(*i*) = 1. If a major power does not offer arguments to account for its uses of armed force in an incident, *i*, then COORD(*i*) = 2. If the primary disagreement addressed by a major power's legal arguments in an incident, *i*, is over the determination of facts, then COORD(*i*) = 3.

We begin by comparing the observations of COORD with the observable implications of the prudential restraint model and the realist model. As shown in Table 2.6, in 107 out of 142 cases (75.4 percent) in which major powers offered legal arguments for their uses of armed force, the primary disagreements addressed were over the inclusivity, priority, interpretation, or application of legal rules.[13] This data supports both the prudential restraint model and the realist model, because according to both models the primary disagreements addressed by the major powers' arguments are likely to be over the inclusivity, priority, interpretation, or application of legal rules.

To evaluate these implications in comparison with those derived from the liberal model and the communal obligation model, the variables TIME_ON and REGIME are used once again. These variables represent the major powers offering the arguments examined above. The test here will be whether or not coordination among the major powers is a function of the major powers' regime types and domestic political cultures and/or the length of time that they have held seats as permanent members of the Security Council. As in the previous test, because COORD is an ordinal variable, an ordered probit model is used, with all variables rescaled to the interval [0,1]. The results are shown in Table 2.7.

According to the liberal model, coordination on the precise meaning of the Charter is more likely to emerge among liberal major powers than

Table 2.6 Disagreements addressed in the arguments offered by major powers ($n = 196$)

Primary area of disagreement	*Number of cases*
Disagreements over the inclusivity, priority, or interpretation of legal rules	50 (25.5%)
Disagreements over the application of legal rules to facts	57 (29.1%)
Disagreements over the determination of facts	35 (17.9%)
Total number of cases in which major powers offered legal arguments	142 (72.4%)

Table 2.7 Coordination among the major powers as a function of their regime types and time as permanent members of the UN Security Council (ordered probit model, $n = 196$)

Variable name	*Coefficient (standard error)*
REGIME	−1.249 (0.328)
TIME_ON	−0.083 (0.279)

Note
Nagelkerke pseudo R-square = 0.086.

among nonliberal major powers. Thus, coordination should be positively correlated with regime type, and the coefficient on REGIME should be positive. This implication, however, is not supported by the data. As shown in Table 2.7, the coefficient on REGIME is negative, with confidence of greater than 99 percent, which is the opposite of what the liberal model suggests.

The reason that the coefficient on REGIME is negative may have something to do with particular characteristics of the Communist government of the Soviet Union. The Soviet Union was involved in most of the incidents involving uses of armed force by a nonliberal major power during the Charter period. According to Ginsburgs (1958: 83), both before and after the ratification of the Charter, Soviet legal arguments were directed simultaneously at other states and at domestic audiences within those states. Ginsburgs argues that these arguments demonstrate a "preoccupation with the facts" rather than "legal hair-splitting," because they were part of a Communist strategy to make Soviet actions "plausible to the masses" across the globe. In other words, regime type may have an effect on how major powers construct their legal arguments, but it is because liberal major powers tend to offer more complex legal arguments than nonliberal major powers do, not because their arguments reflect a gradual emergence of coordination among them. Indeed, the primary disagreements addressed by Soviet legal arguments tended to be over the determination of facts, including those offered for Soviet interventions in Hungary in 1956, in Czechoslovakia in 1968, and in Afghanistan in 1979. In each of these incidents, the Soviet Union claimed that its intervention had followed a request by the government of the state in which it had intervened. By contrast, the primary disagreements addressed by the legal arguments offered by the United States, the United Kingdom, and France were comparatively more likely to be over the inclusivity, priority or interpretation of legal rules, such as those offered for their joint humanitarian intervention in Iraq in 1991, which they claimed was implicitly authorized by the Security Council under resolution 688.

According to the communal obligation model, coordination on the precise meaning of the Charter is likely to emerge among the major powers over time. Thus, coordination should be positively correlated with the length of time that the major powers have held seats as permanent members of the Security Council, and the coefficient on TIME_ON should be positive. This implication is not supported by the data, either. As shown in Table 2.7, the coefficient on TIME_ON is negative, although with confidence of only 23 percent. Based on the evidence, then, the major powers do not appear to be moving toward consensus on the precise meaning of the Charter's prohibition of force.

These results, combined with the results shown above in Table 2.6, provide support for the realist model and the prudential restraint model. According to both these models, the primary disagreements addressed by the major powers' legal arguments are likely to be over the inclusivity, priority, interpretation, or application of legal rules – irrespective of regime type or length of time that they have held seats as permanent members of the Security Council.

Application of claims contained in arguments

A third set of observations addresses the application of claims contained within the arguments offered by the major powers for their uses of armed force. According to hypothesis H_3, major powers will attempt to make their signals of commitment to the existing order credible by including within their arguments claims that are coherent, plausible, and sufficiently restrictive to provide evidence of future restraint. Thus, when formulating an argument for the use of armed force, a major power will attempt to include within that argument claims that apply uniformly to similar cases across time. Decision-makers within the major power will consider claims made in similar situations in the past and claims that might be made in similar situations in the future and will formulate their arguments accordingly, or else attempt to obscure the contradictions between them.

A similar implication derives from the communal obligation model. According to this model, states' beliefs and identities change over time such that they begin to see their actions from the perspective of an international community. They become increasingly concerned with being seen as responsible members of that community and with making claims that are generalizable, impartial, and consistent, as a basis for producing consensus (Johnston 2001: 499–502; Mitzen 2001: 16–17). Thus, decision-makers within the major powers will consider claims that might be made in similar situations in the future and will formulate their arguments accordingly, attempting to accommodate the viewpoints of other states as a means of producing consensus.

Because both the prudential restraint model and the communal obligation model suggest that decision-makers within a major power will consider claims that might be made in the future, policy-making decisions regarding future situations to which current legal arguments might be applied provide mixed support for both models. However, decision-makers' intentions differ according to each model. The prudential restraint model suggests that decision-makers will consider claims that might be made in the future so as to formulate legal arguments that are likely to persuade other states of the legitimacy of actions taken, yet unlikely to hinder future actions, while the communal obligation model suggests that decision-makers will consider claims that might be made in the future so as to formulate legal arguments that are likely to produce consensus through the process of argumentation. Thus, discussions in which participants decide to obscure contradictions with previous claims would support the prudential restraint model, as would situations in which decision-makers offer incentives or use coercive bargaining techniques to gain the acceptance or acquiescence of other states, rather than relying on argumentation to produce consensus. By contrast, discussions in which participants note the viewpoints of other states and attempt to accommodate them in the arguments offered, as a means of producing consensus through argumentation, would support the communal obligation model.

The implication of the realist model is quite different. According to the realist model, major powers offer arguments for actions they have taken in order to generate support for those actions from their domestic constituencies (Krasner 1999: 6; Mearsheimer 2001: 23–7). Because the purpose of these arguments is to generate domestic support and not to signal commitment to the existing order or to produce consensus regarding the precise meaning of the Charter's prohibition of force, major powers will attempt to include within these arguments claims that appeal specifically to domestic audiences. The implication, then, is that decision-makers within a major power will consider the salience of current claims for domestic audiences only and will not consider claims that might be made in similar situations in the future. Discussions in which participants note the usefulness of legal arguments to persuade domestic audiences of the legitimacy of a proposed action but do not also note the usefulness of such arguments to persuade other states of the legitimacy of a proposed action would provide support for this model, as would the absence of any discussions regarding future situations to which current legal arguments might be applied.

According to the liberal model, international law serves as a formal restatement of generally accepted rules that develop through interaction among states having a shared social purpose (McDougal 1960: 339–40; Andrews 1975: 524–5). As states interact, their arguments transmit information that reflects their domestic social identities (Moravcsik 1997: 541–7). By implication, then, when there is a change in a major power's social identity, such as a change in its government or its regime type, its arguments will contain claims that are inconsistent with the arguments it has offered previously. Hence, policy-making discussions in which participants decide to offer arguments that differ from those that policy-makers in

Table 2.8 Observable implications regarding the application of claims comprising the arguments offered by the major powers

Prudential restraint model	Decision-makers within a major power will consider claims made in similar situations in the past and claims that might be made in similar situations in the future and will formulate their arguments accordingly, or else attempt to obscure the contradictions between them.
Realist model	Decision-makers within a major power will consider the salience of current claims for the domestic audience only and will not consider claims that might be made in similar situations in the future.
Liberal model	If there is a change in a major power's government or regime type, then the arguments it offers will contain claims that are inconsistent with its previous arguments.
Communal obligation model	Decision-makers within a major power will consider claims that might be made in similar situations in the future and will formulate their arguments accordingly, attempting to accommodate the viewpoints of other states as a means of producing consensus.

the previous government offered or intended to offer for the same uses of armed force would provide support for this model, particularly if participants reject the previous government's arguments as unsuited to the current government because of differences in values and/or ideology.

These implications (listed in Table 2.8) address policy-making modalities pertaining to the formulation of legal arguments. As such, they are not well suited to the quantitative methods of assessment used in this chapter and will be examined instead in subsequent case-study chapters. Nevertheless, having established the extent to which historical evidence supports hypotheses H_1 and H_2, which pertain to the impact that the Charter has had on the arguments offered by the major powers for their military actions, it is worthwhile next to consider the impact that the Charter has had on the actions themselves, before returning to the process of theory-testing in Chapters 4 through 8.

3

PERSUASION, LEGITIMATION, AND RESTRAINT

As we have seen, the prohibition of force codified in Article 2(4) of the Charter subjects the major powers' military actions to the scrutiny of other states. If states conclude that a major power is only weakly committed to the existing order, or that it has aggressive intentions, then they are likely to respond with resistance to it, because it poses a threat to the existing order and to their relative power positions within that order. Such resistance, whether direct or indirect, inflicts costs on major powers, which they attempt to avoid by offering legal arguments for their actions or engaging in strategies of denial. Offering arguments in this context, however, is not costless, insofar as such arguments impose restraints on the use of armed force that affect the manner and timing of the major powers' military actions. These costs, although they are not readily observable by other states, determine the credibility of the signal that is sent and can have a significant impact on the major powers' military actions, as subsequent chapters demonstrate. To examine these costs, however, we must develop our model further, to encompass the role of the Charter in legitimating the exercise of power and in creating a likelihood of resistance that serves as an implicit enforcement mechanism against major powers that violate it.

The UN Charter and the legitimation of power

The Charter's role in legitimating the exercise of power stems from its underlying purpose of sustaining the existing international order. Most states have remained in agreement that the existing, post-war order is an acceptable form of international order, despite moderate shifts in the balance of power that have occurred since the end of World War II. These states have remained in agreement because the rules included within the Charter to sustain the existing order have been internalized by them, as part of what Bull (1995: 87–9) refers to as a "compact of coexistence" among them. These rules approximate states' interests to such an extent that they have not updated their preferences, despite subsequent shifts in the existing balance of power (Watson 1992: 323–4).

Because states have remained in agreement regarding the existing order, it can be said to have attained legitimacy (Watson 1992: 315; Morgenthau and Thompson 1993: 102). Its legitimacy, however, is not based on states' beliefs, but rather habit and rational calculation (Hyde 1983: 391–400). States have concluded that the marginal utility they might obtain within a different international order is insignificant in comparison with the utility that they derive from the existing order, and that a peaceful change in the existing order is unlikely because states that would be made worse off by such a change are unlikely to consent to it (Krasner 1982: 186–7; Young 1982: 292–3). Because of its general conformity with established practices that serve a shared interest, states remain willing to accept the existing order and the rules necessary to sustain it, even if those rules diverge slightly from their particular interests (Sugden 1989: 90–2).

Actions are legitimate to the extent that they can be reasonably justified according to such rules, that is, to the extent that they can be accompanied by arguments that rationally and persuasively demonstrate those actions' accordance with the underlying purpose of rules that serve a shared interest. Actions can be understood as reasonably justified to the extent that the arguments that accompany them elicit responses expressive of acceptance by other states – irrespective of those states' particular motivations for accepting them. The legitimacy of an action, then, is not a matter of states' beliefs regarding the rightness of the action, nor is it a matter of any collective decision by an authoritative body. Rather, it is the extent of the action's congruence with rules that provide the basis for its justification, as indicated by the extent to which states express their acceptance of it, as opposed merely to acquiescing in it or rejecting it (Fisher 1978: 55; Beetham 1991: 11–20, 82–9).[1]

States' acceptance of an action indicates that they have been persuaded that the action is reasonably justified, because they have concluded that the arguments accompanying it were likely to have been offered in good faith and that those arguments contain claims that are sufficiently restrictive to meet their minimum thresholds. They may disagree with the action itself, because it is not in accord with their particular understandings of the Charter or with their particular beliefs regarding morality or fairness, but they are willing to accept the action as reasonably justified, nonetheless. Conversely, states' resistance to a major power indicates that they have not been persuaded that the action is reasonably justified. They have concluded either that the arguments accompanying the action were likely to have been offered in bad faith or that the claims comprising those arguments are not sufficiently restrictive to meet their minimum thresholds.

Whether or not states agree with an action, their acceptance of it confers legitimacy on it, with each state's acceptance conferring additional legitimacy on it (Beetham 1991: 18). States may express their acceptance by public statements and diplomatic exchanges supporting the major power that engaged in it. They may offer arguments of their own to account for a major power's use of force and/or cast votes favorable to that major power within a multilateral institution. They also may participate in the action by providing assistance or logistical support.

By contrast, states' resistance to a major power withholds legitimacy from its actions. Cumulatively, such resistance to a major power can erode the legitimacy conferred on its actions by other states (Beetham 1991: 18–19). States respond with resistance to a major power by offering counter-arguments and accompanying those counter-arguments with actions intended to inflict costs on the major power they are resisting. States may do so indirectly, through diplomatic means, or directly, through economic or political-military means. These include various acts of retorsion and acts of reprisal (Schachter 1984b: 231; Boyle 1985: 177–8).[2]

Indirect resistance includes withdrawing diplomatic representatives from a major power or expelling that major power's diplomatic representatives, canceling scheduled visits or talks with it, suspending or terminating treaties unrelated to the actions it has taken, or attempting to isolate it diplomatically by withdrawing support for it in multilateral institutions (Voeten 2002: 730–3). Direct means of resistance inflict costs more directly on a major power, by economic or political-military means. Economic means of resistance include tariffs, trade restrictions, financial restrictions, and embargoes (Bowett 1972: 7–11). However, such actions are seldom used against major powers (except by other major powers), because they can be significantly more costly to the state that uses them than they are to the major power against which they are directed (Hirschman 1980: 13–34; Pape 1997: 106–10). Less powerful states, then, are more likely to use political-military means of resistance. These may include suspending or terminating treaties related to the actions the major power has taken, especially bilateral treaties addressing issues such as basing rights, maintenance and refueling rights, or transit and overflight rights – areas in which a major power is likely to place a higher marginal value on cooperation than less powerful states do (Voeten 2005: 549–50). They also may include providing assistance to its adversaries (both state and non-state actors), engaging in covert acts of reprisal, or joining a balancing coalition against it (Pape 2005: 36–7).

Expressions of acceptance and resistance occur frequently within the Security Council, because states are legally obligated to report actions involving the use of armed force to the Security Council (UN Charter, Art. 51, 53). Within the Security Council, states may indicate their acceptance of a major power's actions by offering arguments and/or by casting votes that are favorable to it. They may resist a major power by offering counter-arguments and by casting votes that are unfavorable to it. Seven distinct outcomes are possible.[3] First, the Security Council may approve a resolution that explicitly authorizes a major power's actions (explicit authorization). Second, the Security Council may approve a resolution that implicitly authorizes a major power's actions (implicit authorization).[4] Third, the Security Council may take no action on the matter (no action). Fourth, a major power may apply its veto to defeat a proposed Security Council resolution condemning its actions, although the resolution lacks the necessary votes to pass, irrespective of the major power veto (incidental veto). Fifth, a major power may apply its veto to defeat a proposed Security Council resolution, and other major powers may apply their veto also or abstain from voting (multiple-negative veto). Sixth, a major power may apply its veto to defeat a proposed Security Council resolution, with one or more non-permanent members of the Security Council concurring (near-sole veto). Finally, a major power may apply its veto to defeat a proposed Security Council resolution, with no other members of the Security Council concurring (sole veto).

These outcomes affect the legitimacy of a major power's actions. Expressions of acceptance confer legitimacy on the actions of a major power, while expressions of resistance withhold legitimacy from those actions. The Security Council, however, is not an instrument of collective legitimation in the way that Caron (1993: 555–62) argues. Legitimation within the Security Council occurs cumulatively, not collectively. Each state's acceptance confers additional legitimacy on the actions, while each state's resistance erodes such legitimacy. Nevertheless, to the extent that the Security Council represents the pooled judgments of a broad sampling of states, dissent within the Security Council signals to other states that there is reason to conclude that a major power's actions were not reasonably justified. It provides reason for states to reach conclusions similar to those reached by the members of the Security Council and to respond with resistance (Schachter 1964: 962), thereby withholding legitimacy from those actions. By casting a vote that is unfavorable to a major power, then, a state not only indicates that it disapproves of the actions taken and that it remains unpersuaded that those actions were reasonably justified, it also increases the likelihood that other states will reach similar conclusions. Accordingly, when offering arguments within the Security Council, a major power prefers one of the no-veto outcomes (explicit authorization, implicit authorization, or no action) or the incidental-veto outcome, because these outcomes suggest that it succeeded in persuading most members of the Security Council that its arguably-illegal actions are reasonably justified under the Charter. Outside of explicit authorization, which defines actions as clearly legal, the implicit authorization outcome is most preferable, because it suggests that the actions lie close to the clearly legal category of behavior (see Figure 3.1). Nevertheless, under any of these four outcomes, states will be unlikely to downgrade their beliefs regarding a major power's continuing commitment to the existing order.

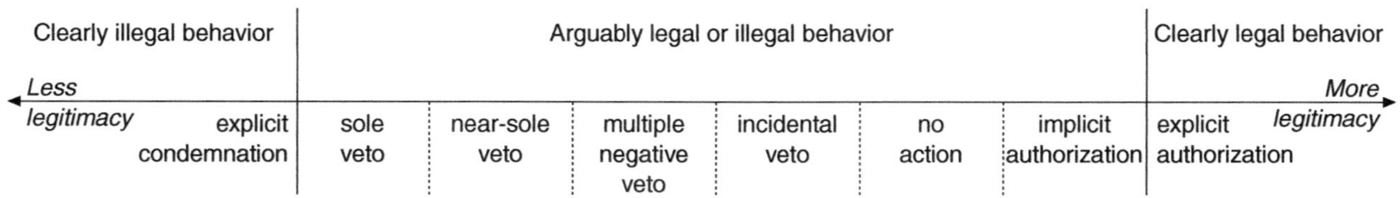

Figure 3.1 Legitimacy and Security Council outcomes.

If the no-veto or incidental-veto outcomes are unreachable, then a major power will attempt to persuade other major powers to vote with it so as to achieve a multiple-negative veto and thereby to avoid "the stigma of exercising a sole veto (or near-sole veto)" (Padelford 1948: 233). The multiple-negative veto suggests that the major power was successful in persuading some members of the Security Council that its actions were reasonably justified. Under any of these outcomes, states will be less likely to downgrade their prior beliefs regarding a major power's commitment to the existing order than they would be under the sole veto or near-sole veto outcomes. Under the sole veto or near-sole veto outcomes, by contrast, states are likely to downgrade their prior beliefs regarding a major power's commitment to the existing order, because the major power was unable to persuade most members of the Security Council that its actions were reasonably justified. These outcomes, then, are least preferable, because they suggest that the arguably illegal actions lie close to the clearly illegal category of behavior.

It is in this manner that the Security Council contributes to the process of legitimation. Dissent within the Security Council provides reason for other states to conclude that the actions of a major power are not reasonably justified, and therefore reason to respond with resistance to that major power. Such dissent also provides information to major powers about the likelihood of resistance against them. As Voeten (2005: 541–4) argues, decisions within the Security Council serve as focal points in a coordination dilemma faced by states with diverging interests in resisting a major power. Although states face different incentives for resisting a major power, Security Council approval or disapproval can provide a specific equilibrium, such that states will be more likely to respond with resistance to a major power if the Security Council disapproves of the major power's actions than if it does not.

The UN Charter and the anticipated likelihood of resistance

States adjust their policy choices according to the potential costs and benefits associated with resistance by various means. If the potential costs of resistance against a major power are high, then states may respond with indirect resistance, casting unfavorable votes in the Security Council but not accompanying those votes with more direct resistance through economic or political military means. Indirect resistance is more likely than direct resistance because it has lower costs; nevertheless, states have incentives to respond with direct resistance against a major power if they perceive that major power as a threat to the existing order, because in threatening the existing order the major power also threatens those states' relative power positions within the existing order. It is this perception of threat that provides an incentive for states to resist a major power through economic or political-military means rather than "free-riding" (Olson 1971) on other states.

States may perceive a major power as threatening if they conclude that it is likely to have aggressive intentions, that is, if they conclude that the major power is likely to be a revisionist major power that uses armed force in an effort to alter or to overturn the existing order. Such a major power no longer accepts the existing order because the balance of power has shifted or because it is unsatisfied with the existing balance of power and seeks to alter it (Schweller 1996: 112–16). It poses a threat to states that are in agreement regarding the existing order, because the existing order helps to preserve those states' relative power positions. The capabilities of a major power with aggressive intentions would enable it to achieve its goal of altering the existing order (or perhaps even overturning it), when less powerful states would fail. States, then, are likely to respond with direct resistance against a major power that they believe to have aggressive intentions.

States also may respond with direct resistance against a major power that they have concluded has only a weak commitment to the existing order. A major power with a weak commitment to the existing order may pose a threat because, although it does not intend to alter or to overturn the existing order, it might not exercise restraint sufficient to preserve the existing order. If it fails to exercise such restraint, it poses a threat both to the existing order and to states' relative power positions within that order. Explanatory hypothesis H_4 follows:

> H_4: If there is a binding legal obligation to sustain the existing international order by refraining from the use of armed force, then states are likely to respond with resistance against a major power whose actions and accompanying arguments suggest that it is only weakly committed or no longer committed to the existing order.

Acquiescence and legal counter-arguments

Rather than responding with acceptance or resistance to a major power's military actions, however, a state may respond instead with acquiescence, offering a counter-argument condemning the actions taken but not accompanying that counter-argument with diplomatic, economic, or political-military means of resistance. Within the Security Council, a state may acquiesce to an action by offering a counter-argument but ultimately casting a vote that is favorable to the major power that engaged in that action, or else abstaining from voting (Claude Jr. 1966: 374). Acquiescence indicates disapproval of an action, but it is an ambiguous response.

It may indicate a state has concluded that an action is reasonably justified, but it is unwilling to respond in a manner that confers legitimacy on that action, because it disagrees with it (Golden 1974: 218). Alternatively, it may indicate a state has concluded that an action is not reasonably justified, but it has calculated that the anticipated payoff from resistance is negative, because it is allied with the major power that engaged in the action, or because it fears retaliation from that major power, or because of a collective-action problem (D'Amato 1982: 104–6; Christensen and Snyder 1990: 140–6).

Acquiescence is a common response, because resistance is often costly, and international legal arguments are inherently conducive to counter-arguments. As Koskenniemi (1989: 43–9) notes, international legal arguments propound particular understandings of law that states present as simultaneously embodying both rules and practice. Consequently, arguments offered to justify uses of armed force are susceptible to counter-arguments that characterize them as purely descriptive accounts of international politics (based solely on state practice). These arguments, in turn, are susceptible to further counter-arguments that characterize them as purely prescriptive accounts of international politics (based solely on a narrow interpretation of codified rules).

Because international legal arguments are inherently susceptible to counter-arguments, it is not difficult for states to offer counter-arguments in bad faith, that is, counter-arguments that misrepresent their particular understandings of law. For example, major powers are unlikely to be threatened by actions that are confined to an area within which another major power has preponderant interest, or that involve limited operations against weak states and are unlikely to be repeated, because such actions are unlikely to enhance the relative power of the major power that engages in them. Nevertheless, because such actions are at least arguably illegal and are potentially threatening to less powerful states, these states may expect the major powers to offer counter-arguments condemning such actions. They may downgrade their prior beliefs regarding major powers that fail to offer counter-arguments, because the absence of counter-arguments suggests that the major powers are willing to accept the arbitrary use of armed force against less powerful states (Franck and Weisband 1971: 5). To prevent this from occurring, a major power may offer counter-arguments in response to actions that it does not perceive as threatening to the existing order, and in doing so, may misrepresent its understanding of the Charter.[5] It also may cast an unfavorable vote in the Security Council, although it will be unlikely to respond with other, more direct means of resistance outside of the Security Council. If a sole-veto or near-sole veto is likely, it may acquiesce, accompanying its unfavorable counter-argument with a favorable vote, or else abstain from voting. Similarly, even if they do not perceive a major power's actions as threatening to the existing order, less powerful states may offer counter-arguments and cast votes that are unfavorable, so as to restrain its actions by withholding legitimacy from them. In doing so, these states misrepresent their particular understandings of the Charter, although they, too, are unlikely to offer direct resistance through economic or political-military means. In pursuing a "double-standard" between acceptance of actions in one instance and resistance to similar actions in another instance (Franck 1984: 812), they use international law as a "weapon" in a contest of verbal sparring among states with which they disagree for political, historical, or strategic reasons (Hoffmann 1968: 41–3).

In either of these situations, the counter-arguments offered are likely to be vague, because in most instances the states offering them do not intend to be bound by them. Their counter-arguments are not intended to communicate their actual understandings of the Charter, but rather to indicate their disapproval of the actions in question. Hence, these counter-arguments are not subject to the same persuasiveness criteria as arguments offered to account for arguably-illegal uses of armed force, because in assessing a major power's uses of armed force, other states are more concerned with the level of dissent within the Security Council than the particularities of the counter-arguments offered by various states to communicate their dissent.

Resistance as enforcement

Major powers cannot know with certainty how other states will respond to their military actions. States might accept the actions, acquiesce in them, or respond with resistance to them, directly or indirectly. The anticipated likelihood of such resistance serves as an implicit means of enforcing the Charter's prohibition of force. States have incentive to respond with direct resistance against a major power that they believe threatens the existing order. However, to the extent that they are uncertain about its intentions or the long-term consequences of its actions, they might conclude that the major power is not a threat to the existing order and thus have incentive to respond with acquiescence or indirect resistance, rather than direct resistance. Because of the complexity of events, states cannot predict with certainty the long-term effects that particular actions might have on the stability of the existing order, and thus perceptions of threat vary from state to state (see Figure 3.2).

Less powerful states cannot coerce a major power, but by resisting it they can increase the economic and military resources that it must expend in order to achieve its foreign-policy goals (Pape 2005: 17), especially if their resistance is coordinated (Voeten 2005: 541–2). As Beetham (1991: 28) notes, "[w]hen the powerful have to concentrate most of their efforts on maintaining order, they are less able to achieve other goals; their power

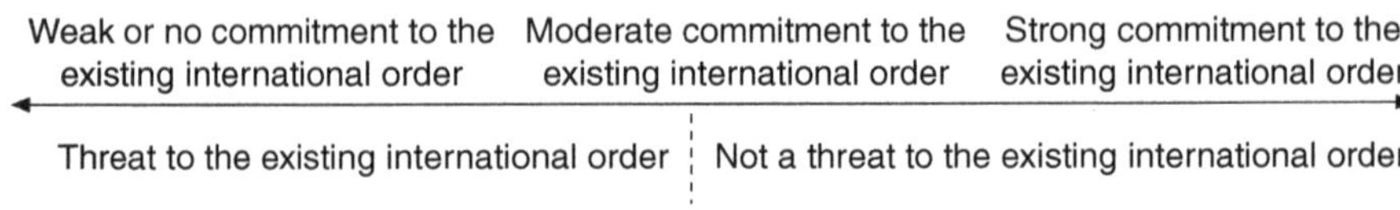

Figure 3.2 Assessing threats to the existing international order.

is to that extent less effective." A major power, then, is unlikely to undertake arguably illegal actions without concluding in some measure that such actions are necessary and attempting to offer persuasive legal arguments to account for them.

To the extent that a major power offers arguments in good faith, it communicates a particular understanding of law, and to the extent that its arguments contain restrictive claims, they provide a basis for other states to infer future restraint. However, because states are unable to ascertain with certainty whether a major power's arguments were offered in good faith or in bad faith, and because states assess arguments, in part, based upon the uniform application of the claims comprising them, an account is persuasive only if previous and subsequent actions accord with the claims that comprise the argument offered (Henkin 1979: 45; Schachter 1984c: 1623). A major power cannot acquire a signaling reputation, because its arguments provide only limited information regarding its understanding of the Charter's prohibition of force and its actions provide only a weak signal of its continuing commitment to the existing order (Jervis 1970: 80–1; Spence 1973: 355–6; Kreps and Wilson 1982: 275–6). Nevertheless, if a major power acts in a manner that seems to contradict its previous claims, then its actions are likely to induce other states to downgrade their prior beliefs regarding its commitment to the existing order and to respond with resistance to it.

Because the process of argumentation is intertemporal, the legal arguments offered by a major power have costs indirectly associated with them. The claims that comprise these arguments place restraints upon the major power that offered them by limiting the options available to it for military actions that can be justified without contradicting its previous claims and thereby undermining the persuasiveness of the account it has provided and the credibility of the signal it has sent. These claims constrain the manner and timing of its military actions by defining the Charter's parameters to proscribe actions taken under specific conditions (Henkin 1979: 29–30, 45). States are likely to respond with resistance to actions taken under these conditions, not necessarily because they disapprove of the actions themselves (although they might), but because the actions contradict claims contained within the major power's previous arguments and therefore suggest that the major power is not committed to the existing order and may have aggressive intentions.[6]

To reduce the likelihood of such resistance, a major power may exercise prudential restraint by altering the manner and timing of its military actions so that they are in accordance with its legal claims or an existing Security Council resolution (Schachter 1986: 123). It may wait to act until specific circumstances obtain, perhaps deploying military units but ordering them not to engage until circumstances obtain that provide a legal pretext for using armed force (Tillema and Van Wingen 1982: 238–40). In the meantime, it may seek to create the circumstances necessary for such a pretext (O'Connell 1975: 55–65; Shannon 2000: 306). Alternatively, it may engage in diplomacy in an attempt to obtain a permissive Security Council resolution or other authorization under Chapter VIII of the Charter. All things being equal, a permissive Security Council resolution is preferable, because it may allow the major power to avoid having to provide a detailed account for its actions in the current situation, which might restrain its actions in subsequent situations. Moreover, it moves the status quo point such that the major power's use of armed force will be scrutinized in comparison to the text of the resolution rather than the text of the Charter.

Denial and rhetorical evasion[7]

In making these decisions, major powers weigh the benefits of legitimation against the costs of altering the manner and timing of their military actions to conform to previous claims or an existing Security Council resolution. Legitimation is instrumentally valuable, insofar as it reduces the likelihood and severity of resistance against a major power in response to the arguments it offers, thereby reducing the costs that might be inflicted on it because of the actions it has taken. However, significant benefits might accrue from taking actions that contradict previous claims. Thus, if a major power is unable to justify its actions according to its previous claims or a permissive Security Council resolution, or if it believes that such a resolution is unlikely, then it may take actions that contradict its previous claims and have little or no basis in an existing Security Council resolution. But it does so at a cost to itself. Because of its veto, the major power needs not anticipate UN-authorized enforcement action against it, but it must anticipate resistance from states that perceive its actions as threatening. Such resistance imposes costs by increasing the economic and military resources that it must expend to achieve its foreign-policy goals (Hoffmann 1968: 42).

To minimize the costs of contradicting its previous claims, a major power may use strategies of denial and rhetorical evasion. A strategy of denial attempts to remove contradictions between arguments and actions by obscuring the actions that contradict previous claims. It involves acting covertly while denying the occurrence of the actions, the extent of the actions, or responsibility for the actions (Henkin 1979: 32). If covert action is not possible or is undesirable, a state may choose a strategy of rhetorical evasion. Rhetorical evasion attempts to remove contradictions between arguments and actions by obscuring the claims that the actions contradict. It involves reinterpreting previous claims to allow the actions taken in a subsequent incident. Because providing an account for an action characterizes that action as part of a limited category of legal behavior, legal claims influence the manner in which previous actions are understood (Schauer 1987: 573–7). Rhetorical evasion attempts to distinguish a current situation from a previous situation and thereby to remove the constraints placed on current actions by a previous claim.

Rhetorical evasion is preferable if previous claims were not communicated clearly, because obscure claims facilitate efforts to distinguish the present from the past. Legal arguments, however, are not infinitely manipulable. They contain parameter definitions that proscribe certain actions, and even if those definitions are intentionally vague, radical reinterpretation cannot obliterate them (Schachter 1986: 119–21; Franck 1988: 715). Indeed, if a major power offers an argument that radically reinterprets its previous claims, then other states are likely to conclude that its arguments were offered in bad faith, because they are incoherent. Accordingly, major powers attempt to include within their arguments claims that are vague and minimally restrictive, so as to avoid having to reinterpret previous arguments in a manner that is likely to elicit resistance from other states (Hoffmann 1968: 42; Boyle 1985: 167). To be persuasive, however, the claims that these arguments contain must be sufficiently restrictive to elicit response of acceptance or acquiescence from most states (Schachter 1991: 46–50). Thus, while major powers attempt to leave the maximum leeway for reinterpretation, they are limited by the signal thresholds of other states, which they attempt to meet by making claims that place at least some restrictions on their future actions. If a major power miscalculates and includes within its arguments claims that are not sufficiently restrictive to meet the signal thresholds of most states, it may add more restrictive claims to its arguments in an attempt to make its signal more credible. Explanatory hypothesis H_5 follows.

H_5: If there is a binding legal obligation to sustain the existing international order by refraining from the use of armed force, then major powers will attempt to reduce the likelihood of resistance by other states in response to their arguably illegal actions by altering the manner and timing of those actions or else engaging in strategies of denial or rhetorical evasion.

Empirical analysis

Having expanded our model to encompass the role of the Charter in legitimating the exercise of power and in creating a likelihood of resistance that serves as an implicit enforcement mechanism, we can continue the process of theory testing. As before, the units of observation are incidents (Willard 1988) in which major powers decided to use armed force within or against other states between October 1945 and October 2003.

Application of claims contained in counter-arguments

A fourth set of observations used in testing addresses the major powers' responses to uses of armed force by other major powers. These responses are indicators of the universality with which the major powers apply the claims contained within the counter-arguments they offer in response to such actions. According to hypothesis H_2, major powers have incentive to misrepresent their actual understandings of law in an attempt to disaffirm the unlawfulness of actions that, in general, might threaten the existing order but that they believe necessary to maintain their own relative power positions within that order. According to hypothesis H_4, states are likely to respond with resistance against a major power whose actions and accompanying arguments suggest that it is only weakly committed or no longer committed to the existing order. In some instances, however, states may conclude that, despite its arguably illegal actions, a major power does not pose a threat to the existing order. Specifically, if a major power uses armed force within a region in which it has preponderant interest, then other major powers are unlikely to conclude that its actions are threatening to the existing order. They are, therefore, unlikely to respond with direct resistance to it, although they are unlikely to respond with acceptance either, because doing so might signal to other states that the major powers have a tacit agreement among themselves regarding spheres of influence, and hence that none of them are truly committed to the existing order. Consequently, the claims comprising the counter-arguments offered in response to uses of armed force by another major power are unlikely to apply universally. Major powers will be less likely to respond with acceptance or direct resistance to uses of armed force in regions in which another major power has preponderant interest and more likely to respond with acquiescence or indirect resistance than if the actions occurred elsewhere.

Competing implications follow from the other models we have examined. According to the realist model, major powers offer counter-arguments to convey their will to other states, accompanied by threats or actions that alter those states' cost–benefit calculations (Hasenclever *et al.* 1997: 104–9). Because the claims contained within these counter-arguments vary according to the relative power of the target state, they do not apply universally. Thus, counter-arguments directed at another major power will contain claims that vary according to whether or not the incidents occurred within a region in which that major power has preponderant interest, irrespective of the signal such counter-arguments might send to less powerful states regarding the major powers' tacit acceptance of spheres of influence. Major powers will be more likely to respond with acceptance or acquiescence to uses of armed force by another major power within a region in which it has preponderant interest and less likely to respond with direct or indirect resistance than if the actions occurred elsewhere.

According to the liberal model, international law serves as a formal restatement of generally accepted rules that develop through interaction among states having a shared social purpose. Because states use international law to support the realization of shared values within the international system (McDougal 1960: 339–40, 350; Andrews 1975: 524–5), counter-arguments offered by a major power will vary according to the domestic social identity of the major power to which they are directed. Thus, major powers with similar regime types will be more likely to respond to each other's arguments with acceptance or acquiescence and less likely to respond to each other's arguments with direct or indirect resistance than major powers with different regime types.

According to the communal obligation model, states gradually come to see their actions from the perspective of an international community and become increasingly concerned with making claims that are generalizable, impartial, and consistent (Johnston 2001: 499–502; Mitzen 2005: 411). Thus, the major powers' responses to uses of armed force by another major power will vary only according to the actions' accordance with accepted rules of international law. They will not vary according to that major power's regime type or whether it acted within a region in which it has preponderant interest.[8] These observable implications are listed in Table 3.1.

We begin by evaluating this implication of the prudential restraint model, which requires coding observations of two additional variables. The first variable, RESPONSE, is coded to represent each major power's response to uses of armed force by another major power. As we have seen, a major power may respond with acceptance, acquiescence, indirect resistance, direct resistance by economic means, direct resistance by political-military means, or it may offer no response at all. Accordingly, observations of RESPONSE are coded as follows, in order of increasing resistance. If a major power, *m*, responds to another major power's use of armed force in an incident, *i*, with acceptance, then RESPONSE(*i, m*) = 0. If a major power, *m*, offers no response to another major power's use of armed force in an incident, *i*, then RESPONSE(*i, m*) = 1. If a major power, *m*, responds to another major power's use of armed force in an incident, *i*,

Table 3.1 Observable implications regarding the application of the claims comprising the counter-arguments offered by the major powers

Prudential restraint model	In response to uses of armed force in a region in which another major power has preponderant interest, major powers will be less likely to respond with acceptance or direct resistance and more likely to respond with acquiescence or indirect resistance than if the actions occurred elsewhere.
Realist model	In response to uses of armed force in a region in which another major power has preponderant interest, major powers will be more likely to respond with acceptance or acquiescence and less likely to respond with direct or indirect resistance than if the actions occurred elsewhere.
Liberal model	Major powers with similar regime types will be more likely to respond to each other's arguments with acceptance or acquiescence and less likely to respond with direct or indirect resistance than major powers with different regime types.
Communal obligation model	Major powers' responses to uses of armed force by another major power will not vary according to that major power's regime type or whether it acted within a region in which it has preponderant interest.

with acquiescence, then RESPONSE(i, m) = 2. If a major power, m, responds to another major power's use of armed force in an incident, i, with indirect resistance, then RESPONSE(i, m) = 3. If a major power, m, responds to another major power's use of armed force in an incident, i, with direct resistance through economic means, then RESPONSE(i, m) = 4. If a major power, m, responds to another major power's use of armed force in an incident, i, with direct resistance through political-military means, then RESPONSE(i, m) = 5.

The second variable, REGION, is coded to represent whether a major power has preponderant interest in the geographical region in which it used armed force. For the United States, the region of preponderant interest is defined to include the states of Central America and the Caribbean, as well as former overseas territories, such as the Philippines. For the Soviet Union, the region of preponderant interest is defined to include the member-states of the Warsaw Pact, while for Russia it is defined to include the member-states of the Commonwealth of Independent States. For the United Kingdom and France, the region of preponderant interest is defined to include all former overseas territories and colonies, with the exception of "settler colonies," such as Canada, Australia, and New Zealand. For

China, the region of preponderant interest includes the states of the Korean Peninsula and Southeast Asia. Observations of REGION are coded dichotomously as follows. If a major power uses armed force in an incident, *i*, within a region in which it has preponderant interest, then REGION(*i*) = 1. If a major power uses armed force in an incident, *i*, within a region in which it does not have preponderant interest, then REGION(*i*) = 0.

Because the prudential restraint model implies a nonlinear relationship between these variables, a cross-tabulation analysis is used and the results are shown in Table 3.2. As shown in the table, major powers were more likely to respond with acquiescence (22.6 percent vs. 21.6 percent) or indirect resistance (26.3 percent vs. 9.8 percent) to uses of armed force by another major power within a region in which it has preponderant interest than to uses of armed force occurring elsewhere. They were less likely to respond with acceptance (41.4 percent vs. 56.4 percent) or direct resistance (9.8 percent vs. 12.3 percent) to uses of armed force by another major power within a region in which it has preponderant interest than to uses of armed force occurring elsewhere. This inverted U-shaped relationship is consistent with the prudential restraint model.[9]

To evaluate the prudential restraint model in comparison with the other models, observations of an additional variable, DIFF_REGIME, are coded to represent the difference in regime types between the major power offering an argument for its uses of armed force and the major power responding to that use of armed force. Using observations of the variable REGIME, coded above to represent a major power's regime type, observations of DIFF_REGIME are coded as DIFF_REGIME(*i*, *m*) = Abs[REGIME(*i*) − REGIME(*m*)], where REGIME(*i*) is the observation of the variable REGIME for the major power using armed force in an incident, *i*, and REGIME(*m*) is the observation of the variable REGIME for a major power, *m*, responding to that use of armed force. Coded as the difference between the observations of REGIME for two major powers, DIFF_REGIME represents the difference in regime type between those two major powers. Pairs of major powers for

Table 3.2 Major powers' responses to uses of armed force by another major power (cross tabulation, $n = 337$)

	Acceptance	*Acquiescence*	*Indirect resistance*	*Direct resistance*	*Total*
Within area of preponderant interest	55 (41.4%)	30 (22.6%)	35 (26.3%)	13 (9.8%)	133 (100%)
Outside area of preponderant interest	115 (56.4%)	44 (21.6%)	20 (9.8%)	25 (12.3%)	204 (100%)

Note
Chi square = 47.83 (df = 3).

which DIFF_REGIME takes on smaller values have regimes that are more similar than pairs of major powers for which DIFF_REGIME takes on larger values.

Observations of two control variables are coded as well. The first variable, NATO, controls for joint NATO membership. During the Cold War, because of the threat of global communism, NATO members tended to support each other's actions throughout the world. Thus, they were less likely to respond with resistance to actions taken by fellow NATO members than they were to respond with resistance to actions taken by other major powers. Accordingly, observations of NATO are coded dichotomously, as follows. If a member of NATO is responding to a use of armed force by another member of NATO in an incident, *i*, then NATO(*i*) = 1. For all other incidents, NATO(*i*) = 0.

An interaction of NATO and COLD_WAR controls for the effects of joint NATO membership during the Cold War. Recall that COLD_WAR is coded as 1 during the Cold War and 0 after the Cold War, and thus the interaction of NATO and COLD_WAR cancels out the effect of joint NATO membership after the Cold War. The variable COLD_WAR also is used by itself to control for changes caused by the end of the Cold War. As rivals and adversaries during the Cold War, some major powers were less likely to respond to other major powers' arguments and actions with acceptance and more likely to respond with resistance than they were after the Cold War. The variable COLD_WAR controls for this effect.

Another variable, COVERT, controls for actions taken covertly. Covert actions are actions for which a major power attempts to conceal its participation or responsibility from other states. If a major power succeeds in its attempt to conceal, then other states will not be aware that the actions occurred, or that the major power participated in them, or that it was responsible for them (unless those states participated in those actions also). Even if a major power is aware of those actions, to the extent that other states remain unaware of them, it is not necessary for that major power to offer a response to those actions as a signal of its commitment to the existing order. The variable COVERT controls for these effects, with observations coded dichotomously, as follows. If a major power acts covertly in an incident, *i*, then COVERT(*i*) = 1. For all other incidents, COVERT(*i*) = 0.

The test here will be whether a major power's response to a use of armed force by another major power is a function of whether or not the action occurred within an area in which a major power has preponderant interest, whether or not the action was taken by a major power with a similar regime type, whether or not the action was taken covertly, whether or not the action was taken during the Cold War, and whether or not the action was taken by a fellow member of NATO. As before, an ordered probit model is used with all variables rescaled to the interval [0,1]. The results are shown in Table 3.3.

Table 3.3 Major power resistance to uses of armed force as a function of difference in regime type and region in which they occurred (ordered probit model, $n = 714$)

Variable name	*Coefficient (standard error)*
REGION	0.135 (0.085)
DIFF_REGIME	1.344 (0.158)
COLD_WAR	0.673 (0.122)
NATO*COLD_WAR	−0.052 (0.156)
COVERT	0.040 (0.082)

Note
Nagelkerke pseudo R-square = 0.282.

According to the realist model, major powers are unlikely to respond with resistance to uses of armed force by another major power in a region in which that major power has preponderant interest. Thus, resistance should be inversely correlated with spheres of influence, and the coefficient on REGION should be negative. However, this implication is not supported by the data. As shown in Table 3.3, the coefficient on REGION is positive with confidence of 89 percent, which is the opposite of what the realist model suggests. Recall, however, from Table 3.2 above that the relationship between RESPONSE and REGION is not linear, but rather U-shaped. The reason these variables appear to be directly correlated in the probit analysis is that, as one moves from a region in which a major power does not have a preponderant interest (i.e., REGION(i) = 0) to one in which it does (i.e., REGION(i) = 1), the probability of acceptance decreases dramatically and the probability of indirect resistance increases dramatically. Although the probability of acquiescence also increases and the probability of direct resistance also decreases, the magnitude of these changes is much smaller, such that the relationship between the two variables is reasonably approximated by a line with a positive slope, although the relationship is not strictly linear.

According to the liberal model, major powers with different regime types will be less likely to respond to each other's arguments with acceptance or acquiescence than major powers with similar regime types. Thus, resistance should be positively correlated with differences in regime type, and the coefficient on DIFF_REGIME should be positive. As shown in Table 3.3, this implication is supported by the data. Even while controlling for the effects of the Cold War and joint NATO membership, the coefficient on DIFF_REGIME is positive with confidence of greater than 99 percent. This finding suggests that major powers with similar regime types are more likely to respond favorably to each other's uses of armed force than to uses of armed force by other major powers, although this might simply be an artifact of the Cold War, with US and British interests remaining closely aligned and French interests gradually diverging from them (Huntington 1999: 42).

According to the communal obligation model, the major powers' responses to uses of armed force will vary only according to the actions' accordance with accepted rules of international law. Thus, resistance should not be correlated with spheres of influence or with differences in regime type. But as we have seen, this implication is not supported by the data. The major powers' responses to uses of armed force by another major power are a function of both the region in which the actions occurred and the regime type of the major power that engaged in them.

Effects on decision-making processes and outcomes

Note also from Table 3.3 that the coefficient on the control variable COVERT is positive rather than negative (as might be expected), although with confidence of only 47 percent. This finding suggests that resistance might be positively correlated with covert action. Consistent with hypothesis H_5, major powers are likely to act covertly if they anticipate direct resistance from other states, and when such actions are discovered they generally evoke resistance. Hypothesis H_5, however, suggests a range of available policy options in addition to covert action. According to this hypothesis, major powers will attempt to reduce the likelihood of resistance from other states in response to their arguably illegal actions by altering the manner and timing of those actions or else engaging in strategies of denial or rhetorical evasion. Thus, decision-makers within a major power will consider the anticipated likelihood and severity of resistance by other states, and both decision-making processes and outcomes will reflect such consideration. Decision-makers will be concerned with other states' assessments of the major power's commitment to the existing order, specifically that perceived violations of the Charter will lead other states to conclude that the major power is not committed to the existing order and that its unrestrained actions signal its aggressive intentions. Accordingly, a major power is likely to wait for circumstances that might reduce the likelihood and severity of such resistance and/or seek to create those circumstances. Alternatively, it may choose to act covertly and deny the occurrence of the actions, the extent of those actions, or responsibility for them. If decision-makers within a major power conclude that the arguments offered do not meet the signal thresholds of other states, then they may clarify those arguments by adding more restrictive claims to them.

Policy-making discussions regarding how other states might respond to the major powers' military actions, given the arguments offered for those actions, provide mixed support for both the prudential restraint model and the communal obligation model, because both models suggest that decision-makers will consider the responses of other states to the arguments offered. However, the concerns of the policy-makers engaged in such discussions differ according to each model. The prudential restraint model suggests that policy-makers will be concerned with other states' assessment of the major power's commitment to its legal obligations under the Charter and its intentions regarding the existing order, while the communal obligation model suggests that policy-makers will be concerned with other states' judgments of the major power's acceptance of communal values or its understanding of its communal responsibilities. According to the communal obligation model, states come to see their actions from the perspective of an international community and develop a capacity and an inclination for approaching problems collectively as they becoming increasingly concerned with being seen as responsible members of the international community (Mitzen 2001: 47–8, 66–77). Thus, decision-makers within a major power will consider the anticipated likelihood of condemnation resulting from other states' judgments that the major power acted in an unprincipled manner. The major powers therefore will become increasingly unlikely to use armed force without seeking authorization or approval from the Security Council, and they will evoke increasingly less dissent within the Security Council when they do so (Hurd 2000: 46–50; Mitzen 2001: 66–80, 91–3).

By contrast, the realist model suggests that, when considering the possible use of armed force, decision-makers within a major power will consider only the relative power of potential adversaries within the region in which the major power might use armed force and will not consider other states' responses to the arguments offered. A major power will use or not use armed force to achieve its interests based solely on the balance of forces within the region. In other words, the Charter's prohibition of force will have no effect upon decision-making processes and outcomes within the major powers.

According to the liberal model, international law penetrates into states' domestic legal systems and thereby reconstitutes their domestic social identities such that they are inclined to comply with international law (Koh 1997: 2654–5). The process is most effective in liberal states, because they are democratic and have a domestic political culture premised upon the rule of law (Henkin 1979: 315; Slaughter 1995: 513–20). Thus, international law will become entrenched in the domestic policy-making procedures of liberal major powers, such that decisions regarding the use of armed force will require the approval of domestic legal advisors and uses of armed force by liberal major powers generally will evoke less dissent within the Security Council than uses of armed force by nonliberal major powers do.

Because many of these implications (listed in Table 3.4) are best suited to qualitative methods of assessment, they will be examined in the case-study chapters that follow. However, we can evaluate certain implications

Table 3.4 Observable implications regarding the impact of the UN Charter on the major powers' decision-making processes and outcomes

Prudential restraint model	Decision-makers within a major power will be concerned that perceived violations of the Charter will lead other states to conclude that the major power is not committed to the existing order and respond with resistance to it. The major power will be likely to wait for and/or seek to create circumstances that provide a legal pretext for its actions or else act covertly.
Realist model	Decision-makers within a major power will consider only the relative power of potential adversaries within the region in which the major power might use armed force. In other words, the Charter's prohibition of force will have no effect upon decision-making processes and outcomes within the major powers.
Liberal model	Decision-makers within liberal major powers will require the approval of domestic legal advisors before deciding to use armed force. Accordingly, uses of armed force by liberal major powers generally will evoke less dissent within the Security Council than uses of armed force by nonliberal major powers do.
Communal obligation model	Decision-makers within a major power will become increasingly concerned with other states' judgments of the major power's acceptance of communal values or its understanding of its communal responsibilities. The major powers will become increasingly unlikely to use armed force without seeking authorization or approval from the Security Council and will evoke increasingly less dissent within the Security Council when they do so.

of the communal obligation model and the liberal model using quantitative methods. To evaluate these implications, observations of a variable, DISSENT, are coded to represent the level of dissent within the Security Council in response to a major power's use of armed force.[10] Observations of DISSENT are coded as follows, in order of increasing dissent. If the Security Council approves a resolution that explicitly authorizes a major power's actions in an incident, *i*, then DISSENT(i) = 0. If the Security Council approves a resolution that implicitly authorizes a major power's actions in an incident, *i*, or if a proposed resolution that explicitly authorizes its actions fails because of a sole veto or near-sole veto, then DISSENT(i) = 1. If the Security Council takes no action regarding a major power's actions in an incident, *i*, then DISSENT(i) = 2. If a proposed Security

Council resolution condemning the actions of a major power in an incident, *i*, lacks the necessary votes, irrespective of the major power's veto, then DISSENT(*i*) = 3. If the Security Council approves a resolution condemning the actions of a major power in an incident, *i*, then DISSENT(*i*) = 4. If the major power uses its veto to defeat a proposed Security Council resolution condemning its actions in an incident, *i*, and other major powers also use their veto or abstain from voting, then DISSENT(*i*) = 5. If the major power uses its veto to defeat a proposed Security Council resolution condemning its actions in an incident, *i*, and one or more non-permanent members of the Security Council concurs, then DISSENT(*i*) = 6. If the major power uses its veto to defeat a proposed Security Council resolution condemning its actions in an incident, *i*, and no other members of the Security Council concur, then DISSENT(*i*) = 7.

As before, the variable COLD_WAR is used to control for the end of the Cold War, which brought about a reduction of tensions between the Soviet Union and the other major powers. Because the level of dissent within the Security Council is likely to reflect this reduction in tension, another variable, COLD_WAR, is used to control for the effects of this exogenous change. The variable COVERT is used again, also, because the Security Council cannot address the actions of a major power if those actions remain concealed.

The test here will be whether the level of dissent within the Security Council is a function of the regime type of the major power that used armed force, the length of time that major power has held a seat as a permanent member of the Security Council, whether or not the actions occurred during the Cold War, and whether or not those actions were taken covertly. Because DISSENT is an ordinal variable, an ordered probit model is used, with all variables rescaled to the interval [0,1]. The results are shown in Table 3.5.

According to the liberal model, uses of armed force by liberal major powers will require the approval of domestic legal advisors and will evoke less dissent within the Security Council than uses of armed force by nonlib-

Table 3.5 Dissent within the Security Council as a function of a major power's regime type and time as a permanent member of the Security Council (ordered probit model, $n = 196$)

Variable name	*Coefficient (standard error)*
REGIME	−0.669 (0.349)
TIME_ON	0.806 (0.540)
COLD_WAR	1.358 (0.329)
COVERT	−0.027 (0.164)

Note
Nagelkerke pseudo R-square = 0.188.

eral major powers will. Thus, dissent within the Security Council should be inversely correlated with regime type, and the coefficient on REGIME should be negative. This implication is weakly supported by the data. As shown in Table 3.5, the coefficient on REGIME is negative, but with confidence of only 90 percent, which is less than the 95 percent confidence level typically used in tests such as this. It may be that liberal major powers evoke less dissent within the Security Council than nonliberal major powers do, but it is unclear from the data.

According to the communal obligation model, over time the major powers will become increasingly less likely to use armed force without seeking authorization or approval from the Security Council and will evoke increasingly less dissent within the Security Council when they do so. Thus, dissent within the Security Council should be inversely correlated with the length of time that a major power has held a seat as a permanent member of the Security Council, and the coefficient on TIME_ON should be negative. However, this implication is not supported by the data. Controlling for the end of the Cold War, the coefficient on TIME_ON is positive, although with confidence of only 86 percent. This suggests that, if anything, there is a trend toward *increasing* dissent in the Security Council. If this is so, it might be a reflection of increasingly divergent interests among the major powers or perhaps a response to emerging US dominance. These possibilities are examined in the concluding chapter of this book.

To evaluate the remaining implications, the chapters that follow use process-tracing, a within-case method of "structured, focused comparison" that tests comparable predictions of competing theories by asking "standardized general questions" regarding causal mechanisms in each case examined (George and McKeown 1985: 35–7, 41–2). Because this method uses a smaller number of observations than quantitative methods of assessment require, it is particularly suited to testing the remaining implications, which address policy-making modalities within the major powers. Such assessment also serves as a necessary supplement to large-n analysis. Large-n testing provides systematic examination of correlations between variables. Case studies, however, provide more direct examination of the causal logic of each model (Russett 1974: 17–20) and the explanation each provides for the functioning of the Charter as a restraint on state action.

4

THE IMPACT OF THE UN CHARTER ON US MILITARY INTERVENTION IN THE CARIBBEAN REGION, 1953–61

US military intervention in the Caribbean region during the period from 1953 through 1961 included the overthrow of the government of Jacobo Arbenz in Guatemala and the attempted overthrow of the governments of Fidel Castro in Cuba and Rafael Trujillo in the Dominican Republic. According to the prudential restraint model, when contemplating military interventions such as these, decision-makers within a major power will be concerned that perceived violations of the Charter will lead other states to conclude that the major power is no longer committed to the existing order and respond with resistance to it. Thus, when formulating arguments for uses of armed force, decision-makers will consider claims made in similar situations in the past and claims that might be made in similar situations in the future and will formulate their arguments accordingly – or else attempt to obscure the contradictions between them – in an attempt to provide a persuasive account for the actions taken. Moreover, the major power will be likely to wait for and/or seek to create circumstances that provide a legal pretext for its actions or else act covertly and deny the occurrence of the actions, the extent of the actions, or its participation in them, in order to reduce the likelihood of resistance from other states in response to those actions.

As this chapter demonstrates, the prudential restraint model provides a more compelling explanation for US decision-making processes and outcomes in these cases than any of the competing models does. In all three cases, US policy-makers delayed planned military operations to seek Organization of American States (OAS) authorization under Chapter VIII of the UN Charter – despite the risks inherent in such delays – out of concern that Latin American states would perceive the United States as an aggressor and respond with resistance to it. When OAS authorization appeared unlikely, US policy-makers decided to act covertly and deny US involvement. The resulting changes to the manner and timing of these operations contributed to their failure in two of the three cases, prompting the Soviet Union to deploy nuclear weapons to Cuba and creating fears among US policy-makers that unrest in the Dominican Republic would lead to a Communist takeover of the island.

These cases are useful for purposes of theory testing because there is variance both within and among them in key explanatory variables, including the government holding office in the United States, the types of actions taken, the arguments offered for those actions, and other states' responses to those actions. Holding the time period, region, and intervening power constant across these cases controls for contextual variables that otherwise might affect observed outcomes (George and McKeown 1985: 25, 32, 45). In addition, the cases are well documented, with much primary source material having been declassified.[1]

Guatemala, 1953–54

US intervention in Guatemala came in response to the policies of Guatemalan president Jacobo Arbenz, who upon taking office in November 1950 had pursued close ties with the Soviet Union. In March 1952, a National Intelligence Estimate concluded that increasing communist influence in Guatemala adversely affected US interests and constituted "a potential threat to U.S. security" (*FRUS 1952–54*, IV: 1031–7), and in June of that same year, Arbenz expropriated 400,000 acres of uncultivated land owned by the United Fruit Company, a US-based multinational corporation. Soon afterwards, the CIA began to suspect that Guatemala was providing weapons and assistance to communist rebels in Haiti and Costa Rica (*FRUS 1952–54*, IV: 1055–6). Consequently, US President Dwight Eisenhower requested that the State Department begin analyzing possible plans of action for responding to the situation in Guatemala.

A draft policy paper sent to Eisenhower in August 1953 by the State Department's Bureau of Inter-American Affairs exemplified US policy-makers' concerns that perceived violations of US legal commitments under the Charter might "endanger the entire fund of good will the United States has built up ... through its policy of non-intervention." The paper warned that direct military intervention would be likely to evoke resistance from Latin American states, possibly including military arrangements with the Soviet Union, a consequence that the paper characterized as "a disaster for the United States far outweighing the advantage of any success gained" through direct military intervention. If the United States were to intervene in Guatemala, the paper recommended that it do so covertly, collecting a "case record" of "communist penetration" in Guatemala "in order to determine when its nature is such that its presentation would elicit sufficient support from other American Republics" to obtain OAS authorization under Chapter VIII of the UN Charter. Without such authorization, the paper warned, even "secret stimulation and natural support of the overthrow of the Arbenz Government would subject us to serious hazards ... [and] the effects on our relations in this hemisphere could be as disastrous as those produced by open intervention" (*FRUS 1952–54*, IV: 1074–86).

Based upon these conclusions, Eisenhower requested that the CIA begin planning a covert military operation to overthrow the Arbenz government. Both Eisenhower and Secretary of States John Foster Dulles realized that, if the United States were to intervene in Guatemala under the existing circumstances, it would be difficult for US policy-makers to formulate a persuasive legal argument to account for the actions taken. Consequently, Eisenhower ordered that the implementation of the plan be delayed until circumstances obtained under which OAS support seemed likely (Pagedas 1995: 59). Even if OAS support could be obtained, however, Eisenhower preferred that the actions remain covert, because he believed that denial would provide a better account for such actions than the proposed legal justification for them as undertaken in accordance with Chapter VIII of the Charter.

Initially, the costs of delaying the proposed operation were minimal, since the CIA would require several months to complete its training of the rebel force, including the provision of unmarked B-26 bombers and other armaments, as well as the infiltration of the Guatemalan armed forces to encourage its leadership not to support Arbenz in the event of a coup (Immerman 1982: 135–7; Blum 1995: 76). However, these costs began to increase substantially as information regarding the proposed operation began reaching the Guatemalan government in January 1954. In a series of public statements offered over the next several weeks, Guatemalan officials identified various individuals involved in the planned operation as well as the location of the secret training base in Honduras, claiming that the United States was conspiring with Nicaragua and Honduras to overthrow the Guatemalan government (Hilaire 1997: 31–2). In response, State Department officials released a statement declaring that the policy of the United States was "not to intervene in the internal affairs of other nations" and that this policy of nonintervention had "repeatedly been reaffirmed." According to the statement, the claims made by Guatemala regarding US preparations for military intervention were "ridiculous and untrue," part of "an increasingly mendacious propaganda campaign" intended to disrupt the work of the Tenth Inter-American Conference of the OAS, which was scheduled for March (*DSB 1954*, 30: 251–2). The statement's reference to the upcoming OAS meeting was part of US policy-makers' legal strategy of seeking implicit or explicit OAS authorization to "lay the groundwork" for "positive action" against Guatemala. Policy-makers believed that succeeding in this would assist them in persuading other states that the United States had no aggressive intentions and was not "leading a movement against one of its small neighbors" (Schlesinger and Kinzer 1999: 124).

Secretary of State Dulles hoped to obtain from OAS member states "a clear-cut and unmistakable policy determination against the intervention of international communism in the hemisphere . . . declaring their intention to take effective measures, individually and collectively, to combat it" (*DSB 1954*, 30: 634). Although seeking OAS authorization would delay the proposed operation for at least two more months, US policy-makers were willing to accept the consequent risk to the operation because they hoped that obtaining a permissive OAS resolution would increase the persuasiveness of US legal arguments. As Immerman (1982: 143) notes, US policy-makers "considered it essential that they establish the proper international climate," so that if US involvement in the operation were discovered, then other states would be less likely to view the operation as an illegal "surrogate invasion" and respond with resistance to it.

On 6 March, the OAS approved a resolution (commonly referred to as the "Declaration of Caracas"). The resolution declared that "the domination or control of the political institutions of any American state by . . . an extra-continental power would constitute a threat to the sovereignty and political independence of the American States." Under the resolution, member states of the OAS could call for a meeting of consultation "to consider the adoption of measures in accordance with existing treaties," although such measures must be "designed to protect and not to impair the inalienable right of each American State freely to choose its own form of government and economic system and to live its own social and cultural life" (*DSB 1954*, 30: 420). The resolution received nearly unanimous support; however, most states merely acquiesced in possible US military action rather than accepting it, expressing doubts concerning the communist nature of the Arbenz regime and concerns that the resolution might help to legitimize US intervention in other American states (Slater 1967: 118–20; Schlesinger and Kinzer 1999: 144–5). Nevertheless, US policy-makers believed that the Declaration bolstered the legal claim underpinning possible US intervention in Guatemala and that "proceeding along the lines of the Resolution" by requesting a meeting of consultation of the OAS would give armed intervention in Guatemala a "legitimate appearance" and thus reduce the likelihood of resistance from other states (Immerman 1982: 146–50).

While most US policy-makers agreed that it would be difficult to formulate a persuasive legal argument for military intervention in Guatemala without obtaining OAS authorization, they realized that seeking explicit authorization had a "disagreeable and disadvantageous" aspect, insofar as the failure to obtain an OAS resolution after calling a meeting of consultation inevitably would weaken the United States' legal position (*FRUS, 1952–54*, IV: 1102–5). Despite this disadvantage, however, Assistant Secretary of State Henry Holland urged Dulles to continue operating through the OAS, because doing so would provide a firm legal basis for military intervention, while "to move unilaterally in Guatemala . . . would be inconsistent with our treaty obligations and the firm policy which we have followed in this hemisphere" and would suggest that the United States was no longer committed to the UN Charter system (*FRUS 1952–54*, IV: 1107–11). In agreement with Holland's assessment, Dulles recommended to Eisenhower that military operations be delayed yet again while policy-makers sought explicit OAS authorization for intervening in Guatemala (*FRUS 1952–54*, IV: 1102–5).

US policy-makers sought to create a legal pretext for intervention by other means as well, planting caches of Soviet weapons throughout Guatemala. These efforts proved to be a failure, with observers dismissing the "discoveries" of the weapons as a hoax (Schlesinger and Kinzer 1999: 150). Soon afterwards, however, a new set of circumstances obtained that US policy-makers believed would provide a sufficient legal pretext for intervening without awaiting OAS authorization. On 17 May, the State Department announced the discovery of a 2,000-ton shipment of light artillery and small arms aboard a Swedish freighter bound for Guatemala (*DSB 1954*, 30: 835).[2] Because of Guatemala's existing military advantage vis-à-vis Honduras, US policy-makers hoped to argue persuasively that intervention in Guatemala was lawful as collective self-defense of Honduras, in accordance with the Rio Pact. Even so, Eisenhower ordered an additional month's delay to allow Dulles sufficient time to present a new set of legal claims, despite the risk that more weapons shipments would arrive in Guatemala.

In offering arguments to justify the proposed intervention, Dulles emphasized the United States' commitment to the existing order, declaring that the United States would act "under the Rio Pact, and in full conformity with [its] treaty obligations." According to Dulles, Guatemala was a threat to international peace and security in the region, having "made gestures against its neighbors which they deem to be threatening and which have led them to appeal for aid" (*DSB 1954*, 30: 874). In offering these arguments, Dulles attempt to obscure the contradiction of his previous claims, which had implied that OAS authorization was necessary for intervention in Guatemala, by purposely avoiding any further mention of the OAS.[3] On 20 May, he sent a circular telegram to US ambassadors, instructing them to inform their accredited governments of the United States' position that "sudden and significant reinforcement of Guatemalan military power by communist-supplied armament" was a "problem that should be carefully reviewed by each government in light of such Inter-American [treaty] commitments as may be involved." Dulles instructed the ambassadors to "confine [their] reply to statement[s] of [the] genuine and serious nature of our concern" and not to mention prior claims regarding OAS authorization (*FRUS 1952–54*, IV: 1117–18).

Meanwhile, Dulles and Holland turned their attention to the more immediate problem of preventing additional shipments of arms to Guatemala in the days prior to the planned intervention. Holland considered using naval forces to detain and search suspicious vessels bound for Guatemala, justifying these actions under Article 4 of the Rio Pact as necessary to secure the peace and security of the hemisphere against the possible introduction of nuclear weapons into the region. These claims would build upon Dulles' claims of collective self-defense under that same treaty. The State Department Assistant Legal Advisor, however, counseled against this policy, noting that, "[w]hile legally, it might be justified ... it is to be borne in mind that such legislation would create a precedent for similar action by other powers," to the detriment of the United States. The Assistant Legal Advisor recommended a policy of restraint, warning that there were likely to be "consequences of charges of violation of freedom of the seas [and] violation of the sovereignty of the country in whose port they might be found" and speculated that such resistance might even rise to the level of military action (*FRUS 1952–54*, IV: 1113). Deputy Under-Secretary of State Robert Murphy agreed, arguing that such actions likely would prove "very expensive over the longer term" because of the resistance they would evoke from other states (Schlesinger and Kinzer 1999: 161).

Although Holland rejected Murphy's conclusion, he seems to have considered both the risks that Guatemala would receive additional shipments of weapons before the planned intervention and the likelihood of resistance from other states in response to involuntary search and seizure of vessels upon the high seas. His disagreement with Murphy was not over whether states might respond with resistance to such arguably illegal actions, but rather the likelihood and severity of such resistance. Believing resistance to be unlikely in this instance, Holland suggested urging states to divert their ships voluntarily, while authorizing the use of force if necessary to prevent additional arms shipments that would endanger the success of the covert intervention (*FRUS 1952–54*, IV: 1120–2). Attorney General Herbert Brownell, Jr. noted that, although "[s]uch action was in general outside the limits of international law," there was a "well-established exception which permitted interference with vessels of another nation on the high seas if self-defense or self-preservation was clearly involved." Brownell warned, however, that there would be "a division among international lawyers on this question" and that it therefore would be necessary to make a persuasive legal claim that Guatemala was importing arms "well in excess of its self-defense needs" and posing a threat to neighboring states and to the Panama Canal (*FRUS 1952–54*, IV: 1131–5).

Concerned with the effects that these arguments might have on future situations, US policy-makers hoped that they would be able to persuade most foreign-flag states to submit voluntarily to searches, making forcible search and seizure unnecessary. In the event that such actions proved necessary, however, Dulles sent a circular telegram to US ambassadors instructing them to inform their accredited governments of the United States' position that a "Soviet thrust into the Western Hemisphere by establishing and maintaining a communist-controlled state ... would represent a challenge to hemispheric security and peace." By importing large quantities of weapons, Guatemala posed an "increasing threat" to the hemisphere, and additional shipments of arms "would further augment Guatemala's preponderant military position in the area" (*FRUS 1952–54*, IV: 1137–9).

As US-trained rebel forces crossed into Guatemala from Honduras on 18 June, the State Department denied US involvement, claiming that there was "no evidence that indicates this is anything other than a revolt of Guatemalans against the Government" (*DSB 1954*, 30: 982). Guatemala, however, appealed to the Security Council, alleging aggression by Honduras and Nicaragua (UN Doc. S/3232). Henry Cabot Lodge, the US representative to the United Nations, responded by claiming that the situation in Guatemala was not subject to the jurisdiction of the Security Council because it did not involve aggression. According to Lodge, the OAS was the appropriate organization to address the situation, and if the Security Council did not allow the OAS to attempt a peaceful settlement of the dispute between Guatemala and its neighbors, it would "gravely impair the further effectiveness of the United Nations." On 20 June, the Security Council unanimously approved a resolution calling for "the immediate termination of any action likely to cause bloodshed" and requesting states "to abstain ... from rendering assistance to any such action" (UN Doc. S/Res/104), but a vote to retain the matter on the Security Council's agenda failed, and the matter was referred to the OAS for consideration.

Because much of the Guatemalan military had remained loyal to Arbenz, the rebel advance stalled near the town of Esquipulas (Pagedas 1995: 61). Eventually, however, strafing from the rebel bombers, combined with misleading radio broadcasts from a series of radio transmitters hidden throughout Guatemala, created panic and disorder sufficient to convince Arbenz to resign. On 30 June, Dulles declared that the situation in Guatemala had been "cured by the Guatemalans themselves," and on 7 July, Colonel Carlos Enrique Castillo Armas was named provisional president of Guatemala (*DSB 1954*, 31: 44). The operation thus achieved its objective of overthrowing the Arbenz government, despite having been undertaken covertly and delayed repeatedly – all part of the US attempt to send a credible signal of its commitment to the existing international order.

Not all states were persuaded by US legal arguments, however. When the OAS convened a special meeting to consider a proposal for a fact-finding mission, Argentina, Chile, Ecuador, and Uruguay alleged US involvement in Guatemala and characterized US actions as aggression (Blum 1995: 79). Although the United States was able to block the proposal until 5 July, when Guatemala reported to the OAS that a dispute no longer existed (Immerman 1982: 173), the cases examined below suggest that these states may have downgraded their prior beliefs regarding the US commitment to the existing order.

Cuba, 1959–61

US policy-makers faced a similar situation in Cuba five years later, following the January 1959 overthrow of the Cuban government of Fulgencio Batista by rebels under the leadership of Fidel Castro. Soon after taking office, the Castro government began pursuing close ties to the Soviet Union and expropriating foreign property in Cuba. On 17 March 1960, Eisenhower approved preliminary plans for invading Cuba to prevent the establishment of a communist government there (*FRUS 1958–60*, VI: 850–1).

As in the Guatemala case, US policy-makers expressed concern that perceived violations of the United States' legal commitments under the Charter might evoke resistance from other states, but noted that an OAS resolution recognizing a provisional government in Cuba would provide a "fig leaf" for direct US military intervention, which could then be justified as having been undertaken in accordance with Chapter VIII of the Charter (*FRUS 1961–63*, X: 46–52). According to a Department of Defense study, in the absence of such a resolution, unless Cuba attacked the US naval base at Guantánamo, there would lack a sufficient legal pretext for direct military intervention, and acting without such a pretext would evoke a "long period of world condemnation" that would have "enormous implications" for future US policy (*FRUS 1961–63*, X: 36–40). Accordingly, Eisenhower ordered that the operation be covert and that it be delayed until a suitable legal pretext obtained (Higgins 1987: 35; Kornbluh 1998: 269–70).

The initial costs of delaying the proposed operation were minimal, since the CIA would require several months to complete the training of the rebel forces in Guatemala, including the provision of unmarked B-26 bombers and other weapons not readily traceable to the United States, as well as the dropping of supplies to rebel forces already in Cuba. These costs began to increase, however, as the invasion plan grew more complex and news stories concerning the operation began appearing in newspapers throughout Guatemala (Wyden 1979: 35–8, 45–64). Moreover, as the summer progressed and Cuban forces began apprehending rebels and intercepting the supplies being dropped into Cuba, the CIA began losing confidence in the success of the mission, noting that the Castro government was growing stronger as Soviet military assistance continued (Kornbluh 1998: 76–7,

151). Nevertheless, despite the increased risk that the proposed operation would fail, US policy-makers continued to delay its implementation, awaiting a legal pretext for military intervention.

In July 1960, Cuba brought the matter to the attention of the Security Council, claiming that the United States had offered protection to Cuban rebels and illegally had sent aircraft into Cuban airspace, creating a "grave situation endangering international peace and security" (UN Doc. S/4378). The United States responded by emphasizing its commitment to upholding its legal obligations under the Charter and claiming that it had "no aggressive purposes against Cuba." It rejected the claims made by Cuba and argued, as before, that the proper forum to discuss the matter was the OAS (UN Doc. S/4388). On 19 July, the Security Council approved a resolution "to adjourn the consideration of [the matter] pending the receipt of a report from the Organization of American States" and urging "all other States to refrain from any action which might increase the existing tensions between Cuba and the United States" (UN Doc. S/Res/144).

As in the Guatemala case, US policy-makers' strategy focused on obtaining an OAS resolution implicitly or explicitly authorizing military action under Chapter VIII of the UN Charter (Gleijeses 1995: 5). On 29 August, the OAS approved a US-sponsored resolution condemning "the intervention or threat of intervention by an extracontinental power in the affairs of the American Republics" and declaring that "the acceptance of a threat of extracontinental intervention by any American state endangers American solidarity and security" (*DSB 1960*, 43: 408). The resolution, however, made explicit reference to "the principle of non-intervention by any American state in the internal or external affairs of other American states," while excluding language evoking a meeting of consultation to address "threats to peace and security" under Article 53 of the Charter, which the United States specifically had sought to have included (Hilaire 1997: 44). Viewed in light of the Guatemalan intervention, then, the resolution (commonly referred to as the Declaration of San José) represented indirect resistance from Latin American states unwilling to accept further US military intervention under the existing circumstances. Although they condemned Soviet interference in Cuba, many states offered arguments critical of US policy as well (Slater 1967: 146–8).

The failure to obtain a more permissive resolution was a significant setback for the United States, insofar as the CIA had concluded several months previously that overthrowing the Cuban government would require a direct military assault involving more forces than would be available from among the rebels being trained in Guatemala (Wyden 1979: 68–75; Gleijeses 1995: 9–10). The proposed solution had been to fly in a provisional government that the United States would recognize and that would then request military assistance (*FRUS 1961–63*, X: 10–16). The

Declaration of San José made OAS recognition of such a government – the "fig leaf" that Eisenhower needed – unlikely.

Upon taking office in January 1961, President John F. Kennedy and his advisors immediately began formulating a response to the situation in Cuba. Expressing concern regarding the possibility of resistance from other states in response to arguably illegal US military actions, Secretary of State Dean Rusk requested a study of "the effects of covert U.S. action in Cuba on the rest of the world" (*FRUS 1961–63*, X: 52–3). Other US policy-makers echoed this concern (Gleijeses 1995: 28). Presidential Advisor Arthur Schlesinger, who opposed the operation, urged Kennedy to avoid any actions that the United States could not plausibly deny and to formulate persuasive legal arguments so that other states would not "assume that our action is provoked by a threat to something other than our security." Schlesinger made specific reference to other states' assessments of US intentions based on its actions and the legal arguments accompanying them and cautioned that the United States might be labeled an "aggressor," just as the Soviet Union had been in Hungary[4] (*FRUS 1961–63*, X: 186–9, 196–203). Under-Secretary of State Chester Bowles argued that acting in defiance of the United States' legal obligations under the Charter "would deal a blow" to a system that is "the condition not only of a lawful and orderly world, but of the mobilization of our own power." Such restraint was necessary to ensure the continuation of the UN Charter system (*FRUS 1961–63*, X: 178–81).

Because of concerns such as these, Kennedy decided to act as Eisenhower had. Authorizing the creation of a provisional Cuban government, Kennedy ordered that the proposed operation remain covert so as not to appear to be a US-led invasion (Kornbluh 1998: 288). Kennedy also ordered that the invasion, which was scheduled to take place in February, be delayed to allow time for US policy-makers to make another attempt at obtaining OAS authorization, although he instructed Rusk that these efforts "should proceed as quickly as possible" (*FRUS 1961–63*, X: 65; Schlesinger Jr. 1965: 181–5).

This additional delay further increased the costs and risks associated with the proposed operation. Eisenhower had concluded that the operation must take place "not later than 1 March 1961" because of the expected delivery of additional arms to Cuba that month and because of pressure from Guatemala regarding the training bases located there (*FRUS 1961–63*, X: 10–16). In late 1960, the CIA had reported that Cuban rebels in Guatemala "were getting seriously restive and threatening to get out of hand before they could be committed," and that following a military revolt sparked by the rebels in November, the Guatemalan government was urging the United States to "take [them] away" (Gleijeses 1995: 15, 27; Kornbluh 1998: 54). Kennedy received a similar report from the CIA in early March, which noted that the rebels' morale could "not be maintained if their commitment to action is long delayed." Following the mutiny that had occurred in late January, it would be "infeasible" to keep them in Guatemala much longer (Kornbluh 1998: 119).

The question of how much longer to delay the proposed operation thus prompted sharp disagreement among US policy-makers, although their discussions continued to examine the likelihood and severity of resistance from other states in response to arguably illegal US actions. Adolph Berle, Chief of the State Department's Latin American Task Force, argued that the United States could not continue to "delay or drift" because doing so would allow Cuba to acquire "a large military capability which can only be reduced by war." Assistant Secretary of State Thomas Mann disagreed, acknowledging the time constraints but arguing that the United States inevitably would be committed once the invasion took place and would require legal backing by the OAS or else face "very grave" consequences. Awaiting OAS authorization would delay the operation until 31 March at the earliest, but the delay was necessary to provide "a defensible position in the UN" and to make support of the provisional government "possible with some degree of legality," thereby bolstering the United States' position "in the eyes of the hemisphere" (*FRUS 1961–63*, X: 81–9).

Mann reiterated this position in a memorandum to Rusk, arguing that direct intervention by the United States "would be in violation of Article 2, paragraph 4, and Article 51 of the Charter of the United Nations, Articles 18 and 25 of the Charter of the Organization of American States, and Article 1 of the Rio Treaty," and as a consequence Cuba "could be expected to call on the other American States . . . to assist them in repelling the attack, and to request the Security Council . . . to take action." Because these states could be expected to pose "impediments to dealing with the Cuban situation," Mann concluded that, although "time is running against us in Cuba in the military sense . . . we should consider proceeding as planned only if we receive strong support for collective action by the two-thirds majority required by the Rio Treaty . . . [for the] recognition of a rebel government" (*FRUS 1961–63*, X: 95–9).[5]

Berle suggested, on the other hand, that if OAS action were necessary, it could follow at the appropriate time, and if at that time the OAS refused to act, the United States could argue that the OAS was "ineffectual as an organization" and that "in order to live up to our responsibilities under the treaties . . . we have no recourse but to take unilateral military action" (*FRUS 1961–63*, X: 89). Berle seemingly was aware of the legal difficulties his proposal would create, not the least of which was the proposal's contradiction of previous US legal claims that regional action through the OAS was necessary for the continued effectiveness of the Charter system, as well as the proposal's effect of precluding this option in similar situations in the future. Indeed, Berle told Kennedy the next day that "it would be impossible, as things stand now" for the United States to intervene in Cuba directly without "being cast in the role of aggressor" (*FRUS 1961–63*, X: 90–91). His disagreement with Mann was not over whether to consider other states' responses to the arguments offered, but rather over how likely the success of the covert action would be and how severe the resistance from other states would be if the covert action did not succeed and the United States found it necessary to intervene in Cuba directly. Berle accepted the CIA's assessment that, although "there would be adverse political repercussions to landing in force," resistance from other states would be "minimal" and "short-lived" if the operation were "quickly successful" (*FRUS 1961–63*, X: 99–107). He believed that further delay would only reduce the likelihood of the operation's success, which in turn would make it more likely that the United States would need to seek OAS authorization for direct intervention. By contrast, proceeding without waiting for OAS authorization would increase the likelihood of the operation's success, and alternatively, the likelihood of a "quick" intervention if the covert operation failed, making it unlikely that the United States would have to argue that the OAS was "ineffectual." Secretary of State Rusk, apparently more cautious than Berle, suggested to Kennedy that "without careful – and successful – diplomatic preparation" within the OAS, intervention in Cuba would "have grave effects upon the U.S. position in Latin America and at the U.N." (*FRUS 1961–63*, X: 90–1).

Agreeing with Rusk, Kennedy delayed the proposed operation until early April, despite warnings from the CIA that "[t]he onset of the rainy season in Guatemala in April would greatly accentuate [the] problem" of morale among the rebels and would make an amphibious landing in Cuba significantly more difficult (Kornbluh 1998: 119). The CIA also had warned that Cuba would have jet capability by late March, once its pilots completed training in Czechoslovakia (*FRUS 1961–63*, X: 81–8), but Kennedy remained unswayed, dispatching Berle on a diplomatic mission to Latin America with instructions to take "careful diplomatic soundings" regarding possible support for OAS action against Cuba (Gleijeses 1995: 21).

To mitigate the costs of this additional delay, US policy-makers considered a blockade to prevent additional shipments of weapons from reaching Cuba. Department of Defense representative Haydn Williams argued that such action would violate existing treaties. Berle added that a blockade "would create more problems for us than it would solve," because other states were likely to respond with resistance to such a clear breach of international law. Accordingly, US policy-makers decided that search and seizure tactics would not be employed on the high seas, but only at ports of call "where local arrangements could be set up without any particular difficulty or risk" (*FRUS 1961–63*, X: 81–8).

On 11 March, Berle reported to Kennedy that OAS support for action against Cuba was unlikely. Kennedy then chose to proceed without OAS authorization, but lacking sufficient legal pretext for direct intervention, he ordered that the invasion plan be changed so that the operation would not "put us in so openly, in view of the world situation" (*FRUS 1961–63*, X: 143). Kennedy forbade US military personnel from direct participation in the invasion, in order to increase the plausibility of the claim that the United States was not involved in it. He also ordered that the landing site be moved from the city of Trinidad to the Bay of Pigs, in order to increase the plausibility of the claim that the rebels were flying from bases within Cuba. Unlike Trinidad, the Bay of Pigs landing site included an airstrip long enough to handle the B-26 bombers that the rebels purportedly would be flying from it, although the geography of the site would make it difficult for the rebels to escape into the mountains if the invasion failed. Finally, Kennedy ordered air strikes to begin two days before the invasion and to escalate gradually – despite the time that this would allow Castro to prepare for the impending invasion – in order to increase the plausibility of the claim that the pilots of the bombers were defectors from the Cuban air force. One of the pilots would land in Florida, announce his "defection" from Cuba, and request asylum in the United States (*FRUS 1961–63*, X: 177). In making these changes, Kennedy ignored warnings from members of the CIA Task Force that an operation of this sort would lack "reasonable expectation" of "a successful conclusion" (Kornbluh 1998: 264).

On 15 April, following the initial air strikes against Cuban airfields, the UN General Assembly met in a Special Emergency Session. Cuba claimed that the United States had committed aggression against its territorial integrity and political independence by sending B-26 bombers into Cuba as a prelude to an invasion by mercenary forces. The United States responded by denying any involvement in the operation and declaring Cuba's claims to be "wholly unfounded" (*UNYB 1961*: 159). The following evening, UN representative Adlai Stevenson sent a sharply-worded telegram to Rusk, expressing concern that perceived violations of the Charter would evoke resistance from other states. Stephenson informed Rusk that he was "[g]reatly disturbed by clear indications ... that bombing incidents in Cuba on Saturday were launched in part at least from outside Cuba" and warned that if US involvement in the operation were discovered, the United States would face an "increasingly hostile atmosphere" at the United Nations (*FRUS 1961–63*, X: 230–2). Stevenson urged Kennedy not to intervene directly in Cuba, arguing that "overt U.S. military support of rebels in [the] absence of [a] legal framework ... would probably be *worse than failure*" because of the resistance it would evoke from other states (*FRUS 1961–63*, X: 295–7, emphasis added).[6]

Stephenson's telegram confirmed US policy-makers' concerns regarding possible resistance from other states, and upon discussing the matter with Rusk, Kennedy immediately canceled plans for further attacks on Cuban airfields (*FRUS 1961–63*, X: 235–7), despite warnings from the CIA that without tactical air support the operation would involve "unacceptable military risks" (Kornbluh 1998: 121). When informed of Kennedy's decision that evening, Deputy CIA Directors Charles Cabell and Richard Bissell went to Rusk's office at the State Department to discuss the matter. Rusk explained to them that "the main consideration" in canceling the air strikes "involved the situation at the United Nations." He informed them of Stevenson's insistence that additional air strikes "would make it impossible for the U.S. position to be sustained" and of Kennedy's conclusion that "such a result was unacceptable." Cabell informed Rusk that the invasion force was landing at that very moment and argued that "failure to make air strikes in the immediate beachhead area first thing in the morning . . . clearly would be disastrous." Rusk replied that the President's decision was final, although he would allow limited air strikes in the immediate beachhead area. At four-thirty the following morning, Cabell requested additional air strikes to prevent the sinking of the ships in the landing force, but Kennedy rejected his request (*FRUS 1961–63*, X: 235–7). Although Kennedy authorized limited air strikes on the beachhead during the night of 18 April, lacking a sufficient legal pretext for direct military intervention, he refused to allow aircrews to fly over Cuban territory (*FRUS 1961–63*, X: 273).

As reports of the invasion's pending failure reached the White House, Attorney General Robert Kennedy urged the President to authorize direct US military intervention to prevent the possible Soviet placement of nuclear weapons in Cuba. The Attorney General suggested that direct intervention could be justified by arguing that Soviet interference in Cuba was a threat to international peace and security in the hemisphere (*FRUS 1961–63*, X: 302–4). Kennedy, however, ordered that the rebels be instructed to "lie low" and that further US assistance "be extended only . . . to assist in survival or evacuation" (*FRUS 1961–63*, X: 315–17). Without US air support, the rebels quickly were defeated. Soon afterwards the Soviet Union began placing nuclear missiles in Cuba, just as Attorney General Robert Kennedy had feared.

Dominican Republic, 1959–61

The overthrow of the Batista government in Cuba had generated worries among US policy-makers not only that Castro would allow Soviet military bases in Cuba, but also that there would be "a domino effect of Castro-like governments" throughout the region (Rabe 1996: 65). These worries intensified following an attempted invasion of the Dominican Republic in June 1959 by a group of Dominican exiles trained and equipped in Cuba. Although military forces loyal to the government of Rafael Trujillo had quelled the invasion, its occurrence demonstrated an increasing level of internal opposition to Trujillo's brutality, leading US policy-makers to conclude that the Trujillo government might be vulnerable to both revolution and invasion (*FRUS 1958–60*, V: 393–406).

In January 1960, the State Department developed a preliminary plan to remove Trujillo and thereby prevent a Cuban-sponsored revolution in the Dominican Republic (*FRUS 1958–60*, VI: 892; Rabe 1996: 65). Although information regarding the State Department's decision-making process in this instance is somewhat limited, the plan's remarkable similarity to the plan being developed for removing Castro from power in Cuba suggests that it was shaped by similar concerns regarding arguably illegal US military intervention evoking resistance from other states. As Secretary of State Christian Herter had reminded US diplomatic and consular staff in August 1959, the "principle of non-intervention and [the] authority of [the] OAS" were "cornerstones of U.S. policy towards Latin America," and the "erosion of these basic concepts ... would result in significant weakening of [the] U.S. position and open up [the] prospect that [the] U.S. would have to direct energies and resources needed elsewhere ... to deal with disorder in [the] Caribbean basin and possibly elsewhere in Latin America" (*FRUS 1958–60*, VI: 310–13). Consistent with these principles, the plan called for the recognition of a provisional government that would request assistance from the United States (*FRUS 1958–60*, V: microfiche doc. DR9; Diederich 1978: 41).

Eisenhower approved the State Department's plan in late March. However, believing that OAS recognition of a provisional government was unlikely, he ordered that US involvement "be kept secret" (*FRUS 1958–60*, V: microfiche doc. DR17). Accordingly, Eisenhower authorized the CIA to begin training Dominican rebels at a secret base in Venezuela, while the State Department worked to gain support for a more general resolution directed against the Dominican Republic (Slater 1967: 192; Diederich 1978: 53).

Recall from above that at this time the State Department also was working to gain support for an OAS resolution directed against Cuba. Venezuelan President Rómulo Betancourt had agreed to support such a resolution, but only after "the Trujillo problem was resolved" (Rabe 1996: 64). Using the situation in Cuba as leverage, Betancourt urged the United States to move more quickly against Trujillo, whom Betancourt alleged to have instigated several bombings and a rebellion in Venezuela (Atkins and Wilson 1972: 282). Eisenhower, however, ordered that the proposed intervention be delayed – despite pressure from Venezuela and reports that the position of the Trujillo government had become "quite precarious" (*FRUS 1958–60*, V: microfiche doc. DR19). As Presidential Advisor Edwin Clark noted in a memorandum to Eisenhower dated 21 April, lacking OAS authorization, it would be necessary to implement the plan under circumstances that "would not place the United States in the role of 'interventionists'" (*FRUS 1958–60*, V: microfiche doc. DR20). Although planes would be ready by mid-May to transport the rebels from Venezuela into the Dominican Republic, no such action would be undertaken under the existing circumstances (*FRUS 1958–60*, V: microfiche doc. DR22).

Several weeks later, however, a new set of circumstances obtained that US policy-makers believed would provide a suitable pretext for direct intervention. Following an assassination attempt against Betancourt by agents of the Trujillo government, the OAS approved a resolution on 20 August condemning the Dominican Republic for "intervention and aggression" in Venezuela (*FRUS 1958–60*, V: microfiche doc. DR26). Secretary of State Herter urged Eisenhower to take advantage of the situation by requesting that the OAS authorize direct military intervention in the Dominican Republic. Herter believed that a resolution could be based on an OAS Peace Commission report from earlier in the year, which had concluded that human rights violations committed by the Trujillo government constituted a threat to international peace and security in the hemisphere because of the refugee flows, rebellions, and retaliations that resulted from them (Slater 1967: 188). According to Herter, the assassination attempt would assist US policy-makers in obtaining an OAS resolution authorizing the use of armed force against the Dominican Republic and provide "a very useful precedent ... for possible later action when the Cuban matter is before us" (Rabe 1996: 67). Former OAS Secretary-General William Manger disagreed, however, noting that the OAS and the larger UN framework were designed to restrain states, not to punish them, and that to suggest otherwise would be detrimental to US interests in the long term (Atkins and Wilson 1972: 114). Most OAS members were similarly reluctant to undermine the basic principle of non-intervention, and Herter's proposal was never put to a vote (Rabe 1996: 67–8).

Soon after the conclusion of the OAS meeting, the CIA began dropping arms and ammunition to rebel groups within the Dominican Republic, using planes painted with DAF markings (Diederich 1978: 53). US policy-makers, however, believed that more direct intervention could not be justified under the existing circumstances. As Assistant Secretary of State Mann explained in a memorandum dated 10 October, insofar as US policy was "limited by ... non-intervention commitments," the absence of a permissive OAS resolution had made "[t]he problem of dealing with Trujillo ... more difficult" (*FRUS 1958–60*, V: microfiche doc. DR27). Full implementation of the plan would again be delayed.

Such delays came at a considerable cost, as they provided time for Trujillo's security forces to infiltrate and destroy most of the rebel groups in the Dominican Republic (Rabe 1996: 68). By November, the State Department's Director of Intelligence and Research warned Herter that "the tide is now running against the United States and the longer the current impasse continues, the more unfavorable to U.S. interests the outcome is likely to be" (*FRUS 1958–60*, V: microfiche doc. DR29). According to reports received from Consul General Henry Dearborn, the rebel groups that remained in the Dominican Republic were "in no way ready to carry on any type of revolutionary activity in the foreseeable future" (Diederich 1978: 45).

Following Dearborn's advice, in January 1961 Eisenhower abandoned the existing plan for supporting rebellion in the Dominican Republic in favor of a preliminary plan for assisting in Trujillo's assassination. The plan involved smuggling sniper rifles, pistols, and other weapons into the Dominican Republic in pieces packaged inside of specially-marked cans of food shipped to an American-owned supermarket (Gall 1963). Dearborn urged haste in implementing the plan, noting that the longer US policy-makers delayed, the more time Trujillo would have for "overturning democratic governments and establishing dictatorships in the Caribbean" (*FRUS 1958–60*, V: microfiche doc. DR28). Betancourt renewed his demands for action as well, promising once again to "head the movement of Latin American countries to dispose of the Castro problem once effective actions were taken against Trujillo" (Rabe 1996: 69).

After assuming office in late January, President Kennedy approved a finalized plan under which the United States would provide assistance to a group of conspirators led by Luís Amiama Tío and Antonio Imbert, who were members of the Trujillo government. According to the plan, Tío and Imbert would assassinate Trujillo, at which time General José Rene Roman Fernandez, Secretary of State for the Armed Forces, would order the execution of the remaining members of the Trujillo family and form a provisional government. If the plot failed, US military forces would intervene and the actions would be justified as self-defense of US nationals in the Dominican Republic (*FRUS 1961–63*, XII: 630–3). The plan thus would enable the United States to account for its actions under the Charter without making reference to the OAS, which US policy-makers now had concluded "was not merely useless but a handicap" (Berle and Jacobs 1973: 744).

Following the failed invasion of Cuba in April, however, Kennedy delayed implementation of this plan as well – despite the risk that Trujillo's security forces would find and arrest the conspirators – out of concern that other states would respond with resistance if US involvement were discovered. Because many states already suspected US involvement in the Bay of Pigs operation, involvement in an assassination attempt soon afterwards would provide additional reason for states to conclude that the United States had aggressive intentions and to respond with resistance to it. Accordingly, the CIA attempted to cancel its delivery of weapons to the conspirators, but the orders did not reach agents in the Dominican Republic until after the weapons already had been delivered (Gall 1963).

Assessing the situation in late May, an NSC Task Force concluded that the United States "ran the risk of being identified with the assassination" and therefore faced possible resistance from other states (*FRUS 1961–63*, XII: 629). Accordingly, Dearborn was instructed to prevent implementation of the assassination plan, which US policy-makers had concluded "would serve very little purpose and expose the United States to the great danger of association with assassination" (Diederich 1978: 96). These instructions echoed concerns previously expressed by Dearborn that the Trujillo government would bring the matter to the attention of the Security Council and the United States would be condemned as an aggressor (*FRUS 1958–60*, V: microfiche doc. DR28).

Nevertheless, against the wishes of US policy-makers, Tío and Imbert carried out the planned assassination the following evening. They failed in their attempts to contact General Roman, however, because he had resumed loyalty to the Trujillo regime when the military refused to obey his orders to effect a coup. Consequently, the regime remained in power, and the conspirators (including General Roman) were executed. Although the Trujillo family fled the island in November, the country remained unstable, and US policy-makers remained fearful of a possible communist takeover. Kennedy ordered the deployment of naval forces to the waters off the coast of the Dominican Republic, but lacking a legal pretext for direct military intervention, he ordered US forces to intervene only in response to a Cuban-sponsored invasion (*FRUS 1961–63*, XII: 647–53).

Assessing the evidence

Consistent with the prudential restraint model, US policy-makers courted a real and considerable risk of failure in an attempt to maintain the persuasiveness of their legal arguments and thereby demonstrate that their actions were not threatening to the existing international order. In each of these cases, US policy-makers delayed planned military operations to seek OAS authorization under Chapter VIII of the UN Charter, and when OAS authorization appeared unlikely, they decided to act covertly and deny US involvement. The resulting changes to the manner and timing of these operations came at considerable cost, leading to failure in two of the three cases and causing US policy-makers to face the possibility of having to invade Cuba in 1962 to remove Soviet nuclear missiles and of having to occupy the Dominican Republic in 1965 to prevent a possible communist takeover.

The willingness of US policy-makers to accept such costs and risks contradicts the realist model, which holds that policy-makers considering possible military action will be concerned only with the relative power and capabilities of potential adversaries in the region. As we have seen in all three cases, US policy-makers expressed concern about the possibility of both direct and indirect resistance from other states and responded accordingly. In 1953, Eisenhower ordered that an operation intended to overthrow the Arbenz government in Guatemala be covert and that it be delayed until a suitable legal pretext obtained. Although he allowed the operation to proceed, following the discovery of a shipment of Soviet arms to Guatemala, Eisenhower delayed its implementation an additional month – despite the risk of additional armaments arriving in Guatemala before the operation could be launched – in order to allow Dulles sufficient time to present a new set of legal claims. In 1960, Eisenhower ordered that a similar operation intended to overthrow the Castro government in Cuba be covert and that it, too, be delayed until a suitable legal pretext obtained. Kennedy delayed the proposed operation even further in 1961 – despite the risk that Cuba would acquire jet capability before the operation could be launched – in order to seek OAS support. In addition, he ordered that the plans be changed so as to make US legal claims more plausible, although doing so further reduced the likelihood of the operation's success. Likewise, Eisenhower delayed proposed military intervention in the Dominican Republic to seek OAS support, and when OAS recognition of a provisional government appeared unlikely, Eisenhower changed the plan from an invasion to an assassination, which Kennedy attempted to delay further in the aftermath of the failed Bay of Pigs invasion.

In each of these instances, policy-makers' main concern was that arguably illegal uses of armed force by the United States might evoke resistance from states threatened by such actions. Contrary to the communal obligation model, policy-makers expressed their concern in terms of perceived violations of US legal commitments under the UN Charter, rather than amorphous conceptualizations of communal values or communal responsibilities. Although Bowles privately lamented the Kennedy administration's lack of "conviction about what is right and what is wrong" regarding possible military action against Cuba, in discussions with fellow policy-makers he urged prudential restraint by noting that such action would be "in clear violation of previous treaty commitments" and that the United States "cannot expect the benefits of this regime of treaties if we are unwilling to accept the limitations it imposes on our freedom to act" (Bowles 1971: 343, 444; *FRUS 1961–63*, X: 178–81). Similarly, although Schlesinger privately expressed concern that military action against Cuba would "spoil the image of the United States in the eyes of the world," he too argued for prudential restraint by making specific reference to other states' assessments of the United States' commitment to its legal obligations under the Charter (*FRUS 1961–63*, X: 186–9, 196–203).

These concerns specifically addressed the likelihood of resistance from less powerful states, sometimes focusing almost exclusively on them, as in January 1961 when Rusk requested a study of possible responses to US military intervention in Cuba. Rusk instructed that the study include "particular reference to the rest of Latin America, the OAS, close NATO allies and *possibly* Soviet and [Chinese] moves" (*FRUS 1961–63*, X: 52–3, emphasis added). Contrary to the realist model, Rusk clearly was concerned with more than just a possible Soviet countermove.

The legal arguments offered to justify US actions in these cases were not directed at domestic audiences, as the realist model suggests; rather, they were directed at other states as signals of the United States' commitment to the existing international order. US policy-makers' attempts to provide persuasive accounts for arguably illegal military actions actually trumped their concerns for domestic public opinion, as was made clear in a State Department memorandum discussing the lack of domestic support for convening a meeting of the OAS prior to initiating military action against the Dominican Republic (*FRUS 1958–60*, V: microfiche doc. DR15). Because they realized that maintaining the persuasiveness of such accounts might restrict subsequent military actions, US policy-makers considered not only present situations but also future situations. For example, policy-makers' assessments of proposed legal justifications regarding Cuba focused not only on the persuasiveness of the arguments offered, but also on the impact that such arguments might have on future US policy options in Laos or Congo (*FRUS 1961–63*, X: 63–4). Similarly, proposed US legal arguments for military action in Guatemala and the Dominican Republic were designed to be used as justifications for subsequent military actions elsewhere.

Domestic legal advisors played only a limited role in these policy-making discussions, however. Contrary to the liberal model, to the extent that US policy-makers consulted legal advisors, their concern was not with the legality of the proposed military actions per se, but rather the anticipated likelihood of resistance in response to such actions. Hence, when considering the possibility of using naval forces to detain and search suspicious vessels bound for Guatemala in May 1954, US policy-makers blithely ignored the conclusion of the State Department Legal Advisor that involuntary search and seizure of foreign-flag vessels "would constitute a violation of international law" (Blum 1995: 76), but gave more serious consideration to the Assistant Legal Advisor's warning that there were likely to be "consequences of charges of violation of freedom of the seas" and that resistance from other states might include possible military action (*FRUS 1952–54*, IV: 1113). And US policy-makers sometimes did not even consult with legal advisors, as when Rusk convened a series of meetings to discuss possible military action against Cuba but invited neither the Attorney General nor the State Department Legal Advisor (Hoyt 1985: 123).

Similarly, domestic political ideology does not seem to have played much of a role in the formulation of policy. Contrary to the liberal model, Kennedy's incoming Democratic administration did not reject legal claims proposed by Eisenhower's Republican administration, despite Schlesinger's urging that Kennedy be careful not to "dissipate all the extraordinary good will" that his administration had acquired because of its "principled concern for human freedom" (*FRUS 1961–63*, X: 92–3). Although Kennedy did change the proposed justification for US military intervention in the Dominican Republic from collective self-defense of an OAS-recognized provisional government to self-defense of US nationals abroad, this change was most likely a consequence of Eisenhower's last-minute change in plans from a US-sponsored invasion to a US-backed assassination rather than a reflection of a distinct political ideology.

In all three cases, US policy-makers attempted to legitimate arguably illegal US actions by attaining a favorable outcome in the UN Security Council and/or the OAS Council of Ministers, even if doing so required the use of coercive bargaining techniques. Contrary to the communal obligation model, US policy-makers did not rely exclusively on argumentation to generate consensus. For example, in March 1954 Dulles made an implicit offer of economic aid in exchange for OAS members' support of the Declaration of Caracas, prompting delegates to note that they had voted in favor of the measure "without the feeling that we were contributing to the adoption of a constructive measure" (Slater 1967: 119; Hilaire 1997: 35). Later, facing resistance from Security Council members, Lodge informed the United Kingdom and France that if they continued to take an "independent line backing Guatemala," then the United States would feel "entirely free" to pursue a similarly independent position "without regard to their position in relation to any such matters as any of their colonial problems in Egypt, Cyprus, etc." (*FRUS 1952–54*, IV: 1184–5).

Concerns about the likelihood of resistance against arguably illegal US actions shaped decision-making processes not only during the initial stages of discussion, but also during the actual implementation of military operations. For example, when Guatemalan rebels became bogged down after the loss of two B-26 bombers to enemy fire, Eisenhower agreed to transfer two additional bombers to them, but only after he was sufficiently satisfied that the transfer could be concealed (Hoyt 1985: 104; Pagedas 1995: 61). By contrast, after the failure of the US-backed assassination plot against Trujillo, Kennedy refused to allow direct US military intervention in the Dominican Republic because there lacked a suitable legal pretext. Likewise, despite the impending failure of the Bay of Pigs operation and the concern that the Soviet Union might attempt to place nuclear missiles in Cuba, Kennedy refused to authorize additional air strikes in the absence of a suitable legal pretext for direct military intervention.[7] As Stevenson suggested to the UN General Assembly two days later, the failure of the Bay of Pigs operation provided "the best evidence of the falsity of the shrill charges of American aggression in Cuba" (*DSB 1961*, 44: 682).

As Stevenson's statement makes clear, the exercise of restraint can entail high costs, but such costs are necessary in order for a major power to provide a credible signal of its commitment to the existing international order. The three cases examined herein demonstrate the extent to which US policy-makers were willing to bear such costs. It remains now to examine the applicability of the model to decision-making processes and outcomes involving other major powers.

5

THE IMPACT OF THE UN CHARTER ON ANGLO-FRENCH MILITARY INTERVENTION IN EGYPT, 1956

In October 1956, Anglo-French military forces intervened in Egypt in an attempt to overthrow the government of Abdel Gamel Nasser. The intervention came in response to the Nasser government's ongoing support of Algerian rebels, its increasing ties to the Soviet Union, and its nationalization of the Suez Canal Company on 27 July 1956. Consistent with the prudential restraint model, although British and French policy-makers believed that the nationalization might provide a legal basis for undertaking military action against Egypt, they delayed the implementation of such action out of concern that other states would perceive the United Kingdom and France as aggressors and respond with resistance to them. Facing resistance in the Security Council and elsewhere, British and French policy-makers relied on an Israeli invasion of Egypt to provide a legal pretext for direct military intervention and confined the operation to the Suez Canal Zone. These changes to the manner and timing of their military actions led to the failure of their attempt to overthrow the Nasser government and contributed to the decline of their influence in the Middle East region.

Similar to the cases examined in the previous chapter, within this case there is variance in the actions taken and the arguments offered for those actions. In addition, there is variance in the intervening powers, which allows for comparison with US decision-making processes and outcomes examined in previous cases, as well as comparison between British and French decision-making processes and outcomes within this one, single case. The case is well documented, with primary source material readily available and supplemented by excellent secondary sources.[1]

Initial stages of military planning

British policy-makers had concluded as early as 1952 that a stoppage of free transit through the canal would have a "disastrous effect" on the British economy because of the shortage of petroleum products that would result (*BDEE 1951–57*, 3.1: 112–13). Prime Minister Anthony Eden, however, viewed the Egypt's nationalization of the Suez Canal Company as "an opportunity," because he believed that it could provide a legal basis for overthrowing the Nasser government (*BDEE 1951–57*, 3.1: 165–8). Accordingly, Eden instructed his Services Chiefs to begin immediate planning for possible military action against Egypt.

Despite the "opportunity" provided by the nationalization, however, British policy-makers were concerned that other states might perceive the United Kingdom as acting contrary to its legal obligations under the UN Charter and respond with resistance to it (Kyle 1991: 148). Cabinet legal advisors warned that the United Kingdom would be "on weak ground" in basing military action on "the narrow argument that Colonel Nasser had acted illegally" (*BDEE 1951–57*, 3.1: 165–8). As characterized by Gerald Fitzmaurice, Senior Legal Advisor to the Foreign Office, "although the Egyptian Government are committing a number of illegalities, none of them ... help us on the central issue" of justifying direct military intervention (Marston 1988: 780). Egypt was in breach of its legal obligations under the Treaty of Constantinople by denying Israeli shipping access to the canal, but it had been since 1951, and the Suez Canal Base Agreement allowed the United Kingdom to reactivate military bases in the Canal Zone only in the event of an armed attack against Egypt (Finch 1957: 377–8). In keeping with legal advisors' recommendations that the case "be presented on wider grounds," Cabinet members decided to justify military action against Egypt by claiming that nationalizing "a company of such an international character as the Suez Canal Company" violated "fundamental principles of international law," and that Egypt's violation of its obligations in administering the canal under the 1888 Treaty of Constantinople resulted in the abrogation of the 1954 Base Agreement between the United Kingdom and Egypt (Carlton 1989: 135; Johnman 2000: 47). As Kyle (1989: 113) notes, although the Cabinet's "most immediate objective was to bring about the downfall of the present Egyptian government," Cabinet members understood that it would be necessary to justify this objective in reference to their longer-term objective of ensuring international control of the Suez Canal.

French Prime Minister Guy Mollet, too, believed that the nationalization of the Suez Canal Company might provide a legal basis for military action. Having concluded already in February 1955 that the Nasser government was supporting Algerian rebels (Crosbie 1974: 57–8), French policy-makers believed that France was "specially threatened" by the consequences that the nationalization might have, "particularly in the Near East and in the oil trade" (*DDF 1956*, II: 167–8). Mollet conferred with Eden by telephone on 27 July and offered French troops to assist in a British-led military operation against Egypt, which he suggested justifying as collective self-defense of Israel in response to Egyptian expansionism

(Crosbie 1974: 68). Although French policy-makers focused somewhat less on matters of legality than their British counterparts, they too were concerned that other states might perceive French military intervention as having been undertaken without regard to international law and respond with resistance to it (Lloyd 1978: 87). As indicated by a telegram from Ambassador Maurice Couve de Murville to Foreign Minister Christian Pineau on 28 July, French policy-makers generally agreed that France should avoid actions that would place it "in an unjustifiable position in the eyes of the world," because such actions might prove costly in the long term by evoking resistance from other states (*DDF 1956,* II: 172–4).

Less keen on military action than their British and French counterparts, US policy-makers proposed a conference to examine international regulation of the canal. At a tripartite meeting on 30 July, French Ambassador Jean Chauvel pressed for quick action, noting that "the longer our decisions take, the more we will allow the Soviets to expand their maneuvers in connection with Colonel Nasser" (*DDF 1956*, II: 189–91). British Foreign Secretary Selwyn Lloyd, however, suggested that an international conference might produce an agreement that could be used to underpin subsequent legal arguments justifying direct military intervention (Bowie 1974: 34, 106). Lloyd's views prevailed, and on 2 August the United Kingdom issued a communiqué claiming that Egypt's actions threatened "the freedom and security of the canal as guaranteed by the Convention of 1888" and inviting signatories to the Convention and other interested states to a conference to be held in London on 16 August. Pineau and Lloyd had hoped to exclude the Soviet Union from the conference, but they recognized that if the Treaty of Constantinople were to be the legal basis for the conference, it would be necessary to invite all parties to attend – including the Soviet Union (Lloyd 1978: 100, 268–70). Although Soviet participation increased the likelihood of an equivocal outcome, Pineau and Lloyd hoped, nonetheless, that the conference would produce a "virtual ultimatum" and that military action could follow the Egyptian government's refusal to accept it (Kyle 1989: 113).

Following the tripartite meeting, Lord Salisbury sent a memorandum to Eden suggesting that any agreement adopted at the conference include "a form of reference to the UN" (Kyle 1991: 165–6). Lloyd agreed, citing a Foreign Office memorandum which had suggested that the arguments offered by the United Kingdom contain restrictive claims emphasizing the "limited goal" of international control of the Suez Canal (Goldsmith 2000: 83–5). Eden, however, feared that an unfavorable outcome in the Security Council would undermine the legitimacy of Anglo-French military actions and retorted "let us keep quiet about the UN." He agreed, nevertheless, to postpone the date of the proposed military operation from 5 September to 20 September, so that the United Kingdom and France would not be seen to be making military preparations during the London Conference, and on

7 August the Foreign Office released a statement denying that the United Kingdom was "threatening to use force or military action against Egypt, nor ... holding an international conference under such threats" (Kyle 1991: 166, 189).

Despite having agreed that Egypt's rejection of a proposal for international control of the canal might increase the persuasiveness of subsequent legal arguments justifying Anglo-French military intervention, most French policy-makers believed that an equally persuasive argument could be made without referring to such a proposal (*DDF 1956*, II: 240–2). Pineau had laid out the French position at the tripartite meeting on 30 July, arguing that direct military intervention could be justified solely in reference to Egypt's illegal nationalization of the Suez Canal Company, its illegal restrictions on freedom of transit through the canal, and its inability to protect foreign nationals working in the Canal Zone (Vaisse 1989: 137). French policy-makers feared that if the proposed London Conference failed to produce a "virtual ultimatum," British policy-makers might not be willing to contemplate direct military intervention. Accordingly, French Defense Minister Maurice Bourgès-Maunoury began planning for separate French military intervention with Israeli assistance (Crosbie 1974: 69), and Pineau sent a circular telegram to French ambassadors on 8 August, outlining a legal justification for such actions. The telegram referred to Nasser's "illegal" nationalization of the Suez Canal Company and France's demand for international operation of the canal in accordance with the Treaty of Constantinople (Vaisse 1989: 136).

French military planners continued to meet with their British counterparts as well. Although British troops already had been deployed to Cyprus in preparation for an invasion of Egypt, both British and French military planners expressed dismay over limitations on military planning that Eden had deemed necessary to maintain the persuasiveness of Anglo-French legal claims. Both the British commander, General Hugh Stockwell, and the French commander, General André Beaufre, had advised Eden that a landing at Alexandria was "soundest from the military point of view" because it would allow Anglo-French military forces to deploy rapidly and advance to Cairo. By contrast, a landing at Port Said would entail "considerable risks," because the capacity of the unloading facilities located there was "only one-third the capacity of those at Alexandria" and the port was attached to the mainland by embankments that could easily be demolished. Nevertheless, Eden urged that the landing take place at Port Said, because he believed that landing at Alexandria would be too indirect an approach to justify legally, given that the canal was the ostensible objective of the operation. Although he allowed them to continue planning for a landing at Alexandria, he ordered that options for a landing at Port Said be included and that planners specify "dates on which the agreed timetable could be modified or delayed" (Beaufre 1969: 29–36, 42–5).

Planning following the first London conference

Delegates convened the London Maritime Conference on 16 August, and on 23 August they approved a plan calling for an international organization to operate, maintain, and develop the Suez Canal under UN auspices. According to the plan (commonly referred to as the "Eighteen-Power Plan"), any threat or use of force to interfere with the operation of the canal would constitute a "threat to the peace" and hence be actionable under the UN Charter (Lucas 1996: 56). Although British and French policy-makers remained divided over possible Security Council involvement, they generally agreed that the plan provided a legal basis for subsequent military action.

British Chancellor Harold Macmillan, who was particularly concerned about the likelihood of resistance against the proposed Anglo-French military operation, met with Lord Salisbury and UN Representative Pierson Dixon on 23 August to consider possible Security Council involvement. Macmillan and Salisbury agreed that any proposed Security Council resolution authorizing the use of force against Egypt was likely to fail and that using armed force after such a resolution failed would "smack of hypocrisy." They also agreed that pursuing authorization by the Security Council would entail considerable risk by delaying the proposed operation and thereby reducing the likelihood of its success. Dixon suggested mitigating these risks by sending a joint letter, along with France, informing the Security Council of the outcome of the London Conference but not requesting that the matter be placed on the Security Council's agenda. According to Dixon, the United Kingdom would then be able to argue that military intervention in Egypt was implicitly authorized by the Security Council's failure to address the matter (Kyle 1991: 203).

Lloyd disagreed with Dixon's suggestion, because he believed that the Security Council would address the matter eventually – regardless of whether or not the United Kingdom referred the matter to it – and thus not referring the matter to the Security Council would only serve to delay the proposed operation even further. According to Lloyd, going to the Security Council would be "full of risks," but not going "would be certain to have consequences of the greatest gravity." In a memorandum dated 27 August, Lloyd suggested that the United Kingdom propose a draft resolution endorsing the Eighteen-Power Plan, and if the Security Council would not approve the resolution, the United Kingdom should argue that "the proceedings were futile and that the UN had shown itself incapable of dealing with the matter" (Kyle 1991: 212–13).

Lloyd's memorandum reflected Foreign Office concerns that direct military intervention in Egypt would have an "extremely adverse" effect on other states' perceptions of the United Kingdom's commitment to its legal obligations under the Charter. As Fitzmaurice had noted in a memorandum dated 13 August, arguably illegal British military actions were likely to evoke resistance from other states and "[t]he repercussions of such a situation may well be very serious, and may be very lasting and far-reaching." Fitzmaurice believed that Egypt was unlikely to do "something that would afford a pretext for armed intervention," and hence British policy-makers must "give [more] thought to how the legal aspects of the matter are presented" (Marston 1988: 784). French policy-makers shared similar concerns, which Pineau had discussed with Lloyd on 24 August. Lloyd had suggested that Security Council consideration of the matter would help to "create a favorable international opinion," and in presenting the Eighteen-Power Plan to the Security Council, they would be "practically sure to obtain seven or maybe eight votes." Pineau noted, however, that it would be necessary to keep military preparations secret to help reduce the likelihood that the Security Council would reject the Eighteen-Power Plan and thereby undermine Anglo-French legal arguments (*DDF 1956*, II: 303–4).

The British Cabinet convened on 28 August to discuss Lloyd's proposal. Minister of Defence Walter Monckton agreed with the proposal and expressed concern regarding the reactions of other states if the United Kingdom acted without UN authorization, including the possible sabotage of British oil installations throughout the Middle East.[2] Salisbury disagreed and suggested that the United Kingdom had a legal basis for intervention without explicit UN authorization if the Security Council could not reach agreement regarding the Eighteen-Power Plan (Carlton 1989: 135–7). The Cabinet, however, sided with Monckton and decided to present a draft resolution to the Security Council. Eden emphasized that a Soviet veto of the proposed resolution would provide implicit authorization for military action against Egypt (Kyle 1991: 212–13).

Meanwhile, British and French military planners were becoming increasingly frustrated over continuing delays in implementing the invasion plan. Intelligence reports indicated that the Egyptian military was mining beaches in the proposed landing zone and placing tanks near the proposed drop zone, prompting French Chief of Staff General Paul Ély to express doubts about the success of the operation (Beaufre 1969: 42–5). Eden, too, was frustrated, noting "[e]very day's postponement is to Nasser's gain and our loss" (*FRUS 1955–57*, XVI: 312). Nevertheless, he continued to delay implementation of the invasion plan to await a suitable legal pretext – which he hoped would come in the form of a Soviet veto.

Although French policy-makers concurred with Eden's assessment regarding the impact of a Soviet veto, they were even more reluctant than he was to delay implementation of the proposed operation to await Security Council action. At a meeting with Lloyd on 5 September, Pineau noted his displeasure with taking the matter to the Security Council without assurances from the United States that it would not abandon the Eighteen-Power Plan and that it would not make an amendment ruling out the use of armed force (Nutting 1967: 59). Lloyd suggested that presenting the Eighteen-Power Plan to the Security Council following Egypt's refusal to accept it would increase the plausibility of Anglo-French legal claims against suspicions that the Plan was merely a pretext for using armed force (Lloyd 1978: 126–7). However, he could give no assurances regarding the United States, having already received a telegram from US Secretary of State John Foster Dulles outlining a proposal for a Suez Canal Users' Association (SCUA) that would employ canal pilots and collect dues independent of the Egyptian government.

Discussing Dulles' proposal on 10 September, Mollet suggested that, as a result of the SCUA, "incidents would arrive quickly" to provide a legal pretext for direct military intervention. Although Eden still favored taking the matter to the Security Council, Mollet believed doing so would indicate skepticism about the SCUA plan and thus increase the risk of a Security Council resolution prohibiting the use of armed force (Kyle 1991: 231–2). British and French policy-makers agreed instead to send a letter notifying the Security Council of the SCUA proposal but to avoid direct Security Council involvement, at least for the time being (*DDF 1956*, II: 367–73, 397–8). Eden ordered that the proposed military operation be delayed until 1 October to accommodate a second London conference, at which the proposed SCUA would be discussed (Beaufre 1969: 62).

Having decided to delay military intervention yet again, British and French policy-makers were running out of time. The proposed operation, code-named Musketeer, could be launched no later than 6 October because of deteriorating weather conditions in the eastern Mediterranean. However, because the plan required 17 days between the order to launch the assault and the actual landing of troops, the decision to launch would have to be made by 19 September. Accordingly, British and French policy-makers approved a backup plan, code-named Musketeer Revise, which could be implemented until the end of October and required only eight days between the order to launch the assault and the actual landing of troops. Rather than landing in force at Alexandria and moving toward Cairo, the plan called for aerial and naval bombardment and a landing of British and French forces at Port Said, just as Eden had urged all along (Lucas 1996: 63).

General Beaufre warned, however, that the backup plan entailed "considerable risks." Because reinforcements could not be landed quickly, Anglo-French amphibious forces would have to break out from the beachhead without armored support and would be exposed to attacks as they traveled single-file along the 12-mile embankment connecting Port Said to the mainland (Beaufre 1969: 502). British and French policy-makers were willing to accept these risks, however, in order to increase the plausibility of their legal claims. They believed that, under the revised plan, they would be able to argue persuasively that they had pursued a peaceful settlement to the dispute and that their actions were intended to secure the canal and not directed against "the territorial integrity and political independence" of Egypt.

Planning following the second London conference

Delegates to the second London conference adopted the SCUA proposal on 19 September, posing a significant legal setback for the United Kingdom and France. As adopted, the SCUA proposal effectively prohibited the use of armed force, and therefore Anglo-French military intervention would not be implicitly authorized by the failure of the Security Council to address the situation in Egypt. It would be necessary, then, for British and French policy-makers to present the matter to the Security Council, where they hoped that it would be accepted by enough states that the expected Soviet veto would give implicit authorization to their joint military intervention (Kyle 1991: 254). Fitzmaurice warned that even if a Soviet veto precluded the Security Council from accepting the SCUA proposal, the Security Council's primary function was to maintain or restore peace and security, and it would "not [have] failed in that duty" by not confirming the SCUA proposal (Johnman 2000: 55). However, concerned with legitimation rather than legality per se, British policy-makers ignored his advice and prepared a letter to be sent to the Security Council. To allow time for the Security Council to meet, Eden postponed the proposed invasion again, from 1 October to 8 October.

Fearing that a settlement based on the SCUA proposal would rule out the use of force against Egypt, on 30 September French policy-makers met with Israeli civilian and military leaders to discuss plans for joint military intervention without British assistance. French policy-makers proposed that Israel act first, in response to Egyptian "aggression," thereby providing a legal pretext for France to intervene to "restore order" and "protect the canal" (Kyle 1991: 266–8).[3] Although General Ély approved the plans, he noted that other states would be more likely to respond with acceptance if France acted with the support of the United Nations, as it had in Korea, than without, as it had in Indo-China (Crosbie 1974: 73; Gaujac 2001: 62).

On 8 October, the Security Council authorized the UN Secretary-General to supervise organized consultation among the United Kingdom, France, and Egypt based on the SCUA proposal. However, as Soviet aircraft and armor continued arriving in Egypt and the weather in the eastern Mediterranean continued to deteriorate, British and French policy-makers were becoming increasingly concerned that additional delays would undermine the success of the proposed military operation. They also were concerned that the longer the Suez Canal continued to function efficiently under Egyptian control, the less persuasive their legal arguments would become (Lloyd 1978: 150). British policy-makers suggested that the SCUA could be argued to be a regional organization, which would allow its members to act under Chapter VIII of the UN Charter in response to Egypt's refusal of free navigation to Israeli shipping during time of peace (Kyle 1991: 282–6). Attorney General Reginald Manningham-Buller warned, however, that "the only force used by Nasser up to date was in relation to the seizure of the Canal Company's property in Egypt," and hence most states were likely to conclude that "the use of that force would not justify the use of force by us" (Johnman 2000: 56).

As talks continued, the Egyptian government began moving toward an agreement based on the SCUA proposal. Fearing that progress in the talks with Egypt would undermine their legal pretext for direct military intervention, French policy-makers decided on 11 October to report unfavorably to the Security Council on the results of the talks and to propose a draft resolution in support of the original Eighteen-Power Plan, with which they hoped to elicit a Soviet veto (*DDF 1956*, II: 569–70; UN Doc. S/3671). British policy-makers acquiesced, hoping as before to attain a majority in the Security Council such that military intervention would have implicit authorization, despite the expected Soviet veto (Nutting 1967: 76–8; Kyle 1991: 281, 287). As it turned out, however, the Soviet veto marked a successful turning point for British and French policy-makers, insofar as states began accepting Anglo-French legal claims and refrained from offering additional legal arguments accusing them of using the UN process as a pretext for military action. As Lloyd reported in a telegram to Eden on 14 October, "[w]e emerge without any result enjoining us against force or to set up a negotiating committee," and with the "changed atmosphere . . . we can count on a more understanding reaction if we have to take extreme measures" (Lucas 1996: 73).

Acting French Foreign Minister Albert Gazier and Deputy Chief of Staff General Maurice Challe presented a plan for such measures to Eden and British Foreign Minister Anthony Nutting that same day. According to the plan, Israel would attack Egypt across the Sinai Peninsula, and once Israeli forces were near the canal, British and French forces would intervene to "protect" the canal and would order both sides to withdraw from it. General Challe argued that no additional legal pretext was necessary, because the nationalization itself was sufficient, as French and British policy-makers initially had argued. Gazier added that, because Egypt had abrogated the Tripartite Declaration,[4] the United Kingdom and France were under no obligation to assist Egypt against outside attack. Nutting, however, disagreed and expressed concern that the proposed military operation would violate the United Kingdom's legal obligations "under the Tripartite Declaration . . . and the UN Charter, plus the 1954 [basing] agreement with Egypt," and as a consequence, the Middle Eastern states would be likely to respond with resistance. According to Nutting, "there would be wide-spread sabotage of oil installations and probably a total stop on oil deliveries to Britain and France" (Nutting 1967: 91–7, 107). Nevertheless, on 16 October Eden approved the proposal, having concluded upon discussing the matter with Mollet that most states would be unlikely to condemn Anglo-French intervention under the proposed circumstances (Lucas 1996: 83; Gaujac 2001: 55). Reporting to the Cabinet on 18 October, Eden noted that Israel was preparing for military action and that he had "reason to believe that if [Israel] made any military move" it would be toward Egypt. The Cabinet decided that, following an Israeli attack on Egypt, the United Kingdom would intervene to protect the canal, justifying its actions based on Egypt's breach of Security Council resolutions regarding Israeli shipping, its illegal seizure of the Suez Canal Company, and its repudiation of the Tripartite Declaration. Public statements would emphasize Security Council consideration of the matter and international support for British and French proposals (Carlton 1989: 140–2).[5]

On 23 October, British, French, and Israeli policy-makers met secretly in Sèvres, France to finalize plans for joint military intervention. Although both Pineau and Lloyd were concerned about the possible reactions of other states to arguably illegal Anglo-French military action against Egypt, they disagreed over how plausible their legal claims would be if such action followed an Israeli invasion of Egypt. Lloyd expressed concern that other states would respond with resistance – both in the Security Council and against British oil installations throughout the Middle East – unless it were clear that Israel had acted first and that the United Kingdom and France had intervened solely to protect the canal (Lloyd 1978: 181–4). He therefore insisted that there be at least 48 hours between the action and the response, because "the pretext must be credible" (Nutting 1967: 102; Kyle 1991: 317–20). Pineau, however, noted Israel's insistence on prompt British air attacks against Egyptian air bases, which Israeli Prime Minister David Ben-Gurion had made a condition for Israel's serving as the "detonator for Musketeer" (Carlton 1989: 66). As a compromise, Eden instructed that the British air attack could occur as soon as Israeli military forces posed what could be perceived as "a clear military threat to the Canal" (Lloyd 1978: 187).

The British Cabinet met on 25 October to finalize legal arguments for direct military intervention. Out of concern that the United Kingdom would be perceived as an aggressor, the Cabinet decided to claim that British actions were in conformity with the UN Charter because the intervention was undertaken "to prevent interference with the free flow of traffic through the Canal, which was an international necessity" (Marston 1988: 799–800). Telegrams were sent to British ambassadors informing them "on the highest legal authority" that the United Kingdom was entitled "under the Charter to take every measure open to them" to halt fighting between Israel and Egypt (Johnman 2000: 59). Monckton expressed concern that presenting an ultimatum would evoke resistance within the Security Council and do "lasting damage" to other states' perceptions of British intentions in the Middle East. Eden, however, emphasized the necessity of conducting the operation in a manner likely to persuade other states that the United Kingdom was "holding the balance between Israel and Egypt" (Carlton 1989: 146–8).

Operation "Musketeer" – phase I

On 29 October, Israeli paratroopers landed near the Mitla Pass in Egypt, and as Israeli forces advanced towards the canal, the United Kingdom and France issued an ultimatum requiring Israeli and Egyptian forces to withdraw ten miles from it.[6] The ultimatum requested that Egypt accept the "temporary occupation by Anglo-French forces of key positions at Port Said, Ismailia, and Suez" and declared that, after 12 hours, if "one or both Governments have not undertaken to comply with the above requests, UK and French forces will intervene in whatever strength may be necessary to secure compliance" (Kyle 1991: 358–9).

In an address to the House of Commons on 30 October, Eden argued that, because the Security Council could be "paralyzed" by the veto of one of the permanent members, states had the right to intervene "in an emergency" to protect the lives of their own nationals in the case of an "imminent threat," without necessarily waiting for an "armed attack." According to Eden, there is nothing in the Charter "which abrogates the right of a Government to take such steps as are essential to protect the lives of their citizens" (Hansard 2003). That afternoon, the United Kingdom and France vetoed a draft resolution calling on all states "to refrain from the use of force or threat of force in the area in any manner inconsistent with the purposes of the United Nations" and "to refrain from giving any military, economic, or financial assets to Israel" (UN Doc. S/3710). In casting its veto, France argued that the Security Council could not condemn Israel, given Egypt's "openly affirmed policy" of annihilating Israel, its interference in French foreign affairs, and its illegal seizure of an international waterway. Although British policy-makers were willing to abstain from voting in order to reduce the likelihood of a Uniting for Peace resolution referring the matter to the General Assembly, the United Kingdom cast its veto along with France in order to prevent France from having to cast a sole veto in the Security Council (*DDF 1956*, III: 105; Johnson 2000: 182). In casting its veto, the United Kingdom argued that there was "no constructive action" that the Security Council could take that would both stop the fighting and safeguard free passage through the canal (*UNYB 1956*: 25–7). The United Kingdom and France also vetoed a draft resolution calling on "all parties concerned immediately to cease fire" and calling upon Israel "immediately to withdraw its armed forces behind the established armistice lines." The matter was then referred to the General Assembly for further consideration (UN Doc. S/3713).

The following day, British and French military forces began bombing Egyptian air bases. As air strikes continued, Pineau sent a circular telegram to French diplomatic representatives throughout the world, instructing them to emphasize France's "long respect for international laws." According to the telegram, France was concerned chiefly with "preserving the Suez Canal . . . from any attack the current conflict can cause" and its joint military action was directed "neither against Egypt, nor against Israel" (*DDF 1956*, III: 123–4). The United Kingdom made similar arguments before the Security Council, emphasizing that its actions were limited and not directed against Egypt's territorial integrity (*UNYB 1956*: 28).

Pineau met with General Ély on 2 November to express concern about the "acute disturbance" French actions had caused around the world. French planes painted with Israeli markings had destroyed Egypt's IL-28 bombers, and a French destroyer had attacked an Egyptian frigate operating near Haifa (Crosbie 1974: 79–80). Pineau believed that, as a consequence of these actions, Middle Eastern states would condemn France as an aggressor and respond with resistance, perhaps by pursuing closer ties to the Soviet Union. Ély responded by noting that the risk had been considered and had been discounted, and suggested that if France had not assisted Israel in this way, Ben Gurion was likely to become impatient and "publicise and exaggerate the agreements made" (Kyle 1989: 128). Nevertheless, Ély recommended that the military operations be accelerated in order to reduce the likelihood of further resistance. Meeting with Eden later that same day, Ély suggested that a small contingent of paratroopers be deployed near the advancing Israeli forces, allowing British and French policy-makers to argue that Anglo-French military forces indeed had placed themselves between the belligerents (Kyle 1991: 420–2). Ély's suggestion quickly became moot, however, as the UN General Assembly approved a resolution urging that "all parties now involved in hostilities in the area should agree to an immediate cease-fire" (UN Doc. A/Res/997).

Operation "Musketeer" – phase II

Following the adoption of the resolution, UN Representative Dixon sent a telegram to Eden noting that "even our closest friends . . . are becoming intensely worried at the possible consequences which might follow if we and the French remain for long in open defiance of the UN." According to Dixon, the "effect of this on the Commonwealth and the whole of the network of Western alliances might be disastrous" (Kyle 1991: 403). The French representative, Bernard Cornut-Gentille, reported similarly on the "permanent and still growing state of crisis" at the United Nations (*DDF 1956*, III: 195–6).

Meeting with the Cabinet on 2 November, Lloyd expressed concern at the likelihood of resistance from other states if the United Kingdom landed troops in Egypt after the General Assembly had called for a ceasefire. Cabinet members concluded, however, that Anglo-French military forces still could occupy key points along the canal, justifying their actions as necessary to prevent the resumption of conflict until a UN force could replace them. The United Kingdom would "act the part of a UN surrogate until the UN took over the job itself" in the hope that "legitimacy would retrospectively be conferred on what the surrogate had done" (Kyle 1991: 428).

In a speech before the House of Commons the following day, Eden laid out the Cabinet's proposal, characterizing the General Assembly resolution as "merely a recommendation" that was not binding. Following the speech, Eden received a telegram from Dixon expressing concern that states in the General Assembly would conclude that the United Kingdom was no longer committed to its legal obligations under the UN Charter and urging Eden not to expand the bombing campaign. Eden responded by ordering that military operations be confined to the Canal Zone, effectively canceling the attempt to overthrow the Nasser government (Kyle 1991: 429–35). Meanwhile, France pressured Israel to impose conditions on its ceasefire acceptance, because Anglo-French military forces had not yet landed in Egypt (Wyllie 1984: 29–30).

On 4 November, the General Assembly approved resolutions requesting the Secretary-General to submit "a plan for setting up … an emergency international United Nations Force to secure and supervise the cessation of hostilities" (UN Doc. A/Res/998) and authorizing the "implementation of the cease-fire and halting of the movement of military forces … not later than twelve hours from the time of the adoption of the present Resolution" (UN Doc. A/Res/999). Following the adoption of these resolutions, Dixon sent a telegram to Eden warning that unless the United Kingdom accepted the ceasefire, it likely would face a General Assembly resolution calling for economic sanctions, including shipments of oil (Johnson 2000: 190). Already, the government of Jordan had forbidden British aircraft from using bases in Jordan to attack Egypt, and Saudi Arabia and Syria had broken diplomatic relations with the United Kingdom and France (*DDF 1956*, III: 171–3). Concerned by these developments, British policymakers noted that it would look "peculiar" if the United Kingdom landed troops in Egypt after the fighting had stopped, since the declared purpose of the intervention was to stop the fighting. They decided, however, that because Israel had refused to withdraw behind the Armistice Line and had rejected a UN peacekeeping force, the operation should proceed as planned, with the landing force justified as "advance elements of the international force or trustees on its behalf" (Kyle 1991: 440–1).

As Anglo-French air forces attacked military targets in Cairo on the morning of 5 November, the General Assembly approved a resolution establishing "a United Nations Command for an emergency international force to secure and supervise the cessation of hostilities" (UN Doc. A/Res/1000). Following the approval of the resolution, Dixon sent a telegram to Eden informing him that the United Kingdom's legal claims were "implausible" to most states and urging him to halt the bombing in an attempt to avoid "collective measures of some kind" against the United Kingdom. Upon receiving the telegram, Eden ordered the immediate cessation of the bombing. Meanwhile, Egypt and Israel informed the Secretary-General of their unconditional acceptance of the ceasefire.

As Anglo-French seaborne forces landed at Port Said the following day, British Cabinet ministers expressed concern about possible resistance from other states, including oil sanctions and perhaps even military intervention by other Arab states (Kyle 1991: 465). Eden was especially concerned about the plausibility of British legal claims for military intervention in Egypt, now that Egypt and Israel had accepted the ceasefire and the United Nations was raising an international peacekeeping force (Eden 1960: 624). In addition, US Secretary of Treasury George Humphrey had presented Macmillan with an ultimatum to accept the ceasefire or else the United States would refuse to provide dollars for oil purchases or support for an IMF loan to prop up the British pound, which was under severe pressure for devaluation as China, India, and other states began selling off their reserves (Wyllie 1984: 38). This pressure prompted Macmillan to argue in favor of the ceasefire, even if doing so meant that the canal might be closed for several months until a UN force was able to reopen it. Cabinet members agreed and decided to accept the ceasefire while arguing that the use of Anglo-French military forces to clear the canal did not constitute "military action" and therefore was not prohibited (Carlton 1989: 153–5). Cabinet members hoped that, as a result of such action, "the operation in the Middle East will increasingly come to be recognized, in retrospect, as a necessary step for the maintenance of world peace rather than an act of aggression" (*BDEE 1951–57*, 3.1: 416).

Following the meeting, Eden phoned Mollet to inform him that the United Kingdom would accept the ceasefire, effective at midnight. Mollet pressed for delay because French forces were dependent upon British logistics, but Eden refused. Mollet ordered French troops to abide by the British-imposed deadline but to advance rapidly until then and attempt to capture Qantara. French troops were four miles short of their objective when the deadline expired (Kyle 1991: 467–76).

Assessing the evidence

Consistent with the prudential restraint model, British and French policy-makers delayed proposed military intervention in Egypt in order to convene two international conferences, which they believed would increase the persuasiveness of legal claims justifying the use of military force. When the results of these conferences undermined the persuasiveness of their claims, British and French policy-makers developed an alternative plan in which an Israeli attack on Egypt would serve as a legal pretext for direct military intervention. Because of diplomatic resistance in the General Assembly, Eden confined military operations to the Canal Zone and accepted a UN-imposed ceasefire within hours of landing troops in Egypt, thereby causing the operation to fail in both its primary objective of overthrowing the Nasser government and its secondary objective of occupying the entire length of the canal and reopening it to shipping.

In making these decisions, British and French policy-makers considered not only the relative power of potential adversaries in the region, as the realist model suggests, but also the likelihood and severity of resistance from other states threatened by the arguably illegal Anglo-French military intervention. During the initial stages of planning, French policy-makers warned against taking actions that would place France "in an unjustifiable position in the eyes of the world" (*DDF 1956*, II: 172–4), while British policy-makers expressed concern that other states might perceive the United Kingdom as an aggressor, acting contrary to its legal obligations under the UN Charter and for purposes other than maintaining the Suez Canal as an international waterway (Kyle 1991: 148). Although French policy-makers agreed to provide direct assistance to Israel by attacking Egypt's bomber force, they did so only because they believed that Ben-Gurion would otherwise leak details of the invasion plan and thereby undermine the persuasiveness of their legal claims (Kyle 1991: 330, 409). When Israel sought to end military operations early, British and French policy-makers attempted to accelerate the proposed timetable for phase II of the operation – despite the military risks of deploying airborne troops without sufficient ground support – in order to increase the plausibility of the claim that they were positioning themselves between the two opposing sides to protect the canal. And when Dixon warned that ongoing air strikes were undermining the plausibility of Anglo-French legal claims, Eden ordered the cessation of bombing, thereby subjecting Anglo-French seaborne forces to house-to-house fighting in Port Said and delaying the use of the port facilities by additional landing forces (Kyle 1991: 453–6, 463).

These concerns specifically addressed the likelihood of resistance from less powerful states. They did not focus primarily or exclusively on other major powers, as the realist model suggests. For example, Cornut-

Gentille's telegram warning of diplomatic resistance at the United Nations made particular reference to "feverish agitation of the Afro-Asian group" (*DDF 1956*, III: 195–6), while British policy-makers focused much of their discussions on the possibility of resistance from Middle Eastern states, including the destruction of British-owned oil pipelines and the denial of British military bases and facilities (*DDF 1956*, III: 171–3). Although the Soviet Union implicitly threatened to attack London and Paris using missiles equipped with "modern destructive weapon[s]," British policy-makers expressed less concern over possible Soviet moves than the "more formidable threat" posed by countries such as India and China, which were selling off their sterling reserves while the United States was refusing to back an IMF loan to prop up the British pound. But according to Eden, neither of these factors was as important as Cabinet members' conclusion that "[o]nce the fighting had ceased, justification for further intervention ceased with it" (Eden 1960: 620–4).

Contrary to the communal obligation model, policy-makers expressed their concerns in terms of perceived violations of British and French legal commitments under the UN Charter, rather than amorphous conceptualizations of communal values or communal obligations. Thus, Pineau's speech to the French National Assembly on 3 August contrasted France's respect for international law with Egypt's disregard for international law (*DIA 1956*: 140–50), while his circular telegram on 1 November emphasized France's "long respect for international law" (*DDF 1956*, III: 123–4). Likewise, Lloyd emphasized that British actions should signal that compliance with the Charter was the "foundation" of its foreign policy (Kyle 1991: 121–31), while the Foreign Office warned that arguably illegal military intervention in Egypt might undermine states' perceptions of the United Kingdom's commitment to its obligations under the UN Charter and other treaties (Johnman 2000: 47).

These arguments were intended to legitimate arguably illegal Anglo-French military actions and not necessarily to generate consensus through deliberation, as the communal obligation model suggests. British and French policy-makers introduced draft Security Council resolutions with the intention of eliciting a Soviet veto, which they hoped to use as a pretext for military intervention (*DDF 1956*, II: 569–70), and they offered subsequent arguments with the intention of obstructing the settlement process, which they feared would prevent Anglo-French military forces from occupying the canal. Rather than deliberation, Eden expected payback from the United States for prior British support and expressed anger afterwards that, while the United Kingdom had "understood" US actions in Guatemala in 1954 and had "done what we could not to hamper them," two years later the United States was "behaving in a precisely contrary manner towards us" (Eden 1960: 566).

Contrary to the liberal model, domestic legal advisors played only a limited role in these policy decisions. French policy-makers do not appear to have consulted with legal advisors at all, while British policy-makers largely ignored their conclusions. For example, when Nutting recommended that Fitzmaurice be invited to discuss the legality of the proposed operation, Eden reportedly responded that "Fitz[maurice] is the last person I want consulted" because "[t]he lawyers are always against our doing anything" (Nutting 1967: 95). Fitzmaurice later complained that he had not been consulted on many of the most important decisions, and noted his concern that "the way in which the matter has been handled on the legal side ... [is] detrimental to the functioning of the Foreign Office" (Johnman 2000: 60–1).

Ultimately, Fitzmaurice proved correct. In complaining about the lack of consultation with Foreign Office legal advisors, he had predicted that, as a result of the United Kingdom's arguably illegal actions, its "position ... [was] bound to be seriously prejudiced" (Johnman 2000: 60–1) – which it was. The failure of British and French policy-makers to exercise sufficient restraint elicited widespread resistance from other states, throughout the Middle East and elsewhere.[7] Such failure, however, does not represent a shortcoming of the prudential restraint model so much as an error in judgment by British and French policy-makers. In assessing the likelihood of resistance from other states, British and French policy-makers miscalculated, much as Soviet policy-makers did during their nearly simultaneous invasion of Hungary, which is examined in the chapter that follows.

6

THE IMPACT OF THE UN CHARTER ON SOVIET MILITARY INTERVENTION IN HUNGARY, 1956

As Anglo-French military forces intervened in Egypt in late 1956, Soviet military forces initiated similar actions against Hungary. An initial operation, intended to quell an uprising by Hungarian dissidents, began on 24 October, while a subsequent operation, intended to overthrow the government of Imre Nagy and keep Hungary in the Warsaw Pact, began on 1 November. Consistent with the prudential restraint model, Soviet policy-makers expressed concern that these arguably illegal military interventions would evoke resistance from other states and altered their actions accordingly. During the initial intervention, reinforcements from outside Hungary were not deployed until after the Hungarian government requested them, and no additional reinforcements were deployed once a ceasefire had been proclaimed. During the subsequent intervention, although Soviet policy-makers arranged for a provisional government to request Soviet military assistance, they concluded afterwards that their failure to exercise sufficient restraint had prompted non-aligned states to downgrade their perceptions of Soviet intentions.

These two cases of Soviet military intervention are useful for purposes of theory testing because they add variance in regime type across cases. Unlike the previous cases, the intervening power in these cases is not a liberal major power, and some might argue not a status quo power, either, although the evidence from these cases suggests otherwise. Although the cases are not as well documented as the previous cases are, primary source material recently has been made available and is supplemented by excellent secondary sources.[1]

Initial stages of military planning

Soviet policy-makers had been fearful of unrest in Hungary since early 1955, when Hungarian Prime Minister Imre Nagy proposed a multiparty government as a solution to attempts by the Hungarian Workers' Party

(HWP) to hinder political and economic reform in Hungary (Békés *et al.* 2002: 60–5). In response to this proposal, HWP First Secretary Mátyás Rákosi removed Nagy from his position as Prime Minister, but as popular resentment grew, Soviet policy-makers became increasingly fearful that the Hungarian government might be overthrown and that Hungary might leave the Warsaw Pact (Kramer 1996: 363). On 13 July 1956, the Central Committee of the Soviet Communist Party (CPSU) sent First Deputy Chairman Anastas Mikoyan to Budapest to stave off the impending crisis. At Mikoyan's suggestion, the HWP removed Rákosi from his position as First Secretary and replaced him with Ernő Gerő. However, Mikoyan reported back to Moscow that the HWP were "losing their grip on power" and that a "parallel center" was forming from "enemy elements operating actively, decisively, and self-confidently" in Hungary (Békés *et al.* 2002: 143–7). Accordingly, Soviet Defense Minister Georgii Zhukov ordered his Deputy Chief of Staff General Mikhail Malinin and General Piotr Lashchenko to prepare a secret plan for responding to large-scale internal disturbances in Hungary. Following the approval of the plan on 20 July, Soviet forces in Hungary were placed on increased alert in anticipation of possible military action (Kramer 1996: 365).

On 23 October, Hungarian dissidents took control of Hungarian Radio facilities in Budapest and broadcast a list of demands for reform (Kirov 1999: 132). Meanwhile, as street protestors shouted "Rákosi into the Danube – Imre Nagy into the government," Hungarian rebels engaged in a coordinated series of attacks on telephone exchanges, printing presses, police stations, munitions factories, and military installations throughout Budapest. Hungarian security forces were quickly overwhelmed (Berecz 1986: 104–5; Kramer 1996: 366).

The Presidium of the CPSU Central Committee met that evening to discuss a report from the Soviet embassy in Budapest that the situation in Hungary was becoming "extremely dangerous" and that Soviet military intervention would be necessary (*CWIHPB 1995*, 5: 53–5). CPSU First Secretary Nikita Khrushchev, who already had ordered several Soviet divisions to prepare for deployment, proposed that the Presidium authorize direct military intervention (Győrkei and Horváth 1999: 10). Zhukov concurred, noting that Gerő already had asked the Soviet military attaché in Budapest to dispatch Soviet troops to suppress the rebellion (*CWIHPB 1995*, 5: 53–5). Mikoyan and others, however, disagreed and suggested that a peaceful solution might yet be possible (*CWIHPB 1996–97*, 8/9: 388–9).

Although they remained divided over the possible use of military force, Presidium members ultimately concluded that they could not approve Gerő's request because it had not come from "the highest Hungarian officials" and therefore was not legal. Khrushchev spoke with Gerő by telephone, informing him that the Soviet Union would approve his request if the Hungarian government presented it in writing. Khrushchev recommended that Prime Minister András Hegedűs convene a meeting of the government to prepare such a request (*CWIHPB 1995*, 5: 53–5). When Gerő responded that such a meeting could not be convened quickly, Khrushchev ordered Zhukov to "redeploy Soviet units into Budapest to assist Hungarian troops and state security forces in the restoration of public order." However, no units from outside of Hungary were to be deployed until a written request was provided (Kramer 1996: 366).[2]

Operation "Wave"

On the morning of 24 October, Soviet military units redeployed from their bases in Hungary to positions around Budapest. That same day, the HWP removed Gerő as First Secretary, replacing him with János Kádar, and demoted Hegedűs to Deputy Prime Minister, replacing him with Imre Nagy. As the fighting continued, Nagy (though not yet sworn in as Prime Minister) declared a state of emergency and announced on Hungarian Radio that he had requested Soviet military forces to intervene in Hungary and restore order. Following the announcement, Soviet military forces from Romania and Ukraine crossed into Hungary to support the troops already deployed to Budapest (Kramer 1996: 366). To increase the persuasiveness of Soviet legal claims, Hegedűs was presented with a backdated request for Soviet military intervention, which he signed on 27 October (Rainer 1993: 104).

Because Soviet military planners had assumed that a show of force would intimidate Hungarian rebels into laying down their arms, Soviet military forces were unprepared for the resistance they faced. Armored units had been deployed without adequate infantry protection, and Hungarian military forces were either unable to provide infantry support or else had defected to the opposing side (Kramer 1996: 366; Győrkei and Horváth 1999: 21). As fighting continued, rebels destroyed Soviet symbols throughout Hungary and called for Hungary's withdrawal from the Warsaw Pact. The HWP Central Committee responded by promising a new national government, economic and political changes, and negotiations regarding the future of the Warsaw Pact. On 28 October, the new government was sworn in; Nagy announced an immediate ceasefire and proposed a negotiated withdrawal of Soviet troops from Hungary (Békés *et al.* 2002: 253–61).

Reporting to the Presidium that day, Khrushchev noted that the uprising had spread to such an extent that Soviet military forces in Hungary were not sufficient to suppress it. Presidium Chairman Kliment Voroshilov urged that additional Soviet military forces be sent to Hungary to form a new government, with their actions justified as a response to foreign interference in Hungary's internal affairs. Premier Nikolai Bulganin disagreed, arguing that the Soviet Union should "adopt a position of support for the current government," because the sending of military forces would "drag us into a dubious venture." Khrushchev concurred, noting that "[t]he English and French are in a real mess in Egypt" and that the Soviet Union "shouldn't get caught in the same company." According to Khrushchev, in pursuing such a policy, the Soviet Union would be "saving face" and thereby reducing the likelihood that other states would respond with resistance, as they had against the United Kingdom and France. Presidium members agreed with Khrushchev and decided to reinforce the Soviet military forces with troops already in Hungary. They would support Nagy's efforts to achieve a political settlement and to negotiate the eventual withdrawal of Soviet forces from Hungary (*CWIHPB 1996–97*, 8/9: 389–92).

Having adopted this policy, Khrushchev noted that it would be necessary to "set Sobolev right at the UN" (*CWIHPB 1996–97*, 8/9: 389–92). Foreign Minister Dmitri Shepilov had instructed UN Representative Arkady Sobolev to argue that the rebellion in Hungary was part of a "fascist movement" and that that the Soviet Union had intervened to assist the government of Hungary in accordance with Article 4 of the 1947 Peace Treaty. However, because Nagy subsequently had referred to the rebellion as a "national-democratic uprising" rather than a "fascist movement," and because Soviet policy-makers now had decided to assist Nagy without using armed force, it would be necessary that Shepilov attempt to maintain the plausibility of Soviet legal claims by obscuring the contradictions between them. Accordingly, Shepilov instructed Sobolev not to mention the Peace Treaty again and to distinguish between a legal "democratic movement" in Hungary and an illegal "fascist movement" that was attempting to take advantage of disorder in Hungary in an attempt to overthrow the lawful government. Similarly, Shepilov instructed Ambassador Yurii Andropov to "speak with the Hungarian leadership about the expedience of publishing an appropriate Hungarian government statement . . . not[ing] that the developments in Hungary are the internal affair of Hungary, and that the counterrevolutionary riot . . . was a result of subversive activity by the imperialist states." According to Shepilov, the statement should claim that "Soviet military forces' participation in suppressing the counterrevolutionary riot is a result of the Hungarian government's request to the government of the USSR to provide assistance in reconstructing the legal order . . . and the Hungarian state's sovereignty." Shepilov instructed that the Hungarian government should protest the introduction of the question in the Security Council and "prepare appropriate materials . . . [and] documents characterizing the Western powers' interference in Hungary's internal affairs which could be used by the Soviet representative discussing this issue" (Békés *et al.* 2002: 270–1).

On 30 October, Hungarian Radio announced the impending withdrawal of the Soviet troops from Budapest, following ceasefire talks.

However, Soviet military forces continued to engage rebels outside of Budapest, reinforced by additional units deployed from bases in the Soviet Union (Talbot 1970: 417). Upon hearing of continued Soviet troop movements, Nagy summoned Andropov and asked him whether it was "true that new Soviet military units are continuing to enter Hungary from the USSR" because "[w]e did not negotiate this." Mikoyan and CPSU Central Committee Secretary Mikhail Suslov sent a report to the Presidium expressing concern that Nagy's protest "could be a turning point in the change in Hungarian policy in the Security Council," insofar as the Soviet Union might be perceived as an aggressor, having violating the ceasefire. They proposed that the Soviet Union "cease sending troops into Hungary, continuing to concentrate them on Soviet territory," even though doing so would delay possible future deployment of Soviet troops in Hungary (*CWIHPB 1995*, 5: 32).

Discussing the report from Mikoyan and Suslov, Khrushchev suggested that the Presidium adopt a declaration on the withdrawal of troops. Two days previously, Khrushchev had asked Shepilov and Central Committee Secretaries Leonid Brezhnev and Piotr Pospelov to prepare a draft of such a declaration, which the Presidium approved that same day. Most members expressed hoped that the declaration would help to extract the Soviet Union from the "onerous position" in which it would find itself if states concluded that its arguably illegal actions signaled aggressive intentions (*CWIHPB 1996–97*, 8/9: 392–3). The declaration, which was published in *Pravda* the following day, declared that Soviet foreign relations were based "on the principles of complete equality, or respect for territorial integrity, state independence and sovereignty, and of noninterference in one another's internal affairs" and that "stationing the troops ... on the territory of another state ... is done ... only with the consent of the state on the territory of which and at the request of which these troops are stationed or it is planned to station them." According to the declaration, Soviet military forces had been instructed "to withdraw ... from the city of Budapest as soon as this is considered necessary by the Hungarian Government" (*DSB 1956*, 35: 745–7).

Operation "Whirlwind"

As Soviet troops completed their withdrawal from Budapest, Nagy announced the end of the one-party system in Hungary and the formation of a coalition government. On 31 October, Nagy sent a letter to Voroshilov requesting "immediate negotiations in connection with the withdrawal of Soviet troops from the entire territory of Hungary" (Békés *et al.* 2002: 316). Nagy's letter, combined with a report from Mikoyan and Suslov that the situation in Hungary was "getting worse," revived fears among Soviet policy-makers that Hungary might leave the Warsaw

Pact (Granville 2004: 72, 85). At a Presidium meeting that same day, Khrushchev urged that the Soviet Union "take the initiative" and intervene in Hungary to overthrow the Nagy government. Khrushchev proposed installing a provisional government headed by HWP First Secretary János Kádár and Hungarian Interior Minister Ferenc Münnich, with which it could negotiate a withdrawal of Soviet troops from Hungary but which would keep Hungary as a member of the Warsaw Pact.[3] The provisional government would request Soviet military assistance, thereby providing a legal pretext for direct intervention. The Presidium approved Khrushchev's proposal and ordered Zhukov to finalize plans for a second military intervention to occur the next day (*CWIHPB 1995*, 5: 32). Upon arriving in Moscow later that evening, Mikoyan objected to the Presidium's decision and expressed his concern that states would perceive the Soviet Union as an aggressor and respond with resistance to it. Khrushchev, however, responded by noting that the decision already had been made and a legal pretext prepared (Schecter and Luchkov 1990: 122).

On 1 November, Soviet military forces in Hungary redeployed to airfields throughout the country, while additional forces crossed into Hungary and assembled at prearranged points (Kirov 1999: 151). Nagy sent a letter of protest to Andropov, who denied that additional Soviet military forces were entering Hungary, claiming that only railway workers were entering Hungary and that Soviet armor was being used only to evacuate wounded soldiers from Budapest (*CWIHPB 1996–97*, 8/9: 395–7). Unsatisfied with Andropov's response, Nagy announced Hungary's withdrawal from the Warsaw Pact. He also sent a letter to the UN Secretary-General requesting recognition of Hungary's neutrality and asking the Security Council "to instruct the Soviet and Hungarian Governments to start the negotiations immediately" on Hungary's withdrawal from the Warsaw Pact (UN Doc. S/3726).

Discussing these developments at a Presidium meeting, Mikoyan reaffirmed his previous argument that military intervention in Hungary was "inappropriate in the current circumstances" and hence the Soviet Union should continue to support the Hungarian government. Zhukov disagreed, arguing that the Soviet Union was "acting on the basis of the Declaration ... [because] the redeployments will bring order," and hence no additional pretext was necessary (*CWIHPB 1996–97*, 8/9: 393–5). Other Presidium members, however, expressed concern once again that other states might perceive the arguably illegal Soviet intervention in Hungary as similar to the British and French intervention in Egypt and respond with resistance (Békés *et al.* 2002: 359–61). In an attempt to maintain the persuasiveness of their legal claims and thereby reduce the likelihood of such resistance, the Presidium decided that the Soviet Union should "hold to" its October 30 declaration, despite Nagy's attempt to use it to their disadvantage in his letter of protest, so that their legal claims would not contradict those contained in the arguments they had offered previously (*CWIHPB 1996–97*, 8/9: 397–8). Despite these efforts, however, the Soviet Union faced widespread resistance within the Security Council the following day, because its statement of 30 October had announced the withdrawal of its troops from Hungary, but Nagy's letter noted that additional troops had entered Hungary. The Soviet Union responded with denial, claiming that it had assisted in suppressing a "counter-revolutionary uprising" against the Hungarian government and that claims regarding additional military forces entering Hungary were "utterly unfounded" (*UNYB 1956*: 68–9).

On the morning of 4 November, additional Soviet military units crossed into Hungary from Romania, as a pre-recorded declaration by Kádár was broadcast on behalf of the "Hungarian Revolutionary Workers' and Peasants' Government." Nagy responded by broadcasting a statement that Soviet military forces had intervened in Hungary "with the obvious intention of overthrowing the lawful, democratic Hungarian Government" and that Hungarian military forces were "in combat" (Békés *et al.* 2002: 383). That same day, the Soviet Union argued before the Security Council that it lacked reliable information on developments in Hungary and vetoed a draft resolution (proposed by the United States) calling upon the Soviet Union to "desist forthwith from any intervention" in Hungary. Following the Soviet veto, the Security Council approved a Uniting for Peace resolution transferring the matter to the General Assembly, which in turn approved a resolution (UN Doc. A/Res/1004) calling upon the Soviet Union to "desist forthwith from . . . any form of intervention in Hungary" and to withdraw its military forces "without delay" (*UNYB 1956*: 69–70). On 7 November, Kádár was sworn in as Prime Minister of Hungary,[4] and on 12 November the Kádár government sent a letter to the UN Secretary General claiming that Hungary had requested Soviet military assistance and that resolution of the matter "lay exclusively within the internal legal competence of the Hungarian State" (UN Doc. A/3341).

Assessing the evidence

Consistent with the prudential restraint model, prior to the initial intervention, Soviet policy-makers expressed concern regarding the likelihood of resistance from other states and attempted to arrange an invitation from the Hungarian government. Although Soviet military forces deployed from their bases in Hungary before receiving such an invitation, Soviet units not already stationed in Hungary were not deployed until Nagy publicly requested Soviet assistance – despite the need for infantry units to protect Soviet armored units already deployed to Budapest – and additional Soviet military forces were ordered to remain where they were once the ceasefire was declared – despite continuing hostilities. As Mikoyan and Suslov's report of 30 October makes clear, contrary to the realist model, Soviet policy-makers were willing to bear considerable costs in order to maintain the persuasiveness of the legal claims justifying Soviet military intervention in Hungary. They were willing not only to sustain the casualties that resulted from the lack of sufficient infantry support, but also to delay possible future deployments of Soviet military forces in Hungary. And they were willing to do so despite having lost confidence in the Hungarian military, which they feared might unite with rebel forces and thereby make it "necessary for Soviet armed forces once again to undertake military operations" in Hungary, on an even larger scale than before (Granville 2004: 66).

Contrary to the communal obligation model, Soviet policy-makers expressed their concerns in terms of perceived violations of Soviet legal commitments under the UN Charter, rather than amorphous conceptualizations of communal values or communal obligations. They noted that military intervention could be legally justified only through a written invitation from the Hungarian government and that it would be necessary to argue before the United Nations that Soviet actions had been undertaken in accordance with the Soviet Union's legal obligations under the UN Charter and the 1947 Peace Treaty with Hungary. At a Presidium meeting on 30 October, after Voroshilov cautioned that a declaration on the withdrawal of Soviet troops from Hungary "must be composed so that we aren't placed into an onerous position" at the Security Council, Shepilov suggested that the declaration emphasize Soviet Union "support [for] the principles of non-interference," while Molotov added that the declaration should mention Soviet compliance with its "treaties with every country." The Declaration that resulted from these discussions made explicit reference to UN Charter principles of "territorial integrity and political independence" and took into account possible legal justifications for future situations in which Soviet military intervention might be necessary (*CWIHPB 1996–97*, 8/9: 392–3).

Although Soviet military forces intervened in Hungary a second time, once it seemed likely that Hungary would withdraw from the Warsaw Pact, Soviet policy-makers made arrangements for a provisional government to request Soviet intervention, and Khrushchev expressed concern that the documents that would be used to justify the second intervention were "poorly prepared" and thus might not be sufficiently persuasive to justify the proposed intervention (*CWIHPB 1996–97*, 8/9: 397–8). A CPSU Committee on Information report later confirmed Khrushchev's fears, noting that India and other non-aligned states had responded with resistance to the Soviet Union's "violation of a condition of the UN Charter" by pursuing closer ties to the United States, which they perceived as providing a "firm[er] guarantee of the maintenance of peace" than the Soviet Union did (*CWIHPB 1994*, 4: 62–4).

7

THE IMPACT OF THE UN CHARTER ON US–BRITISH MILITARY INTERVENTION IN IRAQ, 1990–98

During the period from 1990 through 1998, US and British military forces invaded Iraq and subsequently engaged in a series of smaller military actions, all of which were intended, at least in part, to overthrow the government of Saddam Hussein. These actions came in response to Iraq's invasion of Kuwait in August 1990 and its attempts to develop weapons of mass destruction (WMD). Consistent with the prudential restraint model, US and British policy-makers sought to obtain UN resolutions authorizing enforcement action against Iraq and recognized that maintaining the persuasiveness of legal arguments based on those resolutions would prevent them from expanding their mission explicitly to include the overthrow of the Iraqi government. Consequently, they undertook a series of unsuccessful covert operations intended to accomplish the same purpose. Out of concern that other states would respond with resistance to their arguably illegal military actions, US and British policy-makers delayed and/or canceled several military operations for lack of a sufficient legal pretext, and thus when a major air campaign finally commenced in December 1998, Kurdish and Shi'ite rebels in Iraq no longer believed US and British promises of air support and opted not to take up arms against Saddam's government.

These cases are useful for purposes of theory testing because they occurred during the post-Cold War era, thereby allowing for comparison with previous cases that occurred during the Cold War. They also help to ensure against selection bias, because they include instances in which the UN Security Council gave explicit approval to military action undertaken by a major power. In addition, there is variance both within and among these cases in the actions taken, the arguments offered for those actions, and the governments holding office in both the United States and the United Kingdom. Although not as well documented as the previous cases are, because of their more recent occurrence, these cases can be adequately pieced together using memoirs and secondary sources, which provide a thorough account of US and British decision-making processes and outcomes throughout the period.[1]

Operation "Desert Shield"/Operation "Desert Storm"

Following the invasion of Kuwait on 2 August 1990, US President George H. W. Bush met with his national security advisors to discuss possible US responses. In addition to their fears about Middle East oil supplies, US policy-makers had longstanding concerns about Iraq's biological, chemical, and nuclear weapons programs, which had been in place since the late 1970s (United States Central Intelligence Agency n.d.). Bush informed UN Ambassador Thomas Pickering that he was willing to consider militarily action against Iraq, but before doing so, he wanted to pursue UN involvement, which he believed would assist the United States in "rallying international opposition to the invasion and reversing it." Bush instructed Pickering to work with the government of Kuwait to convene an emergency meeting of the Security Council (Bush and Scowcroft 1998: 303, 316–17; see also Woodward 1991: 226). Meanwhile, having consulted with her Cabinet, British Prime Minister Margaret Thatcher reached nearly the same conclusions as Bush and his advisors had reached, Thatcher suggested that the United States propose a draft Security Council resolution calling for economic sanctions against Iraq (Freedman and Karsh 1993: 75; Thatcher 1993: 816–18). Later that same day, the Security Council unanimously approved a resolution condemning the invasion and demanding that "Iraq withdraw immediately and unconditionally" from Kuwait (UN Doc. S/Res/660).

Although US policy-makers believed that the invasion and subsequent Security Council resolution provided a legal basis for military action, they did not believe that it provided a sufficient legal pretext for overthrowing the Iraqi government. Concerned about the possibility of resistance from other states, US National Security Advisor Brent Scowcroft suggested proceeding along "two tracks," justifying military action as a lawful response to Iraqi aggression while secretly planning to overthrow the Iraqi government as part of such action (Woodward 1991: 237; Graham-Brown 1999: 64). Secretary of State James Baker expressed concern, however, that an attack on Iraq's military forces "could turn things against us unless it is done in conjunction with an Iraqi move into Saudi Arabia." Bush agreed and decided, for the time being, to deploy a defensive force only,[2] despite warnings by CIA Director William Webster that Iraq would not withdraw from Kuwait unless "challenged within the next year" and that the annexation of Kuwait would "fundamentally alter the Persian Gulf region" (Bush and Scowcroft 1998: 322–9). Soon afterwards, Bush signed an intelligence finding authorizing the CIA to recruit Iraqi dissidents to remove Saddam from power (Woodward 1991: 282; Hiro 1992: 113).

On 6 August, the Security Council unanimously approved a resolution calling on states to impose economic sanctions on Iraq (UN Doc. S/Res/661). Meeting with Thatcher that afternoon to discuss the implementation of sanctions, Bush noted that, in the opinion of his legal advisors, a naval blockade was an act of war that had not been explicitly authorized by the Security Council. Thatcher responded by noting that an additional resolution explicitly authorizing the use of armed force "might tie our hands unacceptably" by establishing a precedent that "force could only be used – even in self-defense – when the United Nations approved" (Thatcher 1993: 821–2). She suggested that the United States and the United Kingdom avoid such difficulties by justifying their actions as collective self-defense of Kuwait and Saudi Arabia and not seeking an additional Security Council resolution. Although US policy-makers disagreed with Thatcher's legal assessment, they agreed with her conclusions, and US and British military forces were deployed to Saudi Arabia and Bahrain that very day (Baker 1995: 279; Bush and Scowcroft 1998: 336). In announcing the deployment, Bush argued that US and British military forces would "assist the Saudi Arabian government in the defense of its homeland" (*DSD 1990*, 1: 54–5), while British Foreign Secretary Douglas Hurd added that these forces would "contribute ... to a multinational effort for the collective defense of the territory of Saudi Arabia and other threatened states in the area, and in support of the United Nations embargo" (Freedman and Karsh 1993: 112).

Meeting with Secretary of State Baker on 10 August to discuss a possible naval blockade, Bush expressed concern about the resistance from other states if US naval forces fired on merchant ships during time of peace, given the questionable legality of the blockade under resolution 661. After discussing the matter with Baker, Bush decided that naval forces would not enforce the sanctions until 16 August, so as to allow time for US policy-makers to obtain a formal request for such action from the government of Kuwait (Bush and Scowcroft 1998: 344–5). Following the meeting, Baker released a statement arguing that resolution 661 provided "the legal authority necessary to constitute such an embargo or blockade, provided the request comes from the legitimate government of Kuwait" (Keesing's 1990).

Meanwhile, British naval forces already had begun intercepting and boarding merchant ships en route to and from Iraq, prompting the Soviet Union and France to protest that no state could implement resolution 661 unilaterally. Upon hearing these arguments, British policy-makers expressed concern that members of the Security Council might propose a resolution condemning the United Kingdom's arguably use of armed force. Accordingly, Thatcher ordered a temporary halt to naval enforcement of the sanctions and began to argue as US policy-makers had, justifying the blockade as collective self-defense at the request of Kuwait. On 14 August, the British Foreign Office released a statement arguing that a request from the legitimate government of Kuwait would provide a legal basis for the blockade, even without Security Council approval, and that such a request was expected and would be granted promptly. British policy-makers later supplemented this claim by arguing that British naval forces essentially would be monitoring the observance of the sanctions, and although the United Kingdom would use force, if necessary, it would report any violations of the sanctions to the Security Council (Freedman and Karsh 1993: 145, 455).

On 22 August, as five oil tankers were preparing to depart Iraq, Bush met with his advisors to discuss possible US action. Baker reported resistance from other states in response to British naval actions in the Persian Gulf and suggested that enforcement of the sanctions be delayed further, because US naval action might evoke similar resistance from the Soviet Union and other members of the Security Council (Baker 1995: 286; Bush and Scowcroft 1998: 351–2). Powell agreed, noting that further delay would demonstrate the United States' commitment to the UN Charter and thereby strengthen international support for its actions. Scowcroft disagreed, however, arguing that further delay would only demonstrate a lack of resolve and that seeking a resolution explicitly authorizing the use of armed force would create a precedent that would unduly restrict future US military operations. According to Scowcroft, using armed force after having failed to attain requested UN authorization would be more harmful than using armed force without having sought UN authorization in the first place. Scowcroft reported that he had spoken with British Ambassador Charles Powell who, along with Thatcher, had agreed with his assessment. Bush, however, sided with Baker and decided to delay enforcement of the sanctions and to request explicit UN authorization (Freedman and Karsh 1993: 146–8). On 25 August, the Security Council responded by unanimously approving a resolution calling upon states "co-operating with the Government of Kuwait . . . to use such measures commensurate to the specific circumstances as may be necessary under the authority of the Security Council to halt all inward and outward maritime shipping" (UN Doc. S/Res/665). Following the approval of the resolution, US naval forces began implementing a blockade against Iraq.

Even with the blockade in place, both the CIA and the British Joint Intelligence Committee concluded that sanctions alone were unlikely to lead to the withdrawal of Iraq from Kuwait, and thus armed force would be necessary (Freedman and Karsh 1993: 196, 202). Bush still believed that existing Security Council resolutions provided a firm legal basis for military action, but he was concerned about the possibility of resistance if the United States were perceived as an aggressor for having attacked Iraq without explicit UN authorization or else "some dramatic incident to justify immediate military action." National Security Director Richard

Haass suggested requesting Security Council authorization only if US policy-makers were "fairly certain" that there would be enough votes to approve a resolution authorizing the use of armed force. If not, Haass suggested that the United States justify the use of force based on existing Security Council resolutions, Article 51 of the UN Charter, and a request by the government of Kuwait (Bush and Scowcroft 1998: 353–6). Thatcher, on the other hand, remained opposed to pursuing an additional Security Council resolution under any circumstances. She believed that legal claims of implicit authorization under existing resolutions were sufficiently persuasive and that returning to the Security Council would risk a split vote, which would make such claims less persuasive and evoke even more resistance from other states. Thatcher also was concerned that requesting explicit UN authorization would subject the United States and the United Kingdom to restrictions imposed by the Soviet Union and China and would render future claims based on the inherent right of self-defense under Article 51 less persuasive (Munro 1996: 94, 154). As she argued before an Emergency Session of Parliament on 6 September, "[t]o undertake now to use no military force without the further authority of the Security Council would be to deprive ourselves of a right in international law expressly affirmed by Security Council Resolution 661" (Hansard 2003).

Meeting again on 17 October, Scowcroft argued that obtaining UN authorization to use force in support of the embargo had "set a precedent," which suggested the need for a similar resolution authorizing the use of force to implement resolution 660. Bush concurred, but suggested that a forcible attempt to resupply the US embassy in Kuwait might provoke a response from Iraq that would provide a sufficient legal pretext for military intervention without UN authorization. Thatcher, however, argued that the coalition should not rely on such a provocation, because it might come at an inopportune time. Scowcroft agreed, noting that "if we pounded [Iraq] from the air too soon, before our forces were ready, there could be public pressure to stop all fighting and turn opinion against ever launching a ground campaign." Accordingly, US and British policy-makers decided that they would intervene in Iraq "no later than January or February" and that they would seek a Security Council resolution implicitly or explicitly authorizing such action (Bush and Scowcroft 1998: 382–6; Powell and Persico 1995: 487–8).

In the days that followed, US policy-makers worked on drafting a proposed Security Council resolution. Scowcroft suggested that Iraq be given a deadline to withdraw from Kuwait by the end of the year, when US and British military forces would be in position to launch an invasion. According to Scowcroft, such a deadline would demonstrate US restraint by allowing time for economic sanctions to work. General Colin Powell, the Chairman of the Joint Chiefs of Staff, suggested a slightly later deadline, because US military forces would not be in place until 15 January and because "chances at the UN improve the longer the sanctions have a chance to work." Baker agreed with Powell and Scowcroft and instructed that the draft resolution incorporate the wording of resolution 665, which made reference to "all necessary means," but omit any reference to Article 42 of the UN Charter, which would require that force be used only when the Security Council determined that sanctions had proven "inadequate." According to Undersecretary of State Robert Kimmitt, such a resolution would implicitly authorize the use of armed force against Iraq (Baker 1995: 302–5; Bush and Scowcroft 1998: 392–6). On 29 November, the Security Council approved the resolution, which demanded that Iraq withdraw from Kuwait by 15 January and authorized member states "to use all necessary means to uphold and implement resolution 660 . . . and all subsequent relevant resolutions and to restore international peace and security in the area" (UN Doc. S/Res/678).

As the buildup continued throughout the month of December, Bush met with John Major, the new British Prime Minister, to finalize plans for military action. US and British policy-makers had agreed that, although the removal of Saddam and the elimination of Iraq's nuclear weapons program[3] would be objectives of any proposed military operation, Saddam's removal would not be made an explicit objective of such action, because doing so would "cloud" the basic issue of Iraqi aggression and would be likely to evoke resistance from other states. Instead, they would argue that military force was necessary to reverse Iraqi aggression and that dismantling Iraq's nuclear weapons program was necessary to reduce the likelihood of future aggression (Thatcher 1993: 827; Munro 1996: 158). Powell and US Secretary of Defense Richard Cheney reported that although ground forces would not be in place until early February, air forces would be ready by 15 January, and an air campaign could begin before the ground forces were in place. Accordingly, Bush and Major decided to launch air strikes on the morning of 16 January and to extend the strikes beyond the Kuwait area of operations in order to destroy Iraq's Republic Guard divisions and thereby weaken the Iraqi regime, such that the Iraqi military could then overthrow Saddam. However, so as not to exceed the UN mandate, ground forces would not advance to Baghdad to achieve this purpose (Woodward 1991: 350–2; Major 1999: 225–6).

On 6 January, Bush met with Baker, Scowcroft, Powell, and other advisors to finalize plans for military action. US policy-makers agreed that the initial air strikes should occur in the early morning hours to reduce collateral damage and to allow US and British aircraft to fly in near-total darkness, but they had not agreed on a day. Powell suggested delaying military action for two days following the UN deadline, in order to signal US restraint. Other policy-makers agreed, and 17 January was set as the date for air strikes to begin (Powell and Persico 1995: 502). Baker met with

British Foreign Secretary Douglas Hurd the following day to discuss a French proposal to extend the deadline. Baker and Hurd agreed to reject the proposal, which was linked to a Middle East peace conference, because it imposed conditions on Iraq's withdrawal from Kuwait. Two days later, after meeting with Iraqi Foreign Minister Tariq Aziz in Geneva, Baker announced that a peaceful settlement was unlikely (Hiro 1992: 298).

As coalition aircraft[4] began attacking targets in Iraq on 17 January, US and British policy-makers offered arguments emphasizing the limited objectives of the operation in carrying out the UN mandate. However, included in the target list were "leadership targets," which US and British aircraft attacked in an attempt to assassinate Saddam (Hiro 1992: 362). Major argued, nevertheless, that the objectives of the operation were "clear and limited ... [as] set out in the United Nations Security Council resolutions" (United Kingdom Central Office of Information 1993: 75–6), while Bush argued that the actions had been undertaken so that the "[t]he legitimate government of Kuwait will be restored" and Iraq "will eventually comply will all relevant UN resolutions" (*DSD 1991*, 2: 37–8). Both speeches implied that Iraqi compliance included giving up its "nuclear bomb potential" and its chemical weapons facilities.

On 15 February, Iraq announced that it would comply with the terms of resolution 660, provided that the United States, the United Kingdom, and their allies paid for the reconstruction of Iraq, withdrew all military forces from the region, and negotiated a settlement in Lebanon and the Israeli-occupied territories (UN Doc. S/22229). US and British policy-makers rejected the Iraqi proposal, while reaffirming that they "support[ed] the territorial integrity of Iraq" and had "never targeted or made Saddam Hussein an object of ... this conflict." Bush, however, stated publicly that a possible solution would be for "the Iraqi military and the Iraqi people to take matters into their own hands to force Saddam Hussein ... to step aside and to ... comply with the UN resolutions," prompting British policy-makers to express concern that Bush's statement would undermine the persuasiveness of US and British legal claims regarding the purposes of the military operation (Freedman and Karsh 1993: 410–21).

On 22 February, US policy-makers outlined a proposal giving Iraq until noon the following day to withdraw all of its military forces from Kuwait or face an invasion by coalition ground forces. In doing so, they rejected a Soviet proposal for Iraq to withdraw over the course of three weeks (UN Doc. S/22241), because it would allow Iraq to keep its military forces largely intact, thereby reducing the likelihood that Saddam would be overthrown. Bush announced on 23 February that the conditions of the Soviet proposal did not conform to resolution 660, which demanded "immediate and unconditional withdrawal," and therefore military operations would proceed "as planned" (Hiro 1992: 368–76; see also Bush and Scowcroft 1998: 471–9).

After almost two days of coalition ground operations, Iraq again indicated its acceptance of resolution 660 and agreed to withdraw from Kuwait. In discussing the US response, Baker cautioned that requiring Iraq to abandon its armor would exceed the UN authorization and might evoke resistance from other states. Powell, however, noted that Iraq's reply was not an official response and that coalition forces would require only two more days to destroy most of the Iraqi military, while Bush added that because the reply attached conditions to Iraqi withdrawal, it could be rejected as not being in conformity with "all ... relevant resolutions" and therefore invalid (Freedman and Karsh 1993: 401; see also Bush and Scowcroft 1998: 481–2). UN Representative Pickering informed the Security Council the next day that, although coalition forces would not attack unarmed Iraqi soldiers in retreat, the United States would consider the retreat of combat units to be "movement of war" and therefore "still subject to the rules of war" (Federation of American Scientists 2002a).

With large numbers of Iraqi troops surrendering to coalition ground forces, US and British policy-makers realized that continuing ground operations would contradict previous legal arguments regarding the objections of the military operation (Baker 1995: 436; Powell and Persico 1995: 522). Moreover, a two-day US attack on retreating Iraqi military units heading toward Basra and Umm Qasr had evoked concerns that the Security Council would approve a resolution condemning the continued use of military force. Although General Norman Schwarzkopf reported that some Iraqi Republic Guard units might escape if combat operations were ended too soon, Bush responded that such a risk was "acceptable." Accordingly, on 28 February US and British policy-makers declared the suspension of military operations. Bush called for Iraqi compliance with "all relevant Security Council Resolutions," while Major called for Iraq to "destroy all remaining ballistic missiles and chemical weapons" (Hiro 1992: 392–5).

The Security Council adopted a resolution specifying formal ceasefire terms on 3 April. According to the resolution, "Iraq shall unconditionally accept the destruction, removal, or rendering harmless, under international supervision of ... [a]ll chemical and biological weapons and ... [a]ll ballistic missiles with a range greater than one hundred and fifty kilometres, and ... shall unconditionally agree not to acquire or develop nuclear weapons or nuclear-weapon-usable material." The resolution also required that Iraq submit to UN Special Commission (UNSCOM) and International Atomic Energy Agency (IAEA) weapons inspections (UN Doc. S/Res/687). Although Saddam remained in power, US intelligence estimates concluded that he would be overthrown within one year (Freedman and Karsh 1993: 417).

Operation "Provide Comfort"/Operation "Southern Watch"

Following the end of hostilities, a rebellion broke out among the Kurds in northern Iraq and the Shi'a in southern Iraq. By 24 March, Kurdish *peshmerga* guerrillas controlled all of northern Iraq, prompting a counter-offensive by the Iraqi government. Thousands of Kurdish refugees fled toward Turkey and Iran, which set up emergency camps in an attempt to accommodate them. The Security Council responded on 5 April by adopting a resolution that condemned "the repression of the Iraqi civilian population in many parts of Iraq" and appealed to "all Member States and to all humanitarian organizations to contribute to these humanitarian relief efforts" (UN Doc. S/Res/688).

Following the adoption of the resolution, US and British policy-makers discussed the possibility of direct military intervention to assist the Kurdish and Shi'ite rebellions. Scowcroft warned that such action would be likely to evoke resistance from other states (Bush and Scowcroft 1998: 489–90). As he already had made clear, a coup was "preferred" rather than a rebellion (Graham-Brown 1999: 19). Major, however, proposed that US and British military forces intervene to establish a "safe haven" under UN auspices. A "no-fly" zone north of the 36th parallel would protect the "safe haven," while also providing a legal pretext for coalition forces to attack Mosul and its surrounding air defense facilities. Major argued that if Iraq violated the "safe haven" or the "no-fly" zone, US and British military forces could retaliate, justifying their actions in accordance with resolutions 687 and 688 (Major 1999: 243; Hiro 2001: 171).[5]

US policy-makers initially rejected Major's proposal, out of concern that setting up relief centers on Iraqi soil without its consent would contradict legal claims regarding territorial integrity that were used to justify the use of force against Iraq in the first place. Moreover, because resolution 688 did not explicitly authorize the use of force, US policy-makers believed that such action would be likely to evoke resistance from other states, despite arguments claiming that US actions were consistent with the resolution (Freedman and Karsh 1993: 422–3; Graham-Brown 1999: 26). They concluded, however, that it might be possible to reach some accommodation with the Iraqi government, and on 16 April they joined the United Kingdom in declaring a "safe haven," which British Under-Secretary of State Mark Lennox-Boyd justified as "a temporary measure to meet an immediate and overwhelming humanitarian need" (Warbrick 1991: 973). At a news conference that same day, Bush argued that US and British military forces had acted in a manner "consistent with UN Security Council Resolution 688" (*DSD 1991*, 2: 273). On 18 April, Iraq signed a memorandum of understanding permitting the United Nations to offer humanitarian aid (UN Doc. S/22513), and two days later,

US and British military forces set up a relief camp near the Iraqi town of Zakho.

Despite the implementation of a "no-fly" zone north of the 36th parallel, defeat of the Kurdish and Shi'ite rebellions in March had allowed Saddam to consolidate his power in Iraq, prompting concern among US and British policy-makers that he would not be overthrown as they had hoped. Lacking a sufficient legal pretext for more direct military intervention, Bush authorized a covert operation in northern Iraq "to create the conditions for the removal of Saddam Hussein from power" (Hiro 1992: 417, 2001: 52). The following year, representatives from the US-funded Iraqi National Congress (INC), an umbrella organization of Iraqi resistance groups, met with Secretary of State Baker in Washington, D.C. to report on the repression of the Shi'a in southern Iraq and to advocate a "no-fly" zone similar to the one protecting the Kurds in northern Iraq. US and British policy-makers concluded that attacks against the Shi'a in southern Iraq provided a sufficient legal pretext for imposing a second "no-fly" zone, which could be used to coerce Iraq into cooperating with UNSCOM and IAEA inspectors and to target air-defense systems and weapons production facilities throughout southern Iraq (Graham-Brown 1999: 108; Hiro 2001: 66).[6] Accordingly, they requested a meeting of the Security Council to discuss "alarming and disconcerting" information about Iraq's repression of its Shi'ite population in violation of its obligations under resolution 688 (Aita 1992a).

The Security Council met on 11 August 1992, but adjourned without reaching agreement. Nevertheless, on 26 August Major declared a "no-fly" zone in southern Iraq, which he argued was necessary to ensure the safety of coalition aircraft enforcing resolution 688. The following day, US and British air forces began surveillance operations in Iraq below the 32nd parallel (Aita 1992b). Bush argued that the United States had acted because "the Government of Iraq is failing to meet its obligations under UN Security Council Resolution 688" (*DSD 1992*, 3: 35), while British policy-makers argued that because "[i]nternational law recognizes extreme humanitarian need . . . [w]e are on strong legal as well as humanitarian ground in setting up this 'no fly zone'" (Ramsbothan and Woodhouse 1996: 77–8).

Iraq, however, continued to hinder UN weapons inspectors, and on 11 January 1993 the Security Council released a Presidential Statement declaring that Iraq's actions "constitute[d] an unacceptable and material breach of the relevant provisions of resolution 687" and that "continued defiance" would result in "serious consequences" (UN Doc. S/25091). US and British policy-makers used this statement as a legal pretext to attack Iraqi surface-to-air missile sites throughout the southern "no-fly" zone on 13 January. Four days later, US military forces launched an attack against a nuclear fabrication facility near Baghdad, justifying their actions as having been taken "to help achieve the goals of the United Nations Security Council Resolutions 687, 707, and 715, namely to ensure that Iraq never again acquires weapons of mass destruction" (Federation of American Scientists 2002a). France, which had been participating in patrols of the "no-fly" zones, responded by explicitly dissociating itself from the attacks, which struck a target outside of the southern "no-fly" zone (Weller 1999/2000: 89). On 11 March, France, Russia, and China proposed a Presidential Statement acknowledging Iraqi cooperation with UN inspectors, which US and British policy-makers rejected.

Inspections continued throughout the year, and on 15 October UNSCOM Chairman Rolf Ekéus informed the Security Council that "substantial progress" had been made. On 18 March 1994, France, Russia, and China again proposed an acknowledgment of Iraqi cooperation for inclusion within a Presidential Statement on UN sanctions, which US and British policy-makers again rejected, arguing that sanctions should not be lifted until Iraq complied with all of its obligations, including its human rights obligations under resolution 688. US policy-makers attempted to obscure the contradiction between this argument and previous arguments that had linked sanctions to disarmament by releasing a statement on 20 July arguing that "all relevant resolutions" referred to in resolution 687 included both previous and subsequent resolutions (Hiro 2001: 69–79).

Meanwhile, the US and British intelligence services continued planning the overthrow of Saddam, preparing a coup to take place in June 1996. In January of that year, the CIA planted agents on an UNSCOM inspection team led by Scott Ritter and provided them with equipment for tapping the communications network of the Iraqi intelligence service (Ritter 1999: 143–4; Wurmser 1999: 21–5). To ensure that inspections would continue long enough for Iraqi noncompliance to provide a legal pretext for direct military intervention in support of the planned coup, US and British policy-makers countered Iraqi claims of compliance with continual demands for additional information and documentation regarding its weapons programs (Hiro 2001: 102–5). Their efforts were aided by the defection of General Hussein Kamal Hassan the previous summer. Kamal, who had served as the Iraqi Minister of Technical Industry, provided extensive intelligence on Iraq's efforts to conceal its weapons development programs, although he reported that he had "ordered destruction of all weapons – biological, chemical, missile, nuclear" shortly after the 1990–91 Gulf War (International Atomic Energy Agency 1995).

Because of the intelligence provided by Kamal regarding Iraq's efforts to conceal its weapons programs, on 12 June the Security Council approved a resolution demanding that Iraq give "immediate, unconditional, and unrestricted access" to all sites demanded by UNSCOM inspectors (UN Doc. S/Res/1060). US and British policy-makers had drafted the resolution in the hopes that Iraq would refuse to comply with it and that Ekéus would report Iraq's refusal to the Security Council. Such a report would assist them in persuading the Security Council to declare that Iraq was in "material breach" of its disarmament obligations, providing a legal pretext for military intervention in Iraq in support of the planned coup. However, having inferred that the United States and the United Kingdom were seeking such a pretext, Ekéus negotiated Iraq's acceptance of the resolution on 21 June. While these negotiations were taking place, Iraqi security forces arrested the conspirators involved in the coup plot, which had been discovered by Iraqi intelligence several weeks earlier (Graham-Brown 1999: 117; Hiro 2001: 107–8).

Later that summer, Iraqi military forces again advanced north, beyond the 36th parallel, capturing the town of Irbil and forcing the withdrawal of CIA operatives from the area.[7] British policy-makers suggested that the incident be used as a legal pretext for extending the southern "no-fly" zone, thereby preventing Iraq from training military pilots at air bases in southern Iraq and allowing US and British military forces to probe Iraq's early-warning systems (Graham-Brown 1999: 121; Hiro 2001: 112, 171). Although US policy-makers were concerned that Iraq's actions could not easily be portrayed as hostile, President Bill Clinton agreed with the British proposal, and on 3 September the United States submitted a letter to the Security Council declaring that it would extend the "no-fly" zone in southern Iraq because of Saddam's offensive operations against the Kurdish population of Irbil (UN Doc. S/1996/711).

Later that same day, US military forces attacked Iraqi surface-to-air missile sites in southern Iraq.[8] US Secretary of Defense William Perry justified the actions by claiming that resolutions 678, 687, and 688 implicitly "authorized the United States to organize a coalition to conduct Operation Provide Comfort, which enforced a no-fly zone north of 36 degrees; and later authorized Operation Southern Watch, which enforced a no-fly zone south of 32 degrees" (Federation of American Scientists 2002a). The United Kingdom offered similar arguments in support of these actions. Russia, however, argued that the attacks were an "inappropriate and unacceptable reaction" and urged an end to "all military action threatening the sovereignty and territorial integrity of Iraq" (UN Doc. S/1996/712). China also condemned the attacks, as did most Arab states. France argued that Iraq had not violated any UN resolution by occupying Irbil and announced that it would not participate in patrolling the extended "no-fly" zone in southern Iraq. On 31 December, France added that it would no longer participate in patrolling the "no-fly" zone in northern Iraq (Lockwood 1996; Lockwood and Nundy 1996).[9]

Operation "Desert Thunder"/Operation "Desert Fox"

Meanwhile, the US and British intelligence services had developed a new plan for overthrowing Saddam, which involved providing military aid and training to Kurdish and Shi'ite rebels in Iraq. US and British military forces would provide air cover to facilitate the capture of areas in southern and western Iraq from which to stage a rebellion and would support its advance toward Baghdad. Policy-makers believed that the intelligence gathered through UNSCOM inspections would be useful for planning air strikes on command and control centers in Iraq (Graham-Brown 1999: 117; Wurmser 1999: 37–8; Hiro 2001: 154, 164). However, having concluded that UNSCOM was an "instrument" of the United States and the United Kingdom, Iraq became even less cooperative with UN weapons inspectors in the months that followed (Ritter 1999: 140–1). On 28 October 1997, Iraq declared that it would not allow inspection teams into Iraq until a deadline was established for lifting the sanctions. Iraq also demanded the removal of all US personnel from UNSCOM inspections teams and the cessation of U-2 surveillance flights within Iraq (UN Doc. S/1997/829).

In the weeks that followed, Iraq removed dual-use equipment from monitored sites, demanded that "presidential sites" be excluded from future UNSCOM inspections, and blocked inspections by UNSCOM teams that included US personnel (Lockwood 1997; Weller 1999/2000: 83). In response, US Secretary of State Madeleine Albright and newly-appointed British Foreign Secretary Robin Cook decided to seek a Security Council resolution declaring Iraq to be in "material breach" of its disarmament obligations. Albright and Cook hoped that such a resolution would provide a legal pretext for the use of armed force against Iraq. In preparation for possible military action, both the United States and the United Kingdom ordered the deployment of additional military forces to the Persian Gulf (Bone 1997; Myers 1997). However, following a series of meetings with foreign heads of states, Albright concluded that there would not be sufficient support within the Security Council to obtain such a resolution, and the proposed military operation was delayed indefinitely (LaGuardia 1997; Sherwell 1997; Albright 2003: 277–80).

On 12 January 1998, Iraq again objected to US personnel as part of UNSCOM inspection teams (UN Doc. S/1998/28), and in response, the United States and the United Kingdom deployed additional military forces to the Persian Gulf to "enforce the Security Council's will" (Butcher 1998; Weller 1999/2000: 84). Because Foreign Office legal advisors had concluded that, without a Security Council resolution, the legal authority for using armed force was "unclear," British policy-makers insisted that Albright and Cook seek a new resolution declaring that Iraq was in "further material breach" of resolution 687. British policy-makers quickly concluded, however, that explicit UN authorization was unlikely and began offering arguments that such authorization was unnecessary (Lockwood 1998; Silber 1998). The United States offered similar arguments, reiterating that no additional Security Council resolution would be necessary because Iraq already was in "material breach" of resolution 687 (Weller 1999/2000: 84).

Over the next several days, Albright and Cook again met with foreign heads of state to seek support for military action against Iraq. Concerned that other states might conclude that the proposed air strikes were intended to overthrow Saddam, US and British policy-makers emphasized that the objectives of the operation would be limited, intended to degrade Iraq's potential for launching missiles equipped with chemical or biological warheads. On 14 February, Albright and Cook announced that air strikes would not begin before 18 February in order to allow UN Secretary-General Kofi Annan to visit Baghdad for negotiations. But they warned that any agreement allowing Iraq to continue to violate its disarmament obligations would be unacceptable (Hiro 2001: 137–9). Following Annan's visit, on 23 February Iraq signed a memorandum of understanding with the United Nations, reconfirming "its acceptance of all relevant resolutions of the Security Council," including "immediate, unconditional, and unrestricted access" to all suspected weapons sites (UN Doc. S/1998/166).[10] Nevertheless, the buildup of US and British forces in the Persian Gulf continued, although Cook warned Prime Minister Tony Blair about the need to secure Security Council support to legitimate US and British actions and thereby provide "cover" for the use of military force (Baldwin and Wastell 1998).

On 2 March, the Security Council approved a resolution endorsing the memorandum of understanding and stressing that "any violation would have the severest consequences for Iraq" (UN Doc. S/Res/1154). Although US and British policy-makers had used the threat of veto to preclude the lifting of sanctions before Iraq complied with "all relevant" resolutions, they failed to obtain language authorizing the use of armed force if Iraq violated its agreement with the United Nations. The absence of such language notwithstanding, UN Representative Bill Richardson declared that the resolution provided a "green light" to use force against Iraq if the United States were to decide that Iraq was in "material breach" of its disarmament obligations. Under-Secretary of State Thomas Pickering clarified this claim the following day, arguing that "material breach would mean that the prohibition on the use of force, which arose as a result of the ceasefire [S/Res/687], was no longer in effect" (Lobel and Ratner 1999: 140–1). Likewise, Cook argued that "there was already existing legal authority for military action to enforce the existing understandings from Iraq, and that is not changed by this resolution" (Davies 1998b).

US and British policy-makers agreed that military action against Iraq would have to conclude before the Muslim *hajj* began on 15 March. Because six days of air strikes were planned, this meant that the operation would have to commence no later than 9 March. Accordingly, Albright and Berger met with UNSCOM Chairman Richard Butler and urged him to end inspections no later than 8 March, so that there would be a legal pretext for military action. Butler agreed, but despite the assistance of US and British intelligence, UNSCOM inspectors found nothing to suggest that Iraq was in violation of existing Security Council resolutions. Lacking the legal pretext they had sought, US and British policy-makers again canceled planned air strikes (Ritter 1999: 183–7; Hiro 2001: 142–3).

Over the months that followed, Iraq again restricted monitoring and inspection activities and on 5 August announced that it was suspending cooperation with UNSCOM until the sanctions were lifted (UN Doc. S/1998/718). Although the Security Council approved a resolution on 9 September condemning Iraq's actions and demanding its compliance with its legal obligations (UN Doc. S/Res/1194), Butler reported to the Security Council on 7 October that Iraq again had suspended cooperation and that "considerable uncertainty remained" regarding Iraq's biological weapons (UN Doc. S/1998/920). The Security Council responded on 5 November by unanimously approving another resolution condemning Iraq's decision to end its cooperation with UNSCOM inspectors. The resolution demanded that "Iraq rescind immediately and unconditionally the decision ... to suspend cooperation with the Special Commission" (UN Doc. S/Res/1205). Although members of the Security Council refused to include reference to "material breach" within the text of the resolution, the United Kingdom argued that "the authorization to use force given by the Security Council in 1990 [S/Res/678] may be revived if the Council decides that there has been a sufficiently serious breach of the conditions laid down by the council for the ceasefire [S/Res/687]" and that "the resolution we have just adopted ... has condemned the Iraqi decision to cease cooperation with UNSCOM as a flagrant violation of these obligations" (Weller 1999/2000: 86, 92).

In the days that followed, US Secretary of Defense William Cohen, US National Security Advisor Sandy Berger, and British Foreign Secretary Robin Cook visited foreign heads of state to seek support for military action against Iraq. As before, France, Russia, and China argued that such action required explicit UN authorization (Davies 1998a). Nevertheless, the United Kingdom argued that Iraq's refusal to cooperate with UNSCOM inspectors constituted "a substantial breach of the agreement because it is clear from the evidence that [Iraq] will, if unchecked, try to develop weapons of mass destruction" (Weller 1999/2000: 86). On 13 November, after UN Secretary-General Annan sent a letter to Saddam setting out requirements for cooperating with UNSCOM inspectors (UN Doc. S/1998/1077), Clinton announced that Iraq would face military action the following day if it did not comply with the requirements laid out in Annan's letter (Broder 1998). On 14 November, with US bombers in the air approximately one hour from launching cruise missile strikes, Iraq informed the Secretary-General that it had made "a clear and unconditional decision to resume cooperation with the weapons inspectors" (UN Doc. S/1998/1078). Lacking a suitable legal pretext for military intervention, Clinton immediately canceled the operation.

Soon afterward, Berger met with Butler to plan a new series of weapons inspections, coordinating their efforts so that Butler's report would be released on the proper day to provide a sufficient legal pretext for joint US–British military action. On 13 December, Butler submitted the first draft of his report to Clinton and Berger, who decided that it was too "weak" and proposed revisions to it. The following day, Clinton met with Butler to finalize the changes to the draft (Ritter 1999: 195–6; Hiro 2001: 161). Butler distributed his report to the members of the Security Council on 15 December. According to the report, Iraq had failed to cooperate with UN weapons inspectors, and as a result, UNSCOM was "not able to conduct the work mandated to it by the Security Council" (S/1998/1172).

US and British military forces began bombing Iraq at the same time that Butler was presenting his report to the Security Council (Clinton 2004: 833). As part of the plan developed the previous year, British planes dropped leaflets to encourage rebellion among the Kurds and Shi'a. They refused to participate, however, having concluded from the failure of the United States and the United Kingdom to provide air support following the 1990–91 Gulf War and their repeated failure to do so in recent months that air support was unlikely and that attacking the Iraqi military while it was under attack by foreign military forces would be politically damaging (Hiro 2001: 162–3).

Clinton argued that the action was "consistent with and has been taken in support of numerous UN Security Council resolutions . . . which authorize UN Member States to use 'all necessary means' to . . . establish the terms of the cease-fire mandated by the Council, including those related to the destruction of Iraq's WMD programs." Similarly, Blair argued that Iraq had not complied with its obligations to the UN and that the objectives of the mission were "to degrade the ability of Saddam Hussein to build and use weapons of mass destruction . . . [and] to diminish the threat Saddam Hussein poses to his neighbours by weakening his military capability." Cook added that there was "clear backing in UN resolutions" for military action against Iraq, resolution 1205 having "revived" the authorization to use armed force in resolution 678 (Federation of American Scientists 2002a). France, however, criticized the attacks because of a lack of debate in the Security Council, and discontinued its participation in Operation "Southern Watch" on 31 December (Drozdiak 1998).

Assessing the evidence

As we have seen, US and British policy-makers expressed concern about the possibility of resistance from other states in response to their arguably illegal military actions and sought to obtain UN authorization for those actions. Lacking a sufficient legal pretext for overthrowing the Iraqi government, they agreed to proceed along "two tracks," justifying military operations as consistent with resolution 678 while secretly planning to remove Saddam. The resulting changes to the manner and timing of these operations came at a considerable cost, however. US and British policy-makers had hoped to weaken Saddam's government such that it would be overthrown, but out of concern that the Security Council would condemn their ongoing use of armed force, they suspended military operations after four days of ground combat in February 1991 – even though doing so left three Republican Guard divisions largely intact and Saddam still in power. In June 1996, US and British policy-makers planned a coup against Saddam, but they delayed planned air strikes to allow time for UNSCOM Chairman Rolf Ekéus to negotiate Iraqi acceptance of resolution 1060 – even though doing so allowed time for Iraqi security forces to capture the conspirators and foil the coup plot. Following an assessment by the CIA that there was "little prospect" that Saddam would be overthrown in the near term (Cockburn and Cockburn 1999: 244), US and British policy-makers planned air strikes in support of Kurdish and Shi'ite rebels in Iraq in 1997 and 1998. However, after canceling proposed air strikes three times because Security Council support for such actions seemed unlikely, US and British policy-makers were unable to convince Iraqi Kurds and Shi'a to rebel during Operation "Desert Fox" in December 1998, leaving Saddam in power and UNSCOM inspectors forbidden from returning to Iraq.

In each of these instances, policy-makers' main concern was that arguably illegal uses of armed force would signal a lack of commitment to the existing international order. Policy-makers expressed their concern in terms of perceived violations of legal commitments under the UN Charter, offering arguments that their actions were limited and that they were undertaken in accordance with existing Security Council resolutions. Thus, US and British policy-makers justified air strikes and subsequent ground operations in 1991 as consistent with resolution 678, which authorized states "to use all necessary means to uphold and implement resolution 660 . . . and all subsequent resolutions." Similarly, they justified the implementation of "no-fly" zones in northern and southern Iraq as consistent with resolution 688, which condemned "the repression of the Iraqi civilian population" and called for states to contribution to "humanitarian relief efforts." And they justified subsequent air strikes as necessary to ensure the safety of aircraft monitoring compliance with resolution 688.

These arguments were not directed at domestic audiences, as the realist model suggests, but rather at other states, as signals of commitment to the existing order. Irrespective of domestic-level concerns, US policy-makers delayed naval enforcement of economic sanctions in August 1990 to await explicit UN authorization for the use of force, while British policy-makers, who initially had ordered naval forces to intercept and board merchant ships in the Persian Gulf, suspended such actions to await a formal request from the Kuwaiti government under resolution 661. In making these decisions, both US and British policy-makers considered the anticipated likelihood of resistance from other states and altered their actions accordingly, offering arguments to justify those actions as consistent with existing Security Council resolutions (Pace 1990; Freedman and Karsh 1993: 145). They do not seem to have considered the impact of these arguments on domestic constituencies; indeed, the primary area of disagreement in both the US Congress and the British House of Commons at this time had nothing to do with the legality of naval actions in support of economic sanctions, but rather the amount of time that would be necessary for the sanctions to work and whether or not direct military intervention in Iraq was in the national interest. As Baker (1995: 336) notes, to this point US policy-makers had "done a lousy job" of explaining proposed military action to domestic audiences and "were beginning to pay a political price at home." Accordingly, policy-makers supplemented these arguments with nonlegal claims, specifically claims regarding ineffectiveness of economic sanctions and the impact of the invasion on world oil markets. However, they made these nonlegal claims clearly subordinate to the legal claims used to justify possible military action. For example, when Bush announced the commencement of military operations on 17 January 1991, he claimed that US actions were taken in response to Iraq's refusal to withdraw from Kuwait and its attempts to develop WMD, and only then did he add that the Iraqi invasion had caused damage "to the entire world . . . including to our own economy" (*DSD 1991*, 2: 37–8). Later on, despite widespread domestic support for humanitarian intervention in northern Iraq (Paletz 1994: 284), US policy-makers initially opposed setting up relief centers, out of concern that doing so would violate Iraq's territorial integrity and hence contradict previous legal claims used to justify the use of armed force against Iraq. Afterwards, US and British policy-makers argued that air strikes in and around the "no-fly" zones were taken in accordance with existing Security Council resolutions and not intended to overthrow the Iraqi government – despite widespread domestic support for removing Saddam from power (Mueller 2000: 5–6).

Domestic legal advisors played only a limited role in formulating these policies. For example, when Thatcher ordered British naval units to implement a blockade of Iraq, she asked Foreign and Commonwealth Office legal advisors to review the details of British treaty commitments to Kuwait and Saudi Arabia, apparently ignoring questions regarding the legality of the blockade in the absence of explicit UN authorization (Thatcher 1993: 820). Thatcher also ignored legal advisors' admonitions against forcible removal of a foreign head of state, suggesting to US policy-makers that they use the Iraqi invasion as a legal pretext for actions intended to overthrow Saddam (Munro 1996: 158). Although US Department of Defense lawyers had ruled in 1991 that Saddam was a legitimate target of combat operations because he was a wartime military commander, US policy-makers continued to target him even after combat operations were suspended. To the extent that legal advisors played a role in these decisions at all, then, it would seem to have been simply underscoring the importance of policy-makers' "two tracks" strategy of justifying military action as consistent with existing Security Council resolutions while secretly planning to overthrow the Iraqi government as part of such action. Both US and British policy-makers adhered to this strategy throughout the period – even after the US Congress approved the Iraq Liberation Act, which Clinton characterized as a mandate for the United States to pursue "active application of all relevant United Nations Security Council resolutions" and to make funding "available for assistance to the Iraqi *democratic* opposition" (Federation of American Scientists 2002a, emphasis added).[11]

Domestic political ideology does not seem to have played much of a role, either. Contrary to the liberal model, both US and British policy-makers offered essentially the same legal arguments throughout the period, justifying continued economic sanctions as a lawful response to Iraq's non-compliance with existing Security Council resolutions and justifying continuing attacks on Iraqi air-defense targets as self-defense of aircraft patrolling "no-fly" zones in northern and southern Iraq. Thus, the arguments offered by the Labour government of Tony Blair were essentially the same as those offered by the Conservative governments of Margaret Thatcher and John Major, and the arguments offered by the Democratic government of Bill Clinton were essentially the same as those offered by the Republican government of George H. W. Bush.

What is most striking about these cases, however, is the extent to which US and British policy-makers – irrespective of domestic political ideology – sought to manipulate the Security Council in an attempt to obtain a favorable outcome. As indicated by Bush's request for a "massive" diplomatic effort to align the Security Council against Iraq (Bush and Scowcroft 1998: 316–17) and by Thatcher's concerns regarding a split vote in the Security Council (Munro 1996: 94, 154), both US and British policy-makers were concerned that an unfavorable Security Council outcome would increase the likelihood of resistance from other states. Contrary to the communal obligation model, however, US and British policy-makers did not rely exclusively on argumentation to achieve consensus, but rather offered "diplomatic sweeteners" in exchange for favorable votes on resolution 687 and other resolutions. These included incentives such as financial assistance to Columbia, Ethiopia, Ivory Coast, and Zaire, as well as an offer to remove Cuba from the US State Department's list of states sponsoring terrorism and an invitation for Chinese Foreign Minister Qian Qichen to visit the United States, despite China's violent quelling of Tiananmen Square protests the previous year (Hiro 1992: 257–9; Baker 1995: 305–24). In addition, Secretary of State Baker reportedly promised the Soviet Union that the United States would keep Estonia, Latvia, and Lithuania out of the 1990 Paris summit conference in exchange for a favorable vote on resolution 687 (Weston 1991: 523). As approved by the Security Council, resolution 687 contained an authorization for states to use "all necessary means," but did not specify "armed force." Nevertheless, Baker exercised his authority as President of the Security Council that month to read into the official record that the resolution should be understood to authorize the use of armed force, irrespective of reservations expressed by the Soviet Union and China (Woodward 1991: 333–4; Freedman and Karsh 1993: 233).

US and British policy-makers continued to manipulate the process of deliberation in the Security Council even after hostilities ended, declaring their intention in May 1991 to veto any proposed resolution easing sanctions against Iraq (Caron 1993: 577) and selectively assisting UNSCOM inspectors in 1997 and 1998 in an attempt to create a legal pretext for direct military intervention in Iraq (Hiro 2001: 102–5). In December 1998, US policy-makers went so far as to suggest revisions to the text of Richard Butler's UNSCOM inspections report (Ritter 1999: 195–6; Hiro 2001: 161) and to launch air strikes against Iraq even as the Security Council was convening to review Butler's report. This appears to have been a step too far. In addition to France discontinuing its participation in Operation "Southern Watch," China begin assisting Iraq in the installation of a network of fiber optic cables to improve Iraq's air-defense system and to deprive the United States of its ability to listen in on Iraqi communications (Gertz 2001; Sanger and Myers 2001).

8

THE IMPACT OF THE UN CHARTER ON US–BRITISH MILITARY INTERVENTION IN IRAQ, 1999–2003

US and British air strikes against Iraq continued sporadically throughout 1999 and 2000, destroying suspected weapons sites and command and control facilities. However, consistent with the prudential restraint model, US and British policy-makers delayed the implementation of ongoing plans to overthrow the Iraqi government until a suitable legal pretext obtained. In 2001, presented with a new situation created by the September 11 terrorist attacks, US and British policy-makers decided that the emerging threat of WMD terrorism, combined with Iraq's continued refusal to comply with its disarmament obligations, provided sufficient legal basis for direct military intervention. Nevertheless, to increase the persuasiveness of their legal arguments, they delayed the planned invasion to seek additional UN resolutions authorizing the use of armed force, although ultimately they proceeded without obtaining such authorization.

This case occurs at a time when the balance of power has shifted towards unipolarity, and thus for purposes of theory testing it represents a "hard case." For purposes of policy analysis, it is a necessary case, because it is at the center of ongoing policy debates regarding the continued salience of the UN Charter system. Although the proximity of the events examined herein greatly limits the amount of primary source material that is available, memoirs and news accounts, supplemented by other primary and secondary sources, provide a reasonable and thorough overview of US and British decision-making processes and outcomes throughout the period.[1]

Ongoing planning

Despite the failure of Operation "Desert Fox" in December 1998, US and British policy-makers continued planning the overthrow of Saddam throughout 1999. US National Security Advisor Sandy Berger met with Iraqi National Congress (INC) leaders in May 1999 and reassured them of US policy-makers' "determination to get rid of the Saddam Hussein regime" (Hoagland 1999). However, following Iraq's expulsion of UN weapons inspectors the previous year, there lacked a legal pretext for large-scale use of armed force against Iraq. Accordingly, in December 1999 the United Kingdom proposed a draft resolution establishing a UN Monitoring, Verification, and Inspection Commission (UNMOVIC) to replace UNSCOM (Ritter 1999: 209). The resolution, which the Security Council approved on 17 December, called for Iraq to agree to "a reinforced system of ongoing monitoring and verification" and to "identify additional sites in Iraq to be covered by the reinforced system of ongoing monitoring and verification" (UN Doc. S/Res/1284). Throughout the next year, UNMOVIC attempted to carry out its mandate, but Iraq refused to cooperate.

On 30 January 2001, newly-elected President George W. Bush convened a meeting of US policy-makers to discuss a possible US response. He ordered Secretary of Defense Donald Rumsfeld and Chairman of the Joint Chiefs of Staff General Hugh Shelton to examine military options, including possible deployment of US military forces in northern and southern Iraq. Concerned with the possibility of resistance from other states, Bush suggested that US policy-makers consider building an international coalition similar to the one assembled during the 1990–91 Gulf War. At a follow-up meeting two days later, Rumsfeld argued that the primary objective of any proposed military operation should be the elimination of Iraq's weapons of mass destruction, but he suggested that "going after Saddam" be a part of such operation. Rumsfeld noted that it might be possible to make use of the "no-fly" zones in northern and southern Iraq to aid opposition groups, as the previous administration had done (Suskind 2004: 70–5, 83–5; Woodward 2004: 12).

As a precursor to such action, US and British policy-makers decided to launch a coordinated attack against the new Iraqi air-defense system, which was nearing completion. According to a CIA report, Iraq was about to connect its system to a fiber optic network that had been installed with Chinese assistance. Once completed, the system would pose a threat to US and British aircraft patrolling the southern "no-fly" zone. Although destroying the network would require attacking targets outside of the "no-fly" zone, US policy-makers agreed that such actions could be justified as self-defense of military forces patrolling the "no-fly" zone, consistent with existing Security Council resolutions. As US and British planes launched air strikes on 16 February, US policy-makers argued that the attacks were intended "to degrade Iraq's ability to threaten coalition aircraft enforcing United Nations mandates" and to elicit Iraqi compliance with Security Council resolution 687 and subsequent resolutions (Federation of American Scientists 2002a). British policy-makers added that the actions were consistent with "humanitarian provisions" of existing Security Council resolutions (LaGuardia and Harnden 2001).

Following these attacks, US and British aircraft increased the frequency of their patrols in the northern and southern "no-fly" zones, and US policy-makers worked to update plans by the Clinton administration to overthrow Saddam using Iraqi opposition groups (Woodward 2004: 21). Plans changed dramatically, however, following terrorist attacks on the twin office towers of the World Trade Center and on the headquarters of the US Department of Defense on 11 September 2001.

Planning following the September 11 terrorist attacks

On 12 September, CIA Director George Tenet presented US policy-makers with evidence suggesting that the al-Qaeda terrorist organization was responsible for the previous day's terrorist attacks. Bush proposed that the United States undertake a general "war on terror," making "no distinction" between terrorists and "those who harbor them," but he expressed concern that such a mission would not be sufficiently restrictive to elicit acceptance from other states. Secretary of State Colin Powell agreed, noting that the Security Council was likely to authorize a mission directed at al-Qaeda in Afghanistan, but that it was unlikely to authorize a broader mission. Rumsfeld, however, urged that US policy-makers "take advantage of the opportunity offered by the terrorist attacks to go after Saddam." According to Rumsfeld, Iraq was determined to acquire weapons of mass destruction, and a war on terrorism would have to target Saddam eventually (Woodward 2002: 48–9). Although Bush deferred a final decision on the matter to focus on the more immediate problem of Afghanistan, following the meeting he spoke with counter-terrorism advisor Richard Clarke, instructing him to "go back over everything ... [to s]ee if Saddam did this ... [or] if he's linked in any way" (Clarke 2004: 32).

At a follow-up meeting three days later, Rumsfeld reiterated his belief that the United States should use the terrorist attacks as a legal pretext to overthrow Saddam. Powell again disagreed, arguing that an attack against Iraq would evoke resistance from other states, which would "view it as bait-and-switch" unless there were "something pinning September 11 on Iraq." Powell suggested that US policy-makers focus on Afghanistan and "[k]eep the Iraq options open if [they could] get the linkages," adding that, by participating in UN-authorized action against Afghanistan, the United States would have "increased its ability to go after Iraq – if we can prove Iraq had a role." Chief of Staff Andrew Card agreed, although he suggested building up forces in the Persian Gulf for use against Iraq but waiting to act until US policy-makers could make a persuasive argument for doing do. Bush agreed with Card and decided that planning for possible military action against Iraq should continue, although he was "not going to strike [Iraq] now ... [because] I don't have the evidence at this point" (Woodward 2002: 81–90, 99). Soon afterward, Bush assigned former CIA Director James Woolsey the task of investigating possible Iraqi involvement in the September 11 attacks and other terrorist attacks, for possible use at the United Nations (Page 2002).

After consulting with potential allies, Vice President Richard Cheney and British Prime Minister Tony Blair concluded that most states would withdraw their support if the objective of the proposed operation were broadened to include targets outside Afghanistan, because there lacked evidence linking Iraq to the September 11 attacks (LaGuardia 2003b; Wintour and Kettle 2003). Bush, upon hearing their reports, concluded that it would be necessary to "be patient about Iraq" while laying out the case for military action against Saddam. To prevent the objective from becoming "confused," Bush canceled planned air-strike targets against Iraqi air-defense sites (Woodward 2002: 107).

Discussions continued during the weeks that followed, and by the end of October, Bush and his advisors had decided to use military force, if necessary, to overthrow Saddam. Rumsfeld believed that US military forces would quickly overwhelm the Iraqi military and thus relatively few forces would be needed. He suggested a "rolling start," striking quickly to deny Iraq the opportunity to use unconventional weapons and thereby precluding the necessity of an extensive buildup of military forces and the formation of an international coalition (Page 2002). Because there lacked evidence linking Saddam to the al-Qaeda organization,[2] Rumsfeld suggested that the United States emphasize Iraqi noncompliance with its disarmament obligations under existing Security Council resolutions (DeYoung and Pincus 2003). US policy-makers concluded, however, that it would be necessary to await events in Iraq that would allow them to formulate a persuasive legal argument for military action as a response to such noncompliance. Until then, they would pursue a "bifurcated policy" of preparing for war with Iraq while continuing to work through the United Nations. In preparation for military action, Bush instructed Rumsfeld to update the Pentagon's existing Iraq war plan (Woodward 2004: 1, 26, 72–3).

Addressing a joint session of Congress on 29 January 2002, Bush identified Iraq, Iran, and North Korea as "an axis of evil" and suggested that "Iraq continues ... to support terror." According to Bush, Iraq had "agreed to international inspection – then kicked out the inspectors," which suggested that it "has something to hide." Bush noted that he would "not wait on events, while dangers gather," and would "not permit the world's most dangerous regimes to threaten us with the world's most destructive weapons" (The White House 2003). The following month, Bush instructed the CIA and the Department of Defense to coordinate their plans for overthrowing Saddam. CIA Director Tenet had noted that it would be necessary to commit US ground forces, because Iraqi opposition groups no longer believed promises of US air support. Accordingly, US policy-makers worked over the next several weeks to finalize plans for direct US military intervention, to begin as early as June 2002. Vice President Cheney visited the Middle East to elicit support for such actions and concluded that it would be better to justify military action as having been undertaken in accordance with existing Security Council resolutions than to risk an unfavorable vote on a new resolution explicitly authorizing such action (Hiro 2004: 31–2; Woodward 2004: 60–4, 98–9).

British policy-makers were engaged in similar planning, having concluded that covert support of opposition groups in Iraq would have "a very low prospect of success" because failed promises of air support to the Iraqi Kurds and Shi'a "remain vivid." Accordingly, British policy-makers proposed a "full-scale ground campaign" to take place in late autumn 2002 or early spring 2003. They noted, however, that a successful operation would require the use of military bases in either Jordan or Saudi Arabia. To reduce the likelihood of resistance from these states, as well as from "China, France, and particularly Russia[,] who have the ability to block action in the UN Security Council," British policy-makers sought to develop a persuasive legal argument that Iraq "was in breach of its obligations regarding WMD, and ballistic missiles" and thereby convince the Security Council to "revive the authorisation to use force in [resolution] 678" (*DSM* 08/03/2002).

US National Security Advisor Condoleezza Rice met with British Foreign Policy Advisor David Manning on 12 March to exchange ideas. Rice noted that US policy-makers had not yet decided on "a legal base [*sic*]" for justifying direct military intervention in Iraq (*DSM* 14/03/2002). Although US and British policy-makers agreed on "the need to wrongfoot Saddam, on the inspectors and the UN SCRs," they disagreed on how it should be done. At a follow-up meeting on 17 March, US Deputy Secretary of Defense Paul Wolfowitz suggested that "it was absurd to deny the link between terrorism and Saddam." British policy-makers, however, concluded that US efforts to establish such a link were "so far frankly unconvincing." They proposed instead publishing a white paper that "would make the case against Saddam," based on Iraq's illegal WMD programs, although they did not want to publish it until they could "ensure that the figures are accurate and consistent with those of the US" (*DSM* 18/03/2002, 22/03/2002).

Blair met with Bush in early April to coordinate plans for military action. Prior to the meeting, British Foreign Secretary Jack Straw had informed Blair that there was still "a long way to go" toward formulating a "justification for military action in terms of international law." Straw suggested that Iraq's "flagrant breach of international legal obligations imposed on it by the UNSC provides us with the core of a strategy" and that "if the argument is to be won, the whole case . . . needs to be narrated with reference to the international rule of law" (*DSM* 25/03/2002).

Accordingly, Blair urged Bush to seek a new resolution to help elicit support from other states and thereby "maximise his case" (Kampfner 2004: 168). Based on his earlier conversation with Straw, Blair suggested that the resolution include "a demand for unfettered readmission of weapons inspectors," which would provide a legal basis for subsequent military action (*DSM* 25/03/2002). Bush apparently agreed, and ordered that the proposed date for combat operations be delayed until December, to allow time to seek such a resolution and to take advantage of optimal military and weather conditions in Iraq (Page 2002; Woodward 2004: 99–101). Upon returning to the United Kingdom, Blair met with Treasury officials to incorporate the planned invasion into their financial calculations (Kampfner 2004: 169). Shortly thereafter, US and British special forces secretly began deploying to Kurdish-controlled areas in northern Iraq, while additional forces secretly stashed equipment throughout western Iraq and US and British planes began dropping leaflets encouraging the Kurds and Shi'a to rebel (Hiro 2004: 33, 68; Woodward 2004: 109, 140–4).

Some time in May, British Foreign Office legal advisors presented Blair with a memorandum assessing the legality of direct military intervention in Iraq. The memorandum confirmed Blair's preference for a new Security Council resolution, noting that "violation of Iraq's obligations which undermines the basis of the cease-fire in resolution 687 (1991) can revise the authorisation to use force in resolution 678 (1990)," but "it is for the [Security] Council to assess whether any such breach of those obligations has occurred." According to the memorandum, although the United Kingdom had argued previously that resolution 1205, which condemned Iraq's decision to end cooperation with UNSCOM inspectors, "had the effect of causing the authorisation to use force in resolution 678 (1991) to revive," these arguments were "controversial" and were unlikely to be accepted by other states if offered as justification subsequent military operations (*DSM* 21/07/2002). Concerned about the likelihood of resistance against the proposed invasion, Blair sent Manning to Washington to reiterate his belief that military action without a new resolution would put the United Kingdom in an "extremely difficult position" (Kampfner 2004: 191–3).

On 22 July, Blair circulated a Cabinet briefing paper which argued that "[r]egime change per se is not a proper basis for military action under international law ... [b]ut regime change could result from action that is otherwise lawful." According to the briefing paper, "[i]n the absence of UN authorisation, there will be problems in securing the support of NATO and EU partners" as well as states within the region, and thus it would be "necessary to *create* conditions in which we could legally support military action" in order to reduce the likelihood of resistance from other states and thereby enhance "the prospects of success" (emphasis added). The paper suggested that the United Kingdom prepare a draft Security Council resolution to "set a deadline, leading to an ultimatum" that would create a legal pretext for direct military intervention. It concluded, however, by noting that "for climactic reasons, military action would need to start by January 2003," but that "this timescale would present problems," because British policy-makers "would be most unlikely to achieve a legal base [*sic*] for military action by January 2003" (*DSM* 22/07/2002). At a Cabinet meeting the following day, Cabinet ministers remarked that, although "intelligence and facts were being fixed around the policy ... the case was thin" and it would be necessary for the Attorney General to "consider legal advice with FCO/MOD legal advisors" in order to develop a more persuasive set of legal arguments (*DSM* 23/07/2002).

On 4 August, Blair met with Bush and proposed a timetable for Security Council action and the subsequent invasion of Iraq. Blair reiterated that, while US public opinion might accept regime change as a reason for war, a legal justification would be necessary. He suggested that France and Russia could be persuaded to accept a resolution based on "coercive compliance" with enhanced UN inspections. Bush agreed, and ordered that the proposed military operation be delayed until late January or early February (Kampfner 2004: 197–8).

The following day, Bush met with Powell and Rice to discuss these issues further. Powell urged Bush to "make a pitch for a coalition or UN action to do what needs to be done," because otherwise the United States and the United Kingdom would have difficulty securing agreements from other states regarding basing, access, and overflight rights. Like Blair, Powell believed that if a sufficiently persuasive legal argument could be made, Russia and France would acquiesce in military action against Iraq, while undertaking military action without such an argument would evoke resistance and hence "suck the oxygen out of just about everything else the United States was doing, not only in the war on terrorism, but all other diplomatic, defense and intelligence relationships" (Woodward 2002: 156–7, 332–4). According, Bush decided to make Iraq the focus of a speech that he was scheduled to deliver before the UN General Assembly on 12 September, arguing for military action in response to Iraq's defiance of its disarmament obligations under existing Security Council resolutions (Purdum 2003: 42). To strengthen these arguments, Blair suggested that the United Kingdom prepare a report outlining Iraq's failure to comply with its disarmament obligations. The report[3] would demonstrate that it was not only the United States that believed military action against Iraq would be justified under the UN Charter (Hiro 2004: 61–2).

Although Bush had agreed to seek a new resolution authorizing the use of armed force, in finalizing the text of Bush's speech, Cheney argued that seeking such a resolution would "drag out the process" and accomplish little else. He suggested instead seeking a resolution stating that Iraq had violated existing Security Council resolutions and reserving the right of the United States to act unilaterally in response. Powell disagreed, noting that the Security Council was unlikely to declare Iraq to be in violation of its disarmament obligations if doing so would allow the United States to act unilaterally. After further discussion, US policy-makers settled on a compromise whereby the United States would ask the Security Council "to act" but would not request explicit authorization for using armed force (Woodward 2002: 345–7).

Meeting with Bush on 10 September, Blair suggested a new resolution modeled on resolution 1299, which NATO had argued implicitly authorized its use of armed force against Yugoslavia in 1999. Blair believed that legal arguments based on such a resolution would help to build international support for military action against Iraq, even if the resolution did not explicitly authorize the use of armed force. Bush and Blair agreed to propose a four-week deadline for weapons inspections and to attack Iraq as early as December, even if the members of the Security Council refused to approve the proposed resolution (Harnden and Sparrow 2002; LaGuardia 2003b). In a speech before the Trades Union Conference the following day, Blair argued that Saddam was "in breach of twenty-three outstanding UN obligations requiring him to admit inspectors and to disarm" and that "[s]hould the will of the UN be ignored, action will follow" (Office of the British Prime Minister 2003). Meanwhile, British military planners made preparations for sending up to 20,000 British troops to the Persian Gulf (Hollis 2006: 41), and US and British special forces stepped up covert operations in western Iraq (Bodansky 2005: 54–5, 67–8).

That same day, Cheney met with Powell and Rice to discuss the final draft of Bush's speech. Cheney again expressed his concerns regarding the Security Council, noting that requesting a resolution but failing to obtain it would undermine the persuasiveness of US legal claims. Powell, however, was not convinced. Having discussed the matter with Blair, Bush sided with Powell and inserted a line in the speech requesting that the Security Council act upon the matter (Woodward 2002: 347–8). Addressing the UN General Assembly on 12 September, Bush outlined Iraq's violations of existing Security Council resolutions and urged that these resolutions not be "cast aside without consequence." Bush noted that the United States would "work with the UN Security Council for the necessary resolutions," but if these resolutions were not enforced, then "action will be unavoidable" (White House 2003).

On 16 September, Iraq announced that it would accept the return of UN weapons inspectors "without conditions" (Preston and Purdum 2002). Following the announcement, French Foreign Minister Dominique de Villepin met with Powell in New York to discuss possible Security Council action. According to Villepin, two resolutions would be necessary. The first would demand that Iraq promptly disclose its weapons programs and disarm, while the second would authorize the use of armed force if Iraq refused. Powell agreed, but noted that France should not support the first resolution unless it was prepared to support a second resolution also (Purdum 2003: 51; Weisman 2003b). Meanwhile, US and British policy-makers worked together to draft a proposed Security Council resolution declaring Iraq to be in "material breach" of its disarmament obligations. They decided to exclude claims regarding Iraq's support of terrorism, because such claims were not plausible, and also to exclude claims regarding Iraq's human rights violations, because such claims did not derive explicitly from the Charter text (Woodward 2004: 220). Instead, the proposed resolution only referred to Iraq's WMD programs. It required Iraq to provide a detailed account of its weapons programs and to allow weapons inspectors unrestricted access to all sites in Iraq. In addition, it authorized states to use "all necessary means to restore international peace and security" if Iraq did not comply with its disarmament obligations (Purdum 2003: 54).

France had threatened to veto any proposed Security Council resolution that would "envisage a possible recourse to force" because French policy-makers were concerned that such a resolution would be used by the United States and the United Kingdom as implicit authorization for the use of armed force without consulting the Security Council (Wintour and Kettle 2003). However, French policy-makers did not want Iraq to be the beneficiary of disagreement among the permanent members of the Security Council. Consequently, Villepin met with Powell on 2 November and indicated France's willingness to accept a compromise whereby "further material breach" would be understood to mean both failure by Iraq to include complete and factual information in its weapons declaration and failure "to comply fully" with the demands of UNMOVIC weapons inspectors, provided that these failures were reported to the Security Council for "assessment" (Purdum 2003: 61; Shawcross 2004: 117–18).

In reporting his conversation with Villepin, Powell suggested that US policy-makers accept the French proposal. He expressed his belief that such a compromise would be sufficient to gain at least 14 votes in the Security Council and that UNMOVIC Chairman Hans Blix would find evidence of clandestine weapons programs, which would provide a legal pretext for direct military intervention in Iraq (Weisman 2003b; Woodward 2004: 222–3). Bush accepted Powell's suggestion, and on 8 November the Security Council unanimously approved the resolution, which declared that "Iraq has been and remains in material breach of its obligations under relevant resolutions" and stated that if Iraq failed to take advantage of its "final opportunity to comply with its disarmament obligations," it would be "further material breech of [its] obligations" and would face "serious consequences" (UN Doc. S/Res/1441).

Planning following the adoption of resolution 1441

In accordance with the provisions of resolution 1441, on 7 December Iraq presented an 11,790-page declaration of its nuclear, biological, and chemical weapons programs. The United States rejected the declaration the following week, claiming that the declaration did not account for chemical and biological agents missing when UNSCOM inspectors left Iraq in 1998, and that it failed to explain why Iraq had attempted to purchase uranium and high-tech materials intended for uranium enrichment (Sanger and Preston 2002). Two days later, the United Kingdom also denounced the declaration, characterizing it as a "blatant lie" and arguing that "[i]f Saddam persists in this obvious falsehood, it will become clear that he has rejected the pathway to peace laid down in resolution 1441" (LaGuardia and Jones 2002). US policy-makers considered returning to the Security Council immediately and demanding a new resolution declaring that Iraq was in "material breach" of its disarmament obligations, but they decided that doing so would make it appear as though the United States was determined to use armed force against Iraq (Weisman 2003b). Instead, the State Department released a list of deficiencies in the Iraqi weapons declaration on 20 December and declared Iraq to be in "material breach" of its obligations under resolution 1441 and at risk of losing its "last chance" to avoid war (Weisman 2003a).

The following day, Tenet presented Bush, Cheney, and Rumsfeld with evidence that could be used to justify the use of armed force against Iraq. According to Tenet, Iraq had not accounted for 3,200 tons of precursor for chemical weapons and 6,000 artillery shells. It had constructed a large stand for testing missiles and appeared to have cleared soil from around suspected chemical weapons sites. It also had developed an unmanned aerial vehicle (UAV) and may have built mobile weapons laboratories. Tenet declared that arguments based on such evidence would be a "slam dunk," although Bush believed that they would not be sufficiently persuasive. He instructed Tenet to work on developing better arguments, but warned him to "[m]ake sure no one stretches to make our case" (Woodward 2004: 247–50).

Meanwhile, British military planners were becoming impatient. In addition to their concerns about deteriorating weather conditions in late spring, they lacked a timetable to help them prepare for a large-scale operation that would include the mobilization of reserves. Awaiting events at the Security Council, however, British policy-makers refused to specify a date for the commencement of military operations. As Blair informed Defence Secretary Geoff Hoon in late December, "uncertainty ... is inevitable, because at the moment we simply don't know whether Iraq will be found in breach" (Kampfner 2004: 233–4).

At a press conference on 13 January 2003, Blair noted that his "preference" would be for a UN resolution explicitly authorizing military action against Iraq, but that there could not be "an unreasonable or unilateral block on war." He hedged his previous claims by suggesting that intervention would be justified even if the inspectors did not find evidence of WMD in Iraq, because Saddam had obstructed the inspectors' work (Grice 2003). The need for such hedging was reduced on 16 January, however, when UN weapons inspectors found 12 empty 122-mm chemical warheads in Iraq and approximately 2,000 pages of documents regarding uranium enrichment processes.

That same day, Blix proposed a timetable for inspections to be completed by 27 March. Unfortunately for US and British policy-makers, however, military planners recently had finalized operational plans for an invasion to occur in early February. Waiting until late March or early April for Blix's report would delay the proposed invasion and reduce the likelihood of its success, due to excessive heat and frequent sandstorms in the Iraqi desert during the late spring (Kampfner 2004: 274; Woodward 2004: 100). It also would risk intelligence assets on the ground, which US policy-makers had concluded could not remain hidden beyond mid-February (Woodward 2004: 241–3, 254). Consequently, Bush decided that it would be necessary "to put our case down" before the Security Council, appointing a working group to prepare legal arguments for ending the inspections early (Purdum 2003: 69–70). However, Bush also ordered that the proposed invasion be delayed again, until 10 March (Kampfner 2004: 256; Van Natta Jr. 2006).

Concerned that UN weapons inspectors might not find evidence of Iraqi WMD programs in time to launch the invasion, Bush met with Blair on 31 January to discuss policy options. US and British policy-makers agreed that "diplomatic strategy had to be arranged around military planning," but they were unsure how to proceed. Blair suggested proposing a second resolution, which would provide "international cover, especially with the Arabs." Bush agreed, but expressed concern that the invasion already had been delayed twice and that additional delays would reduce the likelihood of attaining the "quick victory" that military planners had envisaged. Bush suggested preparing the second resolution "as soon as possible . . . [which] probably meant after Blix's next report to the Security Council in mid-February." If such a resolution could not be obtained, Bush suggested that US and British policy-makers attempt to create a legal pretext by other means, perhaps by "bring[ing] out a defector who could give a public presentation about Saddam's W.M.D." or "flying a U2 reconnaissance aircraft with fighter cover over Iraq, painted in U.N. colours . . . [and i]f Saddam fired on them, he would be in breach." US and British policy-makers concluded that "the timing [was] very tight" and that they would "need to stay closely alongside Blix . . . and work hard on other members of the Security Council . . . so that we can secure the minimum nine votes when we need them" (Van Natta Jr. 2006).

Meanwhile, Powell finalized the legal arguments that he would be presenting to the Security Council the following month. He conferred with British Foreign Secretary Jack Straw, who expressed concern about the lack of "corroborative evidence" (Hiro 2004: 135). In an attempt to make his claims more plausible, Powell expurgated disputed claims that Iraq had attempted to purchase uranium from Africa and acknowledged that the aluminum tubes imported by Iraq could be used for artillery rockets as well as centrifuges. Powell also decided to include recently intercepted messages indicating that the Iraqi military was attempting to hide illegal weapons from UN inspectors (Dao and Shanker 2003; Purdum 2003: 69–71).

Addressing the Security Council on 5 February, Powell argued that "Iraq is now in further material breach of its obligations" and that the Security Council had "an obligation ... to see that [UN] resolutions are complied with." According to Powell, although "[w]e wrote 1441 ... to try to preserve the peace," Iraq was "concealing ... efforts to produce more weapons of mass destruction" and "never had any intention of complying with this Council's mandate" (UN Doc. S/PV.4701). Following Powell's presentation, Bush announced that the United States "would welcome and support a new resolution which makes clear that the Security Council stands behind its previous demands," but added that resolution 1441 provided the necessary justification for military action even without an additional resolution and that "the United States, along with a growing coalition of nations, is resolved to take whatever action is necessary to defend ourselves and disarm the Iraqi regime" (White House 2003).

At this time, US policy-makers believed that they would be able to obtain the nine votes necessary to approve an additional resolution, with France, Russia, and China abstaining. However, on 7 February French President Jacques Chirac and Chinese President Jiang Zemin indicated to Bush that they favored continuing weapons inspections and were opposed to any use of armed force against Iraq. French Ambassador Jean-David Levitte suggested that "ten or eleven" members of the Security Council accepted France's arguments (Stevenson 2003). Nevertheless, US and British policy-makers continued work on drafting a second resolution, which would declare that Iraq had failed to disarm and must face "serious consequences." Having concluded that France would not support a second resolution under any circumstances, they turned their attention to Russia, which they hoped would accept or at least acquiesce to the proposed resolution. They hoped that China then would follow, in which case it would not be difficult to gain the support from at least five of the six undecided members of the Security Council (Weisman 2003b). Rice met with Blix on 11 February and suggested a list of specific benchmarks to include in his report as a measure of Iraqi compliance with its disarmament obligations (Purdum 2003: 123).

On 14 February, Blix presented a report to the Security Council on the progress of weapons inspections in Iraq. Blix argued that "Iraq had decided in principle to provide cooperation on process," but noted that "immediate, active, and unconditional cooperation" was not "forthcoming." IAEA Chairman Mohamed El Baradei reported that he had "found no evidence of ongoing prohibited nuclear or nuclear-related activities in Iraq," although "a number of issues are still under investigation, and ... we are moving forward with regard to some of them." British Foreign Secretary Straw responded by arguing that "Iraq's proliferation of weapons of mass destruction, of long-range missiles, and its noncompliance with [Security] Council resolutions is a threat to international peace and security," and that "the issue is not whether Iraq had them, but whether Iraq is actively cooperating to get rid of them." He added that "Iraq's material breaches ... are still there ... [and] if we decide to give unlimited time, for little or no cooperation on substance, then the disarmament of Iraq and the peace and security of the international community ... will not get any easier, but very much harder." Powell argued that the Security Council could not "allow this process to be endlessly strung out as Iraq is trying to do right now," and proposed a meeting on 14 March to reconsider the situation (UN Doc. S/PV.4707). Bush ordered that the operation be delayed once again to accommodate such a meeting, despite the urgings of the Joint Chiefs not to delay military action beyond 10 March (Woodward 2004: 319).

On 21 February, Ambassador Levitte met with US Deputy National Security Advisor Stephen Hadley and informed him that, if the United States were to justify the use of force under resolution 1441, then France would not offer resistance, because the resolution was ambiguous enough to provide implicit authorization. However, if the United States were to push for a second resolution explicitly authorizing the use of force, then France would use its veto. Nevertheless, having agreed that US–British legal claims would be more persuasive with a second resolution, US and British policy-makers continued to work on a preparing a draft, which they presented to the Security Council on 24 February (Purdum 2003: 75; Stromseth 2003: 630–1). In the days that followed, US Under-Secretary of State John Bolton traveled to Russia while British Deputy Foreign Minister Valerie Amos traveled to Cameroon, Guinea, and Angola to elicit support for the resolution (Bumiller 2003). Despite a joint statement released by France, Germany, and Russia arguing that conditions for resorting to armed force had not yet obtained and that "the military option should only be a last resort" (Purdum 2003: 76), US and British policy-makers still hoped that, with the support of nine members of the Security Council, France, Russia, and China would abstain from voting (LaGuardia 2003a; Hiro 2004: 159). They called for a vote on the proposed resolution on 11 March, although British policy-makers suggested that the vote be postponed until later in the week, if necessary, to gain nine votes and thereby attain "legitimacy in the eyes of much of the world" (Weisman and Barringer 2003).

Concerned that the proposed resolution might not be approved, Blair asked Attorney General Lord Goldsmith to assess the legality of attacking Iraq without an additional Security Council resolution. In his response, Goldsmith reiterated previous British legal claims that "resolution 687 suspended, but did not terminate the authority to use force in resolution 678" and suggested that "the arguments in support of the revival [of the authority to use force in resolution 678] are stronger following resolution 1441." He noted, however, that while the United States consistently had argued that "whether Iraq is in breach [of the ceasefire conditions of resolution 678] is a matter ... which may ... be assessed by individual Member States," the United Kingdom "has consistently taken the view ... that ... it is for the [Security] Council to assess whether any such breach of those obligations has occurred." Goldsmith concluded that, while "the safest legal course would be to secure the adoption of a further resolution to authorise the use of force ... a reasonable case can be made that resolution 1441 is capable ... of reviving the authorisation in 678 without a further resolution" (*DSM* 07/03/2003). Similarly, State Department Legal Advisor William H. Taft, IV advised Bush that military action against Iraq was legal because "the [Security] Council imposed a series of conditions on Iraq ... as [part] of the cease-fire declared under UNSCR 687" and "Iraq has 'materially breached' those disarmament obligations" (Franck 2003: 611). With these arguments in hand, US and British policy-makers awaited Blix's next inspections report.

On 7 March, Blix reported to the Security Council that "while the numerous initiatives which are now taken by the Iraqi side ... can be seen as active or even proactive, these initiatives ... cannot be said to constitute immediate cooperation, nor do they necessarily cover all areas of relevance." He added, however, that proof of disarmament would "not take years, nor weeks, but months." El Baradei reported that he did not "have any evidence that Iraq has a nuclear weapons program or has revived its defunct nuclear weapons program" and argued that the British claim that Iraq had attempted to purchase uranium from Niger was based on forged documents. He concluded that he would need "at least two to three months" to complete his inspections. In response, Powell argued that Iraq's actions could not be characterized as acceptable cooperation. Guinea and Chile proposed extending the deadline slightly, while Canada proposed a compromise framework with a deadline of 31 March. France, however, argued that it would "not allow a resolution to pass that authorized the automatic use of force," because "imposing a deadline of only a few days would ... merely be seeking a pretext for war" (UN Doc. S/PV.4714).

Still hoping to obtain a second resolution, Blair sent diplomats to the capitals of various Security Council members to lobby for a favorable vote (Cook 2004: 206–7). On 10 March, however, China announced that it would veto the proposed resolution "whatever the circumstances" (Purdum 2003: 77). Russia also declared its intention to veto the proposed resolution, arguing that "no further resolutions of the UN Security Council are necessary" (Harnden *et al.* 2003). Nevertheless, even as late as 12 March, US and British policy-makers believed that they could attain nine votes in the Security Council and that the majority vote implicitly would authorize the use of armed force against Iraq, despite multiple vetoes (Sanger 2003). Although "[t]he diplomatic timetable was now out of step with the military one" (Kampfner 2004: 295), US and British policy-makers considered extending the deadline to 24 March and agreed that, if it appeared that the vote would result in an unfavorable outcome, then the United States would declare that it was withdrawing the proposed resolution (Purdum 2003: 83; Wintour and Kettle 2003; Woodward 2004: 343–7).

Bush and Blair met in the Azores on 16 March to decide whether there was any possibility of attaining a majority of votes in the Security Council. The following morning, British UN Representative Jeremy Greenstock, along with the US representative, John Negroponte, announced that the efforts of "one Council member" (i.e., France) had undermined US and British efforts to unite the Security Council (Barringer 2003). Greenstock left the resolution on the table, however, so that US and British policy-makers could argue against referring the matter to the General Assembly, via a Uniting for Peace resolution, because the Security Council was still "seized" of it (Williams 2006: 263). That same day, Bush declared that because "[t]he United Nations Security Council has not lived up to its responsibilities ... we will rise to ours." Bush demanded that "Saddam Hussein and his sons must leave Iraq within forty-eight hours" and noted that "[t]heir refusal to do so will result in military conflict, commenced at a time of our choosing" (The White House 2003). That night, US military forces began cutting through the barbed-wire fence along Kuwait's border with Iraq (Kampfner 2004: 298), and on 20 March they launched the invasion.

Following the end of combat operations on 1 May, US and British policy-makers commissioned the Iraq Survey Group (ISG) to find evidence of Iraq's illegal WMD programs. According to the ISG's final report, released on 30 September 2004, Iraq had no deployable WMD as of March 2003 and had not produced any since 1991, although it had both the intention and the production capacity to produce large quantities of biological and chemical weapons once international economic sanctions were lifted (Duelfer 2004). Although Iraqi sovereignty was restored in June 2004, significant numbers of US and British military forces remain in Iraq, fighting an ongoing insurgency.

Assessing the evidence

Consistent with the prudential restraint model, US policy-makers decided shortly after the September 11 terrorist attacks to use military force, if necessary, to overthrow Saddam, but to await events that would allow them to formulate persuasive legal arguments for such actions. Accordingly, US and British policy-makers delayed a planned invasion of Iraq in late 2002 to seek a permissive Security Council resolution that condemned Iraq's failure to comply with its disarmament obligations. Following the approval of resolution 1441, they again delayed the proposed invasion in an attempt to obtain a second resolution providing implicit authorization for the use of force. In doing so, however, they courted considerable risk, because delaying the invasion would require that it occur during the heat and sandstorms of late spring, would endanger intelligence assets on the ground in Iraq, and would allow Iraq time to deploy whatever WMD it might have had. Although it is unclear the extent to which US and British policy-makers actually believed that Saddam had WMD, their beliefs undoubtedly were influenced by their realization in 1991 that Iraq's WMD programs were "more substantial and better concealed than we had believed" (Baker 1995: 441) and by an October 2002 National Intelligence Estimate judging that "Iraq has continued its weapons of mass destruction (WMD) programs . . . has chemical and biological weapons . . . [and] if left unchecked . . . probably will have a nuclear weapon during this decade" (Federation of American Scientists 2006).

The willingness of policy-makers to accept such risks contradicts the realist model, which holds that policy-makers considering military action will be concerned only with the relative power and capabilities of potential adversaries. As we have seen, US policy-makers expressed concern that justifying the use of armed force as part of a general war against "terrorism" would not be sufficiently restrictive to persuade other states that the actions taken were reasonably justified, nor would claiming the unilateral right to enforce Iraqi compliance with its disarmament obligations. These concerns stemmed from military assessments that a successful invasion of Iraq would require the use of military bases in either Jordan or Saudi Arabia (*DSM* 08/03/2002), and that an unfavorable outcome in the Security Council would be likely to prompt resistance from these and other states. For this reason, US and British policy-makers concluded in mid-2002 that it would be "necessary to create conditions in which we could legally support military action" and thereby avoid problems in "securing the support of NATO and EU partners" as well as other states within the region (*DSM* 22/07/2002).

Policy-makers expressed these concerns in terms of perceived violations of US and British legal commitments under the Charter. Bush laid out the argument most clearly in a report to Congress on 19 March, claiming that the actions taken against Iraq were "consistent with the UN Charter" because the Security Council, "acting under Chapter VII of the UN Charter, provided that member states ... have the right to use force in Iraq to maintain or restore international peace and security" and because, according to resolution 1441, "Iraq has been and remains in material breach of its obligations under relevant resolutions and would face serious consequences if it failed immediately to disarm" (GlobalSecurity.org 2003). Although Blair broadened such arguments to include moral claims that were intended primarily for domestic audiences, he couched these claims in the terms of overarching legal claims, noting that military action "must be according to the UN mandate" (Kampfner 2004: 273). These arguments also emphasized US and British restraint. For example, before the House of Commons on 18 March, Blair reiterated that after Iraq's false declaration of 8 December "we waited," after the 27 January inspections report "we still waited," after the 14 February inspections report there was "further waiting," all of which indicated that "[o]ur fault has not been impatience" (Office of the British Prime Minister 2003). Likewise, Bush noted that before pressing for war, the United States and the United Kingdom "first went to the United Nations ... to get another resolution ... which was unanimously approved by the Security Council demanding that Saddam Hussein disarm" (White House 2003).

Domestic legal advisors seem to have played only a limited role in the formulation of such policy, however. Although the State Department Legal Advisor went on record to claim that US actions were consistent with the Charter, he does not appear to have been consulted until after the decision to invade Iraq already had been made. In the same manner, British policy-makers bypassed the Foreign Office throughout almost all stages of discussion (Kampfner 2004: 195; Short 2005: 160). Although Blair consulted with Foreign Office legal advisors in early 2002, prior to the Security Council's approval of resolution 1441, he appears to have sought the advice of the Attorney General only when he feared that a second resolution might not be obtained. The advice that he received from Lord Goldsmith suggested that a second resolution would be preferable, although when Goldsmith addressed Parliament on 17 March, he was unequivocal, arguing that because Iraq was in "material breach" of its legal obligations, "the authority to use force under Resolution 678 has revived and so continues today ... all that Resolution 1441 requires is reporting to and discussion by the Security Council of Iraq's failures, but not an express further decision to authorise force" (Hansard 2003). According to Clare Short (2005: 186–7), the full Cabinet never heard the more nuanced version of Goldsmith's legal advice, either. Foreign Office legal advisors disagreed with Goldsmith's conclusions, and Deputy Legal Advisor Elizabeth Wilmhurst resigned in protest (Burns 2003).

US and British policy-makers hoped, nevertheless, to legitimate their arguably illegal use of force against Iraq by obtaining a favorable Security Council outcome. However, contrary to the communal obligation model, they did not rely exclusively on argumentation to achieve consensus and at times did not seem to be trying to achieve consensus. Bush and Blair agreed in September 2002 that they would use military force against Iraq even if the members of the Security Council refused to approve a permissive resolution, and in exchange for supporting resolution 1441, US policy makers offered Russia assistance in recovering the $8 billion debt owed to it by Iraq (Weisman 2003b). After having decided to seek a second resolution in the spring of 2003, Bush noted that the United States "would put its full weight behind efforts to get another resolution and would twist arms and even threaten" (Van Natta Jr. 2006). Accordingly, US policy-makers worked closely with British intelligence personnel to conduct surveillance on UN diplomats from Angola, Cameroon, Chile, Bulgaria, Guinea, and Pakistan in an attempt to gain support for the proposed resolution (Tyler 2004).

Ultimately, US and British policy-makers went ahead with the planned invasion without having convinced even eight of the 15 members of the Security Council that the military action was reasonably justified. Following their decision, US and British policy-makers contacted members of the Security Council and urged them to vote against any proposed resolution condemning military action, so that it would not be necessary for the United States or the United Kingdom to use their vetoes (Woodward 2004: 358). The next chapter addresses the impact of this decision on the future of the UN Charter system.

9

THE CONTINUED SALIENCE OF THE UN CHARTER SYSTEM

The preponderance of evidence presented in the preceding chapters suggests that the major powers remain generally committed to the existing international order, despite moderate shifts in the balance of power that have occurred since the end of World War II. However, recent US military interventions in Kosovo, Afghanistan, and Iraq – when considered together – might suggest otherwise. With the emergence of unipolarity following the end of the Cold War, it may be that the leading power in the system is no longer committed to the existing order, having concluded that the postwar order no longer approximates the underlying balance of power sufficiently to promote US interests, rather than impeding them. With this possibility in mind, this chapter reviews the evidence presented in support of the prudential restraint model and assesses the implications of the model for the continued salience of the UN Charter system.

The UN Charter as a system of prudential restraint

As we have seen, major powers offer arguments to account for the discrepancy between their arguably illegal military actions and states' expectations of strict compliance with the Charter's Article 2(4) prohibition of force. These arguments serve as signals, because they transmit information used by states to assess the major powers' continuing commitment to the existing international order. According to Fearon (1995: 390–401), such arguments can provide credible signals if they are accompanied by actions that have costs exceeding the benefits that would accrue from transmitting false information. By separating one type of state from another, these "costly" signals provide credible information regarding commitments or intentions, whereas "weak" signals, which are unaccompanied by such actions, do not. As Goldsmith and Posner (2005: 167–84) note, however, though states are unlikely to *upgrade* their prior beliefs regarding a major power simply because of an argument it offers, they are likely to *downgrade* their prior beliefs regarding that major power if it acts like an aggressor, unreliable partner, or cheater, and fails to send even a "weak" signal of its commitment to upholding its legal obligations. Sending a "weak" signal, then, may prevent other states from downgrading their prior beliefs regarding the major power that sends it.

The prudential restraint model bridges the gap between these two signaling logics by considering the costs that are indirectly associated with so-called "weak" signals. According to the model, states assess the credibility of a signal according to the perceived likelihood that an argument offered by a major power was offered in good faith, and the extent to which the claims comprising the argument provide a basis for inferring future restraint. Arguments satisfying these criteria define a limited set of actions as legal, thereby reducing the range of actions that a major power can justify without making claims that are no longer coherent. Providing a persuasive account for the use of armed force, then, is not costless, because maintaining its persuasiveness restricts the actions of the major power that provides it. The magnitude of these costs varies according to the restrictiveness of the claims an argument contains; the more restrictive the claims, the more limited the range of justifiable actions, and hence the greater the likelihood that the major power making such claims remains committed to the existing order. States may be unable to observe these costs, however, because restraint is less readily observable than the absence of restraint is, and thus they assess the restrictiveness of a major power's claims according to a minimum threshold (Robinson 1999: 218–20). If a major power offers an argument containing claims that are less restrictive than a state's minimum threshold, that state will remain unpersuaded by the account the argument provides and will have incentive to respond with resistance to the major power, because the major power's actions appear threatening to the existing order and to that state's relative power position within it.

In most cases, the arguments offered by the major powers gave legal claims priority over nonlegal claims derived from principles of morality, justice, fairness, or efficiency – despite the ostensive appeal of such claims to domestic audiences – which suggests that legal arguments are particularly useful for signaling a major power's continuing commitment to the existing order. According to the prudential restraint model, this is because legal arguments correspond to states' background expectations under the Charter, link past actions to future intentions, and most importantly, contain claims derived from a codified framework of law that is inherently sustaining of the existing order. The extant theoretical literature has tended to ignore these characteristics of legal arguments, however. Even Goldsmith and Posner (2005: 95–9, 183), who recognize the role of legal arguments in linking past actions to future intentions, characterize such arguments as unique because they invoke specific rules of interpretation codified in the Vienna Convention on the Law of Treaties – not because of the inherent relationship between law and order that legal arguments invoke.

Johnstone (1991: 380–93) also emphasizes a distinctive process of interpretation, basing his analysis on the concept of a "collective norm-creating body," which he refers to as an "interpretive community." There is, however, little evidence to support Johnstone's assertion that states define "appropriate behavior" collectively. As we have seen, the claims contained within the major powers' legal arguments generally did not reflect an emerging consensus, but rather addressed fundamental areas of disagreement, such as whether or not humanitarian concerns or other ends "consistent with the Purposes of the United Nations" have priority over the Charter's Article 2(4) prohibition of force, whether or not indirect aggression is tantamount to "armed attack" under Article 51, and whether or not existing Security Council Resolutions implicitly authorized the use of armed force in certain situations. This tendency was stable across time, suggesting that even after decades of interaction within the Security Council and elsewhere, the major powers are not converging towards a common understanding of the Charter. Had the major powers internalized an "enduring group framework of shared legal language," as the communal obligation model suggests (Mitzen 2001: 11–20), their disagreements would have become increasingly more likely to address the determination of relevant facts – other, more fundamental areas of disagreement having already been settled.[1]

Nevertheless, such lack of consensus need not undermine the process of signaling. As this book has demonstrated, legal arguments can serve as signals even when major powers act unilaterally and/or propound understandings of law that differ from those of most other states. The prudential restraint model thus complements existing formulations of institutional signaling, which require that the major powers act multilaterally. According to these formulations, major powers attempt to make their signals credible by accruing the costs associated with "channeling power" through an international organization (such as the United Nations), which functions by coordinating military action among the major powers and less powerful states (Abbott and Snidal 1998; Thompson 2001; Weinberger 2003). According to the prudential restraint model, by contrast, major powers attempt to avoid resistance from other states by exercising restraint, altering the manner and timing of their military actions in accordance with the arguments they have offered or intend to offer. They attempt to make their signals credible by accruing the costs associated with the exercise of such restraint, and the Security Council functions by subjecting their military actions to the scrutiny of other states, thereby increasing the likelihood of resistance against unrestrained action. The Security Council can be effective therefore even when there lacks "unanimity of the permanent members" (UN Doc. A/Res/377), because it provides a specific equilibrium to coordinate resistance from less powerful states (Voeten 2005: 541–4).

To reduce the likelihood of such resistance, major powers seek to gain the acceptance or acquiescence of other states in order to obtain favorable Security Council outcomes. Such outcomes are important, insofar as dissent within the Security Council provides reason for other states to conclude that a major power's actions were not reasonably justified and therefore to respond with resistance to those actions. A major power thus prefers a favorable Security Council outcome, because such an outcome suggests that the major power succeeded in persuading most members of the Security Council that its actions are reasonably justified under the Charter – even though such outcome might actually have resulted from coercion or bribery, rather than persuasion.

Understood in this way, the Security Council is not an instrument of collective legitimation, insofar as legitimation within the Security Council occurs cumulatively – not collectively – and is based on rational calculation. It is not a matter of states' beliefs regarding the rightness of an action, nor collective decision by an authoritative body, but rather the extent of the action's congruence with rules that serve a shared interest, as indicated by the extent to which states express their acceptance of it. This interest-based conception of legitimacy allows for consideration of how states' interests affect their particular understandings of law and their actions, rather than implicitly assuming that states respond uniformly to particular arguments and actions according to a collective decision regarding the legitimacy of such actions (Hyde 1983: 391). As we have seen, states do not respond uniformly to particular arguments and actions, and the claims comprising the counter-arguments they offer are unlikely to apply universally. There is, in fact, an inverted U-shaped relationship between the level of resistance to a major power's military actions and whether or not those actions occurred within a region in which that major power has preponderant interest. This relationship suggests that there is a tacit agreement among the major powers regarding spheres of influence, which is not codified in the Charter and which the legal arguments of the major powers belie (Bull 1995: 221). The relationship obtains because the major powers, although unlikely to perceive military actions within another major power's area of preponderant interest as threatening to the existing order, recognize that acceptance of such actions might suggest that the major powers are only weakly committed to the international order instantiated in the Charter. Thus, the major powers are more likely to respond to such actions with acquiescence or indirect resistance than with acceptance or direct resistance.

What is most striking, however, is not the manner in which the major powers responded to military actions undertaken by other major powers, but rather the extent to which they altered the manner and timing of their own military actions – despite the costs and risks of doing so – out of concern that other states would perceive those actions as threatening to the existing order and respond with resistance to them. Hence, policy-makers frequently delayed planned military operations until specific circumstances obtained that provided a legal pretext for using armed force. In some cases, they deployed military units, but ordered them not to engage until such circumstances obtained. In other cases, policy-makers sought to create the circumstances necessary for such a pretext and/or attempted to obtain a permissive Security Council resolution or other authorization under the Charter. In still other cases, policy-makers used armed force without awaiting a legal pretext for acting, but acted covertly while denying the occurrence of the actions, the extent of the actions, or responsibility for those actions. As suggested herein, these decision-making outcomes were part of the major powers' attempts to mitigate the anticipated likelihood and severity of resistance from other states in response to their arguably illegal uses of armed force.

In some cases, delaying planned military operations may have increased the likelihood of a negotiated settlement, even though no such settlement was reached. For example, over the course of several weeks leading up to the Anglo-French invasion of Egypt in 1956, Nasser offered a series of concessions that British policy-makers eventually seemed willing to accept, although French policy-makers were not. Likewise, over the course of several weeks leading up to the US–British invasion of Iraq in 2003, Saddam offered a series of concessions that, in retrospect, might have allowed for eventual completion of the disarmament and inspections process. However, because of faulty intelligence (Gellman 2004) and Saddam's continuing pattern of intransigence, US and British policy-makers concluded that such an outcome was unlikely, and proceeded with the planned invasion. These cases suggest, nevertheless, that the dilatory effects of the Charter in some instances might increase the likelihood of a peaceful settlement by allowing additional time for negotiations. Military preparations during such negotiations enable the major powers to send credible signals of resolve, which further increase the likelihood of a peaceful settlement (Van Evera 1999: 51–2). In a study of international law and crisis processes, Young (2003) has found evidence to support this proposition, although closer examination is necessary to ascertain the manner and extent to which such decision-making outcomes can be attributed to concerns stemming from the Charter framework.[2]

In other cases, however, it is clear that altering the manner and/or timing of proposed military operations contributed directly to the failure of those operations. For example, by confining military operations to the Canal Zone and reducing the duration of those operations, the United Kingdom and France failed to overthrow the government of Egypt in 1956. Similarly, by changing the scope of proposed military operations and limiting direct US involvement in those operations, the United States failed to overthrow the governments of Cuba and the Dominican Republic in 1961. And, by repeatedly delaying and/or canceling proposed air strikes against Iraq, the United Kingdom and the United States failed for more than a decade to instigate the overthrow of Saddam Hussein.

Even when the major powers succeeded, such as the Soviet Union did in Hungary in 1956 and the United States and the United Kingdom did in Iraq in 2003, they accrued high costs in doing so. In the case of Hungary, these costs were paid in blood, with large numbers of casualties sustained due to the deployment of Soviet armor into urban areas without sufficient infantry support.[3] In the case of Iraq, although there was a risk of increased casualties due to adverse weather conditions and the possible use of chemical weapons, most of the costs paid by the United States and the United Kingdom came after the invasion and stemmed less from altering the manner and timing of their invasion plans than from other states' resistance to the invasion as well as the subsequent occupation and reconstruction. According to Brainard and O'Hanlon (2003), the costs of occupation and reconstruction may be as much as $100 billion higher than they would have been if states had been persuaded to respond to the joint US–British military operation with acceptance and had participated directly in it and/or in the ensuing occupation and reconstruction.[4] And this estimate does not include the number of casualties sustained by US and British military forces since the end of combat operations. As this case demonstrates, the costs accrued by altering the manner and timing of proposed military operations may be high, but the costs accrued from other states' resistance to those operations may be even higher – sometimes in the short term as well as in the long term.

The UN Charter and the post-Cold War international order

US and British policy-makers decided to invade Iraq, despite having failed to persuade even eight out of 15 members of the Security Council that their actions were reasonably justified. Facing indirect resistance within the Security Council and elsewhere in the weeks leading up to the invasion, it ought to have been clear to them that such resistance was likely to continue and could prove costly – especially during the ensuing occupation and reconstruction. Did US and British policy-makers underestimate these costs, or were there other factors involved?

As suggested above, it might be that the Charter system is being "eroded," as the gap in military capabilities between the United Sates and the other major powers continues to grow, and that in its place there is emerging a system of "shared hegemony" (Farer 2003: 360). Under such a system, the United States would not seek to overturn the existing order, but rather to create exceptions for itself through permissive Security Council resolutions selectively applied (Byers 2002b: 39; Alvarez 2003:

880). Under this system, the United States would work within the existing Charter framework, if possible, but would slip its legal bonds as necessary, operating within "coalitions of the willing" that include at least one other major power. Although its commitment to the existing order would be lessened, the United States would continue to offer arguments to account for its military actions and thereby attempt to reduce the likelihood of resistance from other states in response to those actions.

To the extent that the Charter system is being "eroded" in this manner, the process would seem to have begun well before the Iraq war, during the Kosovo crisis of 1999. In response to Yugoslav President Slobodan Milosevic's refusal to accept the Rambouillet Peace Agreement, the United States and its NATO allies (including the United Kingdom and France) launched air strikes against Yugoslavia. In justifying these actions, US Secretary of State Madeleine Albright argued that, because there was an agreed "need for compliance" with resolution 1199 (demanding that Yugoslavia "take immediate steps to improve the humanitarian situation" and calling for consideration of "additional measures to maintain or restore peace and stability"), there was no need for "additional resolutions" authorizing the use of armed force (Murphy 1999a: 169). When British Foreign Office legal advisors questioned the legality of bombing Yugoslavia without explicit Security Council authorization, Albright reportedly suggested that British Foreign Secretary Robin Cook "[g]et new lawyers" (Rubin 2000). Two years later, following the September 11 terrorist attacks, the Security Council unanimously approved resolution 1368, which called upon states to "to combat by any means ... threats to international peace and security caused by terrorist attacks." The United States responded to the September 11 attacks by invading Afghanistan, and the President of the Security Council stated afterwards that "the unanimity of support" expressed in resolution 1368 was "absolutely maintained." And when the United States invaded Iraq two years later, it claimed that its actions were consistent with resolution 1441, which declared that Iraq would face "serious consequences" if it remained in "material breach of its obligations under relevant resolutions."

Although military action followed a permissive Security Council resolution in all three cases, this apparent trend does not mark a departure from previous practice. As we have seen, US policy-makers frequently sought to obtain such resolutions – if not from the Security Council, then from the Organization of American States. More to the point, in two of the three cases, policy-makers did not rely on such resolutions as a basis for justifying US actions. Rather, policy-makers provided what Franck (1999: 118) refers to as an "expiating explanation of the special circumstances." In Kosovo, US policy-makers argued that the United States was "upholding [its] values ... and advancing the cause of peace" (Murphy 1999b: 629), while in Afghanistan, US policy-makers argued that military action was taken in self-defense under Article 51 of the Charter, implicitly expanding the definition of "aggression" to include the harboring of terrorists following a large-scale attack against a sovereign state.[5] As Kohen (2003: 224–5) observes, states responded to US military actions in both cases with "deliberate ambiguity," offering "vague statements from a legal perspective" to suggest that "'this time' the action fell within a legal framework." These responses suggest that states generally perceived US actions as having occurred under unique circumstances that were unlikely to be repeated, and therefore that such actions were not threatening to the existing international order, because they were not intended to enhance the relative power of the United States.

By contrast, in the Iraq case US policy-makers claimed what may have appeared to be a generalized exception to the Charter, arguing that in view of Iraq's clandestine WMD programs, requirements of self-defense made it impossible to "wait for the final proof" of such weapons' existence (White House 2003), and that in view of Security Council inaction, the United States had the authority to determine unilaterally when there existed a "material breach" of the obligations specified in previous Security Council resolutions. Thus, while the United States did not run roughshod over the Charter system – in fact delaying the proposed invasion for several months to seek implicit authorization from the Security Council and ultimately justifying the invasion as having been undertaken in accordance with existing Security Council resolutions – states may have responded with resistance simply because they were unwilling to countenance further weakening of the Charter framework by granting the generalized exception claimed by the United States (Farer 2002: 363). France, for example, used diplomacy to undermine possible Security Council support for US actions and joined with Belgium and Germany in blocking NATO plans to send Patriot missile batteries to Turkey in preparation for the invasion. Turkey, in turn, refused to allow the use of its territory for US military forces to invade Iraq from the north, while Russia provided the Iraqi military with intelligence regarding US troop deployments and battle plans (Burns 2006).

Viewed in the absence of a larger context, these incidents are rather misleading. For example, while Turkey refused to allow US forces the use of military bases located in Turkey, it allowed them to use its airspace and sent approximately 10,000 troops into northern Iraq (Winrow 2006: 197). Jordan and Saudi Arabia also allowed US forces to use their airspace, although publicly Saudi Arabia only admitted to allowing US forces the use of a command and control center at Prince Sultan Air Base (Rennie 2003). Moreover, as late as December 2002, France was preparing to assist in the invasion by deploying up to 15,000 troops to the Middle East (Kessler 2004). And once the invasion began, Germany provided US forces with intelligence gathered by German agents in Baghdad. According to

Bernstein and Gordon (2006), "German–American cooperation during the war was continuing, systematic and regular" – hardly the response one would expect if the United States were in fact attempting to create a system of "exceptional rules for itself alone" (Byers 2002b: 39).

A better explanation for recent US actions and other states' responses to those actions requires consideration of additional factors: the "noise" that accompanied US attempts to signal restraint, and the origin of such "noise" – namely, US policy-makers' assessment of an emerging threat not anticipated within the Charter framework. As we have seen, US policy-makers justified the invasion of Iraq by claiming that it was implicitly authorized under resolution 1441. At various times, however, they also included claims of self-defense. For example, Secretary of State Powell's address to the Security Council on 5 February 2003 recalled the language of resolution 1441 that Iraq would face "serious consequences" if it did not comply with its disarmament obligations, but also noted policy-makers' concerns that Iraq's illicit weapons "can be connected to terrorists and terrorist organizations that have no compunction about using such devices against innocent people" (UN Doc. S/PV.4701). By supplementing claims regarding the interpretation of existing Security Council resolutions with claims regarding more fundamental disagreement over the inclusivity of the Charter's Article 51 "inherent right of self-defence," Powell inadvertently created "noise" that obscured the intended signal of continuing US commitment to the existing international order. This was in addition to "noise" already created by Vice President Cheney's assertion that Iraq's "rejection of a viable inspections system, and ... demonstrated hostility ... combine to produce an imperative for preemptive action" (White House 2003), and the September 2002 National Security Strategy, which called for "anticipatory action ... even if uncertainty remains as to the time and place of the enemy's attack" (Bush 2002: 6).

The origin of such "noise," as these statements suggest, is US policy-makers' assessment of the emerging threat posed by terrorism and the proliferation of WMD. As the leading power in the international system, the United States is more sensitive to this emerging threat than the other major powers are, because its extensive interests throughout the world make it a primary target for terrorist attacks. Such attacks would be devastating if undertaken by terrorists armed with WMD. The Charter framework is ill-equipped to deal with this emerging threat, however, because it is built upon assumptions regarding interstate war that are of limited applicability to non-state actors. Unlike interstate wars, impending terrorist attacks are difficult to detect, because the preparations for such attacks are relatively easy to conceal; and it is difficult to respond to such attacks, because terrorists are able to conceal themselves within the civilian population.

Ironically, whatever proposed adaptation of the Charter framework that may be necessary to meet this emerging threat is unlikely to be accepted by other states if it is posed by the leading power in the system (i.e., the United States). This is not because institutional frameworks are inadequate to the task of restraining the major powers, but rather because the actions of the leading power are subject to more intense scrutiny than those of the other major powers, insofar as the leading power has the largest incentive to alter the existing institutional framework in a manner intended to serve its own interests (Pape 2005: 14). States, then, are likely to be suspicious of any attempt by the United States to loosen existing restraints on the use of armed force, because such changes to the existing framework seem prima facie unlikely to serve the interests of other states. As Johnstone (2004: 833) notes, it is not surprising therefore that states had difficulty ascertaining whether US actions in Iraq were part of an effort "to adapt existing ... institutions to new threats" or an effort "to tear down ... those institutions and start again from scratch."

Overcoming this problem will require not only that the United States engage with other major powers and with leading states such as Germany, Japan, and India, but also that less powerful states give more serious attention to the emerging threat of WMD terrorism. Both the General Assembly's recent condemnation of "terrorism in all its forms and manifestations, committed by whomever, wherever and for whatever purposes" (UN Doc. A/Res/60/1), and the United States' recent involvement in multilateral efforts to address proliferation threats posed by Iran and North Korea are important first steps, but much work remains to be done. As this book suggests, continued progress will require a demonstrated willingness by the major powers – and the United States in particular – to restrain the exercise of their power and thereby signal their continuing commitment to basic Charter principles.

APPENDIX A

Case selection and methodology

The units of observation used herein for testing purposes are incidents in which major powers decided to use armed force within or against other states between October 1945 and October 2003. Decisions to use armed force are defined to include the following incidents. First, they include decisions to deploy military units within the land borders or territorial waters of another state for conducting combat operations therein. Combat operations include counter-insurgency action, combat patrol, or offensive maneuver. Second, decisions to use armed force include decisions to attack targets under the control of or within the land borders or territorial waters of another state, provided that such decisions were authorized at a level higher than that of the local military commanders. Third, they include decisions to blockade the ports and/or coasts of another state. Fourth, they include decisions to provide weapons and/or training to armed bands, groups, irregulars, or mercenaries while they are engaged in any of the activities listed above. This definition is adapted from Tillema and Van Wingen's (1982: 223–4, 246) definition of military actions.

The definition excludes the following incidents as units of observation. First, it excludes decisions to participate in UN peacekeeping operations or observer missions under UN command (such as UNPROFOR in the former Yugoslavia or UNEF in the Sinai). Participation in such missions, however, should not be confused with participation in UN-authorized or UN-approved enforcement actions under the command of individual states (such as the US-led intervention in Korea in 1950, the British intervention in Cyprus in 1963, or the French intervention in Rwanda in 1994), which meet the criteria listed above and thus are included as units of observation. Second, it excludes decisions regarding civil and colonial policing or administration (such as French decisions regarding Algeria in the 1950s, British decisions regarding Northern Ireland in the 1970s, or Russian decisions regarding Chechnya in the 1990s) or similar actions in zones of legal occupation (such as Soviet decisions regarding East Berlin in 1953). The legal questions applicable to such incidents are not derived from the Charter's prohibition of force and thus are beyond the scope of this analysis. Third, it excludes decisions to participate in noncombat operations within the land borders or territorial waters of another state, including overflights (such as American U-2 flights over the Soviet Union in the 1950s) and military training exercises (such as yearly US military exercises in Korea). Fourth, it excludes unauthorized or accidental uses of armed force (such as the Soviet downing of a Korean passenger jet in September 1983 or the US downing of an Iranian passenger jet in July 1988) or uses of armed force that result from the application of established rules of engagement rather than planning among key decision-makers (such as the initial skirmishes between the Soviet Union and China along the Ussuri River in March 1969 or US attacks on Libyan aircraft over the Gulf of Sidra in March 1986). Such decisions, however, should not be confused with subsequent decisions made by key policy-makers (such as the decision by the Soviet Union to retaliate against China or the decision by the United States to retaliate against Libya). Finally, it excludes decisions made by China during the Charter period prior to October 1971, during which time China's legal status was disputed, and the Republic of China (i.e., Taiwan) occupied China's seat on the UN Security Council. These incidents are excluded as outliers because of the unique legal questions involved.

Incidents in which two or more major powers acted jointly (such as the United Kingdom and France in Egypt in 1956, and the United States, the United Kingdom, and France in Yugoslavia in 1999) are coded as unique cases for each major power involved. In most cases, however, rather than acting jointly, one or more major powers assisted in actions initiated by another major power (such as the United States assisting France in Chad in 1986 and the United Kingdom assisting the United States in Afghanistan in 2001). These incidents are coded as cases only for the major powers that initiated the action; the actions of the other major powers are coded as responses to that action.

Ongoing incidents in which the mode of action remained the same (such as the intermittent US air strikes against Laos that began in September 1959) are coded as a single case. However, ongoing incidents in which the mode of action changed are coded as multiple cases. For example, US involvement in Korea is coded as three cases. The first case involves the decision to intervene in South Korea on 25 June 1950 to evacuate American citizens. The second case involves the decision to intervene in South Korea on 27 June 1950 in support of the South Korean government. The third case involves the decision to intervene in North Korea on 7 October 1950 to unify the Korean peninsula.

Examining only incidents in which major powers decided to use armed force may appear to be selection bias, because it does not examine incidents in which the major powers decided not to use armed force. However, because the prudential restraint model addresses the manner and timing of military actions and the arguments offered to account for those actions, case selection is not biased by selecting only cases in which the major powers actually used armed force. The appropriate empirical questions are when and how major powers undertake the arguably illegal uses of armed force that they have decided to undertake, and not whether they decide to undertake such actions in the first place. In other words, this book examines how the Charter's prohibition of force affects decision-making processes and outcomes after decision-makers already have decided upon a general plan of action, not how international law affects their earliest deliberations. Moreover, although some competing models focus on the Charter's prohibition of force as a restraint on decision-makers' earliest deliberations, these models also have implications for the effects it has on decision-making processes and outcomes after those earliest deliberations have concluded. If the evidence fails to support these more limited implications regarding decision-making processes and outcomes once decision-makers have decided upon a general plan of action, it is unlikely to support more expansive implications regarding decision-makers' earliest deliberations.

The data collected from these incidents provide a basis for inferring causality, which can be understood as the difference between a realized outcome and the expected counterfactual outcome when an explanatory variable takes on a different value (King *et al.* 1994: 77–8). The causal effect being tested herein is restraint on the actions of major powers that results from the Charter's prohibition of force. Specifically, it is the limits, restrictions, or checks on their actions that obtain because of the Charter's prohibition of force and the legal arguments and counter-arguments associated with it.

Each of the models tested herein suggests a different form of restraint on state action. According to the prudential restraint model, the Charter's prohibition of force creates an anticipated likelihood of resistance against unreasonable action, which elicits prudential restraint from major powers such that they may alter the manner and timing of their military actions in accordance with the arguments that they have offered or intend to offer. According to the realist model, the Charter's prohibition of force does not function as a restraint on the actions of the major powers, but rather serves as a tool by which major powers place coercive restraints on the actions of less powerful states. According to the liberal model, the Charter's prohibition of force elicits domestic-level restraint within the major powers, which varies by the degree to which they have internalized international legal rules into their domestic legal systems. According to the communal obligation model, the legal prohibition of force and the Charter system of which it is a component require participation by the major powers in an international forum (i.e., the UN Security Council) and elicit communal restraint from them as they become increasingly less likely to use armed force without UN authorization or approval.

To infer restraint of each type in incidents involving the use of armed force, the appropriate counterfactuals would be conceptualizations of those incidents in the absence of the Charter's prohibition of force. However, because of the uniqueness and complexity of these events and the many variables involved in them, these counterfactuals would be difficult to construct. Thus, it would be difficult in some cases to conclude by counterfactual analysis whether or not certain incidents demonstrate the type of restraint predicted by each model. Accordingly, this book infers causality by evaluating the causal mechanisms of each model, using both quantitative and qualitative methods. It collects multiple observations from each case and then, using congruence procedures and process-tracing procedures, it assesses the extent to which these observations are consistent with observable implications derived from the prudential restraint model and each of the competing models (George and McKeown 1985: 23–9, 34–8). The qualitative methods supplement the quantitative methods by allowing for more direct examination of the causal logics of each model and consideration of the type of restraint predicted by each model in selected cases.

From each of these models, there derive observable implications that pertain to the restraints that the Charter places on state actions. These observable implications provide evidence with which to test these models, without having to construct counterfactuals for all cases. In addition, because the relationship between the Charter and state restraint in each of these models involves legal argumentation, there also derive from them observable implications that pertain to the particular characteristics of the arguments and counter-arguments offered. These additional implications make the results of the empirical analysis more compelling by providing multiple contexts in which each model might be disproved and providing additional data to compensate for possible ambiguity of results (George and McKeown 1985: 26). As King *et al.* (1994: 24–30, 109–10) note, "the more evidence we can find in various contexts, . . . the more confidence we and others should have in our conclusions."

The cases examined in Chapters 4 through 8 were selected for variance in the key explanatory variables, including the types of actions taken and the arguments offered for those actions. Within some of these cases, there is also variance in the governments holding office. Among them, there is variance in whether actions occurred within areas in which a major power has preponderant interest and whether those actions were taken by a liberal major power or by a nonliberal major power. There is also variance across time, including variance in Cold War and post-Cold War time periods (George and McKeown 1985: 25).

No cases occurring prior to 1950 were examined in these chapters, because during the earliest years of the post-war period the major powers settled many issues stemming from World War II, including admission to the United Nations of states such as Austria, Finland, Italy, Japan, and Mongolia, and civil wars and boundary disputes stemming from the war. In addition, the major powers learned through practice how the UN Charter system would work, most importantly how abstentions and vetoes would work. Excluding cases from the early post-war period allows time for the international system to settle to equilibrium – as assumed by the prudential restraint model – and reduces the likelihood of one of the selected cases being an outlier. For example, the Korean War case is affected in large part by the absence of the Soviet delegate to the Security Council and the controversy over whether the absence of a major power counted as an abstention.

In addition to satisfying the case-selection criteria listed above, these cases were selected, in part, for their historical significance, because it is useful to understand how the Charter's prohibition of force functioned in historically significant cases (Van Evera 1997: 86–7). Most of them are "hard" cases, insofar as they involve uses of armed force that occurred without UN authorization or approval and in response to something other than direct aggression in the form of an armed attack against the intervening power(s). Hence, the presumption in these cases would be that the Charter's prohibition of force did not function as a restraint on the actions of the major powers.

Again, it might seem that, in selecting only cases involving actual uses of armed force, the selection of cases is biased. The cases selected might be exceptional cases in which domestic-level restraint or communal restraint failed, even though such forms of restraint succeeded in other cases in which major powers decided not to use armed force. If the selection of cases were biased in this way, the results would be biased in favor of the prudential restraint model and the realist model. However, although the liberal model and the communal obligation model focus on the Charter's prohibition of force as a restraint on decision-makers' earliest deliberations, these models also have implications for the effects that the Charter has on decision-making processes and outcomes once decision-makers already have decided upon general plans of action – including plans that allow for the possible use of armed force. If the evidence fails to support these more limited implications regarding decision-making processes and outcomes, it is unlikely to support more expansive implications regarding decision-makers' earliest deliberations. Such results also would suggest that, once decision-makers have concluded that the use of force may be necessary to achieve a foreign policy goal, the Charter fails to restrain the major powers in any way, and hence that the Charter fails as a restraint on the actions of the major powers precisely when such restraint is needed most. Nevertheless, to ensure against any such bias, the case selection includes cases during the 1990–91 Gulf War that should be "easy" cases for such models. These cases involve multilateral uses of armed force with authorization from the Security Council. Moreover, because all of the cases selected cover a substantive span of time, included within several of them are incidents in which policy-makers decided not to use armed force, at least for the time being. Examining the reasons for which those decisions were made provides evidence to distinguish between the competing models.

APPENDIX B
Case coding

The following rules were used to code observations of each variable.

CLAIM_TYPE

Observations of the variable CLAIM_TYPE are coded to represent the types of claims contained within the arguments offered by the major powers. These arguments may contain legal claims, nonlegal claims, or both. Observations of CLAIM_TYPE are coded as follows, in order of increasing legality of claims:

CLAIM_TYPE(i) = 0

If the arguments offered by a major power to account for its uses of armed force in an incident, i, contain only nonlegal claims, then CLAIM_TYPE(i) = 0. Nonlegal claims are claims that reference bases for assessing state conduct other than international law or that address the proper locus from which to derive rules to govern state interaction. These include claims of morality, justice, fairness, efficiency, and so forth.

CLAIM_TYPE(i) = 1

If a major power offers no arguments to account for its actions in an incident, i, then CLAIM_TYPE(i) = 1. These include incidents in which a major power announces that an action has occurred or will occur but offers no arguments to account for it.

CLAIM_TYPE(i) = 2

If the arguments offered by a major power to account for its uses of armed force in an incident, i, contain both legal and nonlegal claims, then CLAIM_TYPE(i) = 2. Legal claims are claims that derive from a legal framework and reflect areas of dispute regarding legal rules. They include claims regarding the inclusivity of legal rules, claims regarding priority among legal rules, claims regarding the proper interpretation of legal rules, claims regarding the application of legal rules to facts, and claims regarding the determination of relevant facts.

CLAIM_TYPE(i) = 3

If the arguments offered by a major power to account for its uses of armed force in an incident, i, contain only legal claims, then CLAIM_TYPE(i) = 3. As noted above, legal claims are claims that derive from a legal framework and reflect areas of dispute regarding legal rules. They include claims regarding the inclusivity of legal rules, claims regarding priority among legal rules, claims regarding the proper interpretation of legal rules, claims regarding the application of legal rules to facts, and claims regarding the determination of relevant facts.

COLD_WAR

Observations of the variable COLD_WAR are coded to represent whether or not an incident occurred during the Cold War. For coding purposes, it is assumed that the Cold War began immediately following World War II and that it ended in 1990. Observations of COLD_WAR are coded dichotomously as follows:

COLD_WAR(i) = 0

If an incident i occurred in 1990 or later, then COLD_WAR(i) = 0. In other words, 0 indicates the absence of the Cold War.

COLD_WAR(i) = 1

If an incident i occurred in 1989 or earlier, then COLD_WAR(i) = 1. In other words, 1 indicates the presence of the Cold War.

COORD

Observations of the variable COORD are coded to represent the extent of coordination among the major powers, as indicated by the primary disagreements their legal arguments address. As noted above, legal arguments may contain claims that address five different types of disagreements: (1) disagreements over the inclusivity of legal rules, (2) disagreements over the priority of legal rules, (3) disagreements over the interpretation of legal rules, (4) disagreements over the application of legal rules to facts, and (5) disagreements over the determination of facts.

Simple legal arguments may contain claims that address only one type of disagreement. However, legal arguments that are more complex or conveyed via multiple channels may address several disagreements. The primary disagreement addressed by such arguments is the disagreement that is most frequently addressed, the most consistently addressed, or the most emphasized. Often, but not always, the counter-arguments offered by other states determine the primary disagreement that a major power's arguments address.

To the extent that the major powers are converging towards a shared understanding of law, the primary disagreements that their legal arguments address are more likely to be over the determination of facts than the application of legal rules to facts, or the inclusivity, priority, or interpretation of legal rules, because such disagreements are more fundamental (Boyle 1985: 108–9). Accordingly, observations of COORD are coded as follows, in order of increasing coordination.

COORD(i) = 0

If a major power offers only nonlegal arguments to account for its uses of armed force in an incident, i, then COORD(i) = 0. Legal argument contain claims explicitly derived from the legal framework in which they are offered. Legal arguments regarding the use of armed force contain claims derived from the UN Charter. Nonlegal arguments contain claims that derive from alternative references, such as principles of morality, justice, fairness, efficiency, and so forth.

If the primary disagreement addressed by a major power's legal arguments in an incident, i, is over the inclusivity of legal rules, then COORD(i) = 0. Legal arguments containing claims regarding the inclusivity of legal rules address disagreements over whether or not a particular rule is appropriately included among those rules agreed to be pertinent to a situation. In the context of the Charter, claims of inclusivity address disagreements over whether or not "self-defense" includes actions taken to protect citizens abroad against an imminent or ongoing "armed attack," whether or not actions directed against "the territorial integrity or political independence of any State" include actions taken as reprisals, actions taken to recover lawful territory, and retaliatory actions taken as vindication of legal rights.

If the primary disagreement addressed by a major power's legal arguments in an incident, i, is over the priority of legal rules, then COORD(i) = 0. Legal arguments containing claims regarding priority among legal rules address disagreements over whether or not certain rules have priority over other rules pertinent to a situation. In the context of the Charter, claims of priority address disagreements over whether or not decolonization, humanitarian concerns, self-determination, or other ends "consistent with the Purposes of the United Nations" have priority over the Charter's Article 2(4) prohibition of force.

If the primary disagreement addressed by a major power's legal arguments in an incident, *i*, is over the interpretation of legal rules, then COORD(*i*) = 0. Legal arguments containing claims regarding the proper interpretation of legal rules address disagreements over the extent to which a particular understanding of law accord's with law's underlying purpose. In the context of the Charter, claims of interpretation address disagreements over whether or not indirect aggression is tantamount to "armed attack," whether or not an "armed attack" to which a state has clearly committed itself can be said to have "occurred," and whether or not an existing Security Council Resolution implicitly authorizes the use of armed force.

COORD(*i*) = 1

If the primary disagreement addressed by a major power's legal arguments in an incident, *i*, is over the application of legal rules to facts, then COORD(*i*) = 1. Legal arguments containing claims regarding the application of legal rules to facts address disagreements over whether or not agreed rules apply to a particular set of facts. In the context of the Charter, claims of application address disagreements over whether or not a Security Council resolution was adopted in accordance with the Charter, whether or not uses of armed force were taken in accordance with an existing treaty, and whether or not the party inviting or consenting to the use of armed force within its territory is the legitimate government of that territory.

COORD(*i*) = 2

If a major powers does not offer arguments to account for its uses of armed force in an incident, *i*, then COORD(*i*) = 2. Such incidents are coded as a relatively high level of coordination because they generally involve actions taken covertly (such as interventions in civil wars), which most states would argue are illegal, or other types of actions (such as simple rescues of foreign nationals), which most states would argue are legal. The absence of argument implies a relatively high level of coordination.

COORD(*i*) = 3

If the primary disagreement addressed by a major power's legal arguments in an incident, *i*, is over the determination of facts, then COORD(*i*) = 3. Legal arguments containing claims regarding the determination of facts address disagreements over whether or not certain events transpired or the particular manner or sequence in which they transpired. In the context of the Charter, claims of fact address disagreements over whether or not there exists an agreement between states, whether or not a state used armed force against another state or within its boundaries, whether or not a state used armed force prior to the time at which it claimed a legitimate right to do so, whether or not its actions were taken in response to an existing threat or use of armed force by another state, and whether or not its armed forces are pursuing the objectives claimed.

COVERT

Observations of the variable COVERT are coded to represent whether a major power used armed force covertly. Covert uses of armed force are uses of armed force for which a major power attempts to conceal its participation or responsibility from other states, irrespective of whether that attempt is successful or not. Observations of COVERT are coded dichotomously as follows:

COVERT(i) = 0

If a major power did not use armed force covertly in an incident, i, COVERT(i) = 0.

COVERT(i) = 1

If a major power used armed force covertly in an incident, i, then COVERT(i) = 1.

DIFF_REGIME

Observations of the variable DIFF_REGIME are coded to represent the difference in regime types between the major power offering an argument for its uses of armed force and the major power responding to that use of armed force. Using observations of the variable REGIME, coded to represent a major power's regime type, observations of DIFF_REGIME are coded as DIFF_REGIME(i, m) = Abs[REGIME(i) – REGIME(m)], where REGIME(i) is the observation of the variable REGIME for the major power using armed force in an incident, i, and REGIME(m) is the observation of the variable REGIME for a major power, m, responding to that use of armed force.

DISSENT

Observations of the variable DISSENT are coded to represent the level of dissent within the Security Council regarding a major power's use of armed force. Observations of DISSENT are coded as follows, in order of increasing dissent:

DISSENT(i) = 0

If the Security Council adopts a resolution that explicitly authorizes a major power's actions in an incident, i, then DISSENT(i) = 0. A major power receives explicit authorization for its actions if the Security Council approves a resolution that specifically names a major power and authorizes its actions or if the Security Council approves a resolution that authorizes member states to act in a specific way or to use "all necessary means" to achieve a specific objective.

DISSENT(i) = 1

If the Security Council passes a resolution that implicitly authorizes a major power's actions in an incident, i, or if a resolution that explicitly authorizes its actions fails because of a sole or near-sole veto, then DISSENT(i) = 1. A resolution that implicitly authorizes the actions taken by a major power is one that authorizes actions of the sort taken by that major power without specifically naming it or noting a specific objective.

DISSENT(i) = 2

If the Security Council takes no action regarding a major power's actions in an incident, i, then DISSENT(i) = 2. The Security Council takes no action on a matter if it either fails to consider the matter or else approves a resolution that neither authorizes a major power's actions (either explicitly or implicitly) nor condemns them.

DISSENT(i) = 3

If a Security Council Resolution condemning the actions of a major power in an incident, i, lacks the necessary votes to pass, irrespective of the major power's veto, then DISSENT(i) = 3.

DISSENT(i) = 4

If the Security Council approves a resolution condemning the actions of a major power in an incident, i, then DISSENT(i) = 4. In such instances, a major power abstains from voting rather than casting its veto.

DISSENT(i) = 5

If a major power uses its veto to defeat a Security Council Resolution condemning its actions in an incident, i, and other major powers also use their veto or abstain from voting, then DISSENT(i) = 5.

DISSENT(i) = 6

If a major power uses its veto to defeat a Security Council Resolution condemning its actions in an incident, i, and one or more non-permanent members of the Security Council concurs, then DISSENT(i) = 6.

DISSENT(i) = 7

If a major power uses its veto to defeat a Security Council Resolution condemning its actions in an incident, i, and no other members of the Security Council concur, then DISSENT(i) = 7.

NATO

Observations of the variable NATO are coded to represent whether a major power responding to a use of armed force in an incident, i, is a member of NATO along with the major power that used armed force in that incident. Observations of NATO are coded dichotomously as follows:

NATO(i) = 0

If a major power responding to a use of armed force by another major power in an incident, i, and/or the major power using armed force in that incident are not members of NATO, then NATO(i) = 0.

NATO(i) = 1

If a major power responding to a use of armed force by another major power in an incident, i, and the major power using armed force in that incident are both members of NATO, then NATO(i) = 1.

PRIORITY

Observations of the variable PRIORITY are coded to represent whether or not a major power gives priority to the legal claims contained within the arguments it offers. Observations of PRIORITY are coded dichotomously as follows.

PRIORITY(i) = 0

If the arguments offered by a major power to account for its uses of armed force in an incident, i, contain nonlegal claims only, then PRIORITY(i) = 0.

If a major power initially offers no arguments to account for its uses of armed force in an incident, i, but then does so once its actions are discovered, then PRIORITY(i) = 0.

If the arguments offered by a major power to account for its uses of armed force in an incident, i, consistently include nonlegal claims and fail to distinguish them from legal claims by one of the means listed below, then PRIORITY(i) = 0.

PRIORITY(i) = 1

If the arguments offered by a major power to account for its uses of armed force in an incident, i, contain legal claims only, then PRIORITY(i) = 1.

If the arguments offered by a major power to account for its uses of armed force in an incident, i, consistently enumerate legal claims ahead of nonlegal claims, then PRIORITY(i) = 1.

If the arguments offered by a major power to account for its uses of armed force in an incident, i, include language that makes the nonlegal claims clearly subordinate to the legal claims, then PRIORITY(i) = 1.

If the arguments offered by a major power to account for its uses of armed force in an incident, i, seldom include nonlegal claims, then PRIORITY(i) = 1.

REGIME

Observations of the variable REGIME are coded to represent a major power's regime type and its domestic political culture. Because the liberal model defines a major power as liberal if it is democratically-governed and has a domestic political culture premised upon the rule of law, observations of REGIME are coded according to the average of the scores given to each major power for political rights and civil liberties by Freedom House (2006) for a particular year.

Observations of REGIME are coded as REGIME(i) = 7 – FH(i), where FH(i) denotes the average of the scores for political rights and civil liberties given to a major power by Freedom House during the year in which an incident, i, occurred. These scores range from 1 (most liberal) to 7 (least liberal). Freedom House scores are available for July 1972 through November 2004.

Scores for the United States, the United Kingdom, and France during the period October 1945 through June 1972 are assumed to be the same as those for July 1972. This assumption is sensible, insofar as the scores for these major powers vary only slightly during the period from July 1972 though November 2004. The scores for the Soviet Union following the death of Stalin until July 1972 are assumed to be 6s. This assumption is sensible, insofar as the scores for the Soviet Union during the 1970s are 6s for both political rights and civil liberties. Scores for the Soviet Union during the reign of Stalin are assumed as 7s. This assumption is sensible, also, insofar as the scores given to China from July 1972 through June 1977 and from July 1989 through June 1998 also are 7s.

REGION

Observations of the variable REGION are coded to represent whether a major power has preponderant interest in the region in which it has used armed force. Observations of REGION are coded dichotomously as follows:

REGION(i) = 0

If a major power uses armed force in an incident, i, in a region in which it does not have preponderant interest, then REGION(i) = 0. For the United States, the region of preponderant interest includes the states of Central America and the Caribbean, as well as former overseas territories, such as the Philippines. For the Soviet Union, the region of preponderant interest includes the member-states of the Warsaw Pact. For Russia, the region of preponderant interest includes the member-states of the Commonwealth of Independent States. For the United Kingdom, the region of preponderant interest includes all former overseas island territories and African colonies, with the exception of "settler colonies," such as Canada, Australia, and New Zealand. For France, the region of preponderant interest includes all former overseas island territories and African colonies. For China, the region of preponderant interest includes the states of the Korean peninsula and the states of Southeast Asia.

REGION(i) = 1

If a major power uses armed force in an incident, i, in a region in which it has preponderant interest, then REGION(i) = 1. As noted above, for the United States, the region of preponderant interest includes the states of Central America and the Caribbean, as well as former overseas territories, such as the Philippines. For the Soviet Union, the region of preponderant interest includes the member-states of the Warsaw Pact. For Russia, the region of preponderant interest includes the member-states of the Commonwealth of Independent States. For the United Kingdom, the region of preponderant interest includes all former overseas island territories and African colonies, with the exception of "settler colonies," such as Canada,

Australia, and New Zealand. For France, the region of preponderant interest includes all former overseas island territories and African colonies. For China, the region of preponderant interest includes the states of the Korean peninsula and the states of Southeast Asia.

RESPONSE

Observations of the variable RESPONSE are coded to represent each major power's response to uses of armed force by another major power. A major power may respond with acceptance, acquiescence, indirect resistance, direct resistance by economic means, or direct resistance by political-military means, or it may offer no response. Observations of RESPONSE are coded as follows, in order of increasing resistance:

RESPONSE(i, m) = 0

If a major power, m, responds to another major power's use of armed force in an incident, i, with acceptance, then RESPONSE(i, m) = 0. A major power may respond to another major power's use of armed force with acceptance by making public statements and diplomatic exchanges supporting that major power, by offering arguments of its own to account for the actions taken, by casting votes in multilateral institutions that are favorable to the major power that engaged in those actions, or by joining in those actions by providing assistance or logistical support.

RESPONSE(i, m) = 1

If a major power, m, offers no response to another major power's use of armed force in an incident, i, then RESPONSE(i, m) = 1.

RESPONSE(i, m) = 2

If a major power, m, responds to another major power's use of armed force in an incident, i, with acquiescence, then RESPONSE(i, m) = 2. A major power may respond to another major power's use of armed force with acquiescence by offering counter-arguments to condemn the actions taken but not accompanying those counter-arguments with diplomatic, economic, or political-military means of resistance.

RESPONSE(i, m) = 3

If a major power, m, responds to another major power's use of armed force in an incident, i, with indirect resistance, then RESPONSE(i, m) = 3. A major power may respond to another major power's use of armed force with indirect resistance by withdrawing its diplomatic representatives from that major power, expelling that major power's diplomatic representatives, canceling scheduled visits or talks, suspending or terminating treaties unrelated to the actions taken by the major power, or attempting to isolate it diplomatically by withdrawing support for it in multilateral institutions. Such actions include offering resolutions or casting votes within those multilateral institutions that are unfavorable to that major power.

RESPONSE(*i*, m) = 4

If a major power, m, responds to another major power's use of armed force in an incident, *i*, with direct resistance by economic means, then RESPONSE(*i*, m) = 4. A major power may respond to another major power's use of armed force with direct resistance by economic means through tariffs, trade restrictions, financial restrictions, and embargoes.

RESPONSE(*i*, m) = 5

If a major power, m, responds to another major power's use of armed force in an incident, *i*, with direct resistance by political-military means, then RESPONSE(*i*, m) = 5. A major power may respond to another major power's use of armed force with direct resistance by political-military means through suspending or terminating treaties related to the actions that major power has taken, providing assistance to its adversaries, engaging in covert acts of reprisal against it, or joining a balancing coalition against it.

TIME_ON

Observations of the variable TIME_ON are coded to represent the amount of time that a major power has held a seat as a permanent member of the Security Council. Observations of TIME_ON are coded as TIME_ON(*i*) = m(*i*) / 12, where m(*i*) represents the number of months that a major power has held a seat as a permanent member of the Security Council at the time of an incident, *i*. The United States, the United Kingdom, France, and the Soviet Union/Russia have held seats as permanent members of the Security Council since October 1945. China has held a set as a permanent member of the Security Council since October 1971.

APPENDIX C

Case overview

The following is a brief overview of the 196 cases examined in this study:

1 Soviet Union–Iran (March 1946)
Under the terms of the Tripartite Treaty of 1942, the Soviet Union was required to withdraw its military forces from Iran within six months of the end of World War II. However, Soviet military forces remained past the stipulated deadline and declared an autonomous republic in northern Iran.

2 United Kingdom–Albania (November 1946)
On 12 November 1946, British military forces entered Albanian territorial waters to clear mines after an Albanian shore battery fired on British cruisers and two other British warships struck mines in the Corfu Channel.

3 Soviet Union–Hungary (February 1947)
In February 1947, Soviet military forces secretly provided aid to Hungarian rebels, resulting in a Communist takeover of Hungary.

4 United States–China (March 1949)
In March 1949, US military forces intervened in China to protect the US embassy and to aid in the evacuation of US citizens as Communist forces advanced towards Nanking.

5 United Kingdom–China (April 1949)
In April 1949, British military forces intervened in China to evacuate British and Commonwealth citizens as Communist forces advanced towards Nanking.

6 United States–Albania (May 1950)
In May 1950, the United States and the United Kingdom secretly provided assistance to Albanian rebels as part of a covert plan to overthrow the Albanian government.

7 United Kingdom–Albania (May 1950)
In May 1950, the United States and the United Kingdom secretly provided assistance to Albanian rebels (see above).

8 United States–South Korea (June 1950)
On 25 June 1950, US military forces intervened in South Korea to evacuate US citizens following an invasion from North Korea.

9 United States–South Korea (June 1950)
On 27 June 1950, US military forces intervened in South Korea to assist South Korean forces following an invasion from North Korea.

10 United States–North Korea (October 1950)
On 7 October 1950, US military forces intervened in North Korea to assist South Korean forces that had crossed into North Korea.

11 United Kingdom–Egypt (October 1951)
In October 1951, British military forces took control of the Suez Canal following Egypt's renunciation of a 1936 basing agreement. After Egyptian forces attacked water filtration plants supplying the Canal Zone, British forces demolished Egyptian houses in order to clear access to a water supply. Following attacks on British military vehicles and personnel, British forces attacked an Egyptian police barracks.

12 United States–Guatemala (October 1953)
In October 1953, the United States secretly began providing assistance to Guatemalan rebels as part of a covert plan to overthrow the government of Jacobo Arbenz.

13 United States–China (January 1955)
In January 1955, US military forces intervened in China to evacuate US citizens from the Tachen Islands following bombardment of the islands by Chinese military forces.

14 France–Tunisia (May 1956)
In May 1956, French military forces intervened in Tunisia to quell a separatist rebellion.

15 Soviet Union–Poland (October 1956)
On 19 October 1956, Soviet military forces intervened in Poland to quell an uprising in Poznan prompted by poor economic conditions.

16 Soviet Union–Hungary (October 1956)
On 24 October 1956, Soviet military forces intervened in Hungary to quell an uprising by Hungarian students demanding the withdrawal of Soviet military forces.

17 Soviet Union–Hungary (November 1956)
On 2 November 1956, Soviet military forces intervened in Hungary to overthrow the government of Imre Nagy following Hungary's attempt to withdraw from the Warsaw Pact.

18 United States–Egypt (October 1956)
In October 1956, US military forces intervened in Egypt to evacuate US citizens from Alexandria following an Israeli invasion of Egypt.

19 United Kingdom–Egypt (November 1956)
On 1 November 1956, British and French military forces intervened

in Egypt in response to Egypt's nationalization of the Suez Canal Company.

20 France–Egypt (November 1956)
On 1 November 1956, British and French military forces intervened in Egypt in response to Egypt's nationalization of the Suez Canal Company (see above).

21 France–Morocco (December 1956)
In December 1956, French military forces intervened in Morocco to quell a rebellion.

22 United Kingdom–Yemen (March 1957)
In March 1957, British military forces intervened in Yemen in response to a series of border incidents between Yemen and the southern Arabian protectorates.

23 United Kingdom–Muscat and Oman (July 1957)
In July 1957, British military forces intervened in Muscat and Oman to restore order following a rebellion against Sultan Said bin Taimur.

24 United States–Indonesia (November 1957)
In November 1957, the United States secretly began providing assistance to Indonesian rebels as part of a covert attempt to overthrow the government of Ahmed Sukarno.

25 France–Tunisia (February 1958)
On 8 February 1958, French military forces intervened in Tunisia in response to attacks on French aircraft flying near the Tunisian border.

26 United Kingdom–Yemen (May 1958)
In May 1958, British military forces intervened in Yemen following attacks by Yemeni-backed rebels in Aden.

27 Lebanon (July 1958)
On 15 July 1958, US military forces intervened in Lebanon in support of President Camille Chamoun as fighting broke out between armed groups in Lebanon.

28 United Kingdom–Jordan (July 1958)
On 17 July 1958, British military forces intervened in Jordan in support of King Hussein following a coup against fellow Hashemite ruler King Faisal II of Iraq.

29 United States–Laos (September 1959)
In September 1959, the United States secretly sent arms and personnel to assist the government of Laos against Pathet Lao rebels.

30 France–Cameroon (January 1960)
In January 1960, French military forces intervened in Cameroon to assist the government against Cameroonian People's Party (UPC) rebels.

31 United States–Cuba (March 1960)
In March 1960, the United States secretly began providing assistance

to Cuban rebels as part of a covert attempt to overthrow the government of Fidel Castro.

32 United States–Congo (July 1960)
In July 1960, US military forces intervened in Congo to assist in the evacuation of civilians during a rebellion in Katanga.

33 France–Senegal (August 1960)
In August 1960, French military forces secretly intervened in Senegal in support of President M. Leopold Senghor following the breakdown of the Mali Federation and a possible coup attempt against Senghor.

34 United States–Dominican Republic (April 1961)
In April 1961, the United States secretly began assisting rebels in the Dominican Republic as part of a plan to overthrow the government of Rafael Leonidas Trujillo.

35 United Kingdom–Kuwait (July 1961)
On 3 July 1961, British military forces intervened in Kuwait to protect against a possible Iraqi invasion.

36 France–Tunisia (July 1961)
On 19 July 1961, French military forces intervened in Tunisia to lift a siege on the French naval base at Bizerte.

37 France–Cameroon (October 1961)
In October 1961, French military forces intervened in Cameroon to assist the government against Cameroonian People's Party (UPC) rebels.

38 United States–South Vietnam (November 1961)
In November 1961, US military forces intervened in South Vietnam to assist the government against Viet Cong rebels.

39 France–Mauritania (March 1962)
In March 1962, French military forces intervened in Mauritania following a rebel attack on French military officers.

40 United States–Thailand (May 1962)
On 15 May 1962, US military forces intervened in Thailand to prevent a possible Communist insurgency.

41 France–Congo-Brazzaville (September 1962)
In September 1962, French military forces intervened in Congo-Brazzaville to suppress riots that broke out following a soccer match.

42 France–Gabon (September 1962)
In September 1962, French military forces intervened in Gabon to suppress riots that broke out following a soccer match (see above).

43 United States–Cuba (October 1962)
In October 1962, US naval forces imposed a naval quarantine to prevent the shipment of Soviet nuclear missile components to Cuba.

44 Soviet Union–Yemen (November 1962)
On 26 November 1962, the Soviet Union secretly airlifted Egyptian

military forces into Yemen to assist in a military coup against the government of Muhammad al Badr.

45 France–Congo-Brazzaville (August 1963)
In August 1963, French military forces intervened in Congo-Brazzaville to quell riots.

46 United Kingdom–Malaysia (December 1963)
In December 1963, British military forces intervened in Malaysia to assist the government against North Kalimantan National Army rebels.

47 United Kingdom–Cyprus (December 1963)
In December 1963, British military forces intervened in Cyprus to impose a ceasefire during a civil war.

48 France–Niger (December 1963)
In December 1963, French military forces intervened in Niger to quell a military mutiny prompted by complaints over low pay and the appointment of an unpopular military commander.

49 United Kingdom–Zanzibar (January 1964)
On 17 January 1964, British military forces intervened in Zanzibar to evacuate British citizens following the overthrow of the Sultan.

50 United Kingdom - Tanganyika (January 1964)
On 25 January 1964, British military forces intervened in Tanganyika to quell a military mutiny prompted by complaints over low pay, poor working conditions, and the low number of African officers in the senior ranks.

51 United Kingdom–Uganda (January 1964)
On 25 January 1964, British military forces intervened in Uganda to quell a military mutiny prompted by complaints over low pay and poor working conditions.

52 United Kingdom - Kenya (January 1964)
On 25 January 1964, British military forces intervened in Kenya to quell a military mutiny prompted by complaints over low pay and reports of similar mutinies in Tanganyika and Uganda (see above).

53 France–Gabon (February 1964)
On 18 February 1964, French military forces intervened in Gabon to restore order following the overthrow of Leon M'ba.

54 United Kingdom–Yemen (March 1964)
On 28 March 1964, British military forces intervened in Yemen in retaliation for attacks against the southern Arabian protectorates.

55 United States–North Vietnam (August 1964)
On 4 August 1964, US military forces intervened in North Vietnam in retaliation for alleged attacks against US naval vessels in the Gulf of Tonkin.

56 United States–Congo (November 1964)
On 24 November 1964, US military forces intervened in Congo to

rescue US citizens and foreign nationals being held hostage by rebels in Stanleyville.

57 United States–North Vietnam (February 1965)
On 6 February 1965, US military forces began bombing North Vietnam in an attempt to coerce the North Vietnamese government to end its support for Viet Cong rebels.

58 United States–Dominican Republic (April 1965)
On 28 April 1965, US military forces intervened in the Dominican Republic to restore order following a military coup.

59 United Kingdom–Southern Rhodesia (March 1966)
On 4 March 1966, British military forces established a naval blockade around Mozambique to prevent petroleum from reaching Southern Rhodesia following its Unilateral Declaration of Independence.

60 United States–Congo (July 1967)
In July 1967, US military forces intervened in Congo to assist the government in quelling a revolt in Katanga.

61 United Kingdom–Mauritius (January 1968)
In January 1968, British military forces intervened in Mauritius to quell riots prompted by economic problems.

62 Soviet Union–Czechoslovakia (August 1968)
On 20 August 1968, Soviet military forces invaded Czechoslovakia to overthrow Communist party leader Alexander Dubcek.

63 France–Chad (August 1968)
In August 1968, French military forces intervened in Chad to quell a rebellion.

64 France–Nigeria (August 1968)
In August 1968, France secretly began providing assistance to rebels in the Biafra province of Nigeria.

65 United States–Cambodia (March 1969)
In March 1969, US military forces secretly began bombing Cambodia to quell a communist insurgency.

66 Soviet Union–China (March 1969)
On 15 March 1969, Soviet military forces attacked Chinese troops along the Ussuri River in response to a border incident with China.

67 France–Chad (April 1969)
In April 1969, French military forces intervened in Chad to assist the government in quelling a rebellion.

68 Soviet Union–Sudan (January 1970)
In January 1970, Soviet military forces secretly intervened in Sudan to assist the government against Anya Nya rebels.

69 United States–Cambodia (April 1970)
In April 1970, US military forces intervened in Cambodia to destroy a Viet Cong command base.

70 United Kingdom–Oman (July 1970)
In July 1970, British military forces secretly intervened in Oman to restore order following a coup.

71 France–Niger (August 1973)
In August 1973, French military forces intervened in Niger to prevent a possible military coup against President Hamani Diori.

72 Soviet Union–Israel (October 1973)
In October 1973, Soviet military forces secretly provided logistical support to Arab states fighting against Israel and flew combat missions on their behalf. In addition, Soviet vessels transported a Moroccan expeditionary force to the Syrian front, and after the war, Soviet officers commanded Syrian artillery units along the Syrian front.

73 China–South Vietnam (January 1974)
On 16 January 1974, Chinese naval forces engaged South Vietnamese forces operating near the Paracel Islands, seizing a South Vietnamese garrison and occupying the westernmost islands.

74 United States–Iraq (May 1974)
In May 1974, the United States secretly began providing assistance to Kurdish rebels in Iraq.

75 United Kingdom–Cyprus (July 1974)
On 15 July 1974, British military forces intervened in Cyprus to rescue Archbishop Makarios, following his overthrow by Greek officers in the Cypriot National Guard.

76 United Kingdom–Cyprus (August 1974)
On 14 August 1974, British military forces intervened in Cyprus to rescue British citizens following a Turkish offensive in Cyprus (see above).

77 United States–Cambodia (April 1975)
On 12 April 1975, US military forces intervened in Cambodia to assist in the evacuation of US citizens and foreign nationals from Phnom Penh.

78 United States–South Vietnam (April 1975)
On 29 April 1975, US military forces intervened in South Vietnam to assist in the evacuation of US citizens and foreign nationals from Saigon.

79 United States–Cambodia (May 1975)
On 13 May 1975, US military forces intervened in Cambodia in an attempt to rescue the crew of the merchant ship *Mayaguez*, which had been seized by Cambodian naval forces.

80 France–Comoros (August 1975)
In August 1975, France secretly assisted in the overthrow of Comoros President Ahmed Abdullah.

81 Soviet Union–Angola (November 1975)
In November 1975, the Soviet Union began providing weapons and

training to MPLA rebels in Angola. In January 1976, Soviet transport planes airlifted Cuban troops into Angola.

82 United States–Lebanon (June 1976)
On 28 June 1976, US military forces intervened in Lebanon to evacuate US citizens and foreign nationals from Beirut following a Syrian military intervention.

83 France–Benin (January 1977)
On 16 January 1977, France secretly assisted in the attempted overthrow of Mathreiu Kerakon in Benin.

84 France–Zaire (April 1977)
On 10 April 1977, French military forces provided logistical support to Moroccan forces deployed in Zaire to quell a rebellion.

85 France–Mauritania (May 1977)
On 13 May 1977, French military forces provided logistical support to Moroccan forces deployed in Mauritania to quell a rebellion. Following an attack on railway installations in Mauritania, France began bombing rebel positions.

86 Soviet Union–Ethiopia (November 1977)
In November 1977, Soviet military forces secretly intervened in Ethiopia to assist the government in quelling rebellions in Ogadan and Eritrea.

87 France–Chad (April 1978)
On 16 April 1978, French military forces secretly intervened in Chad to assist the government in quelling a rebellion.

88 Soviet Union–Afghanistan (April 1978)
In April 1978, Soviet military forces secretly provided logistical support to rebels in Afghanistan.

89 France–Comoros (May 1978)
In May 1978, France secretly assisted in the overthrow of Comoros President Ali Solih, replacing him with Ahmed Abdullah (who had been overthrown in 1975).

90 France–Zaire (May 1978)
On 19 May 1978, French military forces intervened in Zaire to rescue French citizens and foreign nationals following a rebellion in the Shaba province.

91 China–Vietnam (February 1979)
On 17 February 1979, Chinese military forces intervened in Vietnam following Vietnam's invasion of Laos and Cambodia and its expulsion of Chinese citizens.

92 Soviet Union–North Yemen (February 1979)
In February 1979, Soviet military forces secretly began providing assistance to National Democratic Front rebels in North Yemen.

93 France–Chad (June 1979)
In June 1979, French military forces intervened in Chad to repel an invasion from Libya.

94 France–Central African Empire (September 1979)
On 20 September 1979, French military forces intervened in the Central African Empire to assist in the overthrow of Emperor Bokassa.

95 Soviet Union–Afghanistan (December 1979)
On 27 December 1979, Soviet military forces intervened in Afghanistan following the overthrow of Nur Muhammad Taraki.

96 France–Tunisia (January 1980)
On 28 January 1980, French military forces intervened in Tunisia to assist in quelling a rebellion.

97 United States–Iran (April 1980)
On 24 April 1980, US military forces intervened in Iran in an attempt to rescue hostages that had been seized at the US embassy in Tehran and US consulates in Tabriz and Shiraz.

98 United Kingdom–Gambia (July 1981)
In July 1981, British military forces secretly intervened in Gambia to rescue British hostages and to assist military forces from Senegal in restoring President Jawara following a coup.

99 United States–Nicaragua (August 1981)
In August 1981, the United States secretly began providing assistance to Nicaraguan rebels. In October 1983, the CIA organized attacks against petroleum storage facilities in Nicaragua, and in January 1984 the CIA organized an operation to mine Nicaraguan harbors.

100 France–Seychelles (November 1981)
In November 1981, French military forces intervened in the Seychelles following a coup attempt against President Albert René.

101 Soviet Union–Poland (December 1981)
On 13 December 1981, Soviet military forces secretly intervened in Poland, establishing a military council headed by General Wojciech Jaruzelski.

102 United Kingdom–Argentina (April 1982)
On 12 April 1982, British military forces deployed to the Falkland Islands in response to an Argentinian invasion of the islands.

103 United States–Lebanon (September 1982)
On 19 September 1982, US and French military forces deployed to Lebanon following a massacre of refugees by the Lebanese Phalangist Party.

104 France–Lebanon (September 1982)
On 19 September 1982, US and French military forces deployed to Lebanon as part of a multinational force (see above).

105 United States–Syria (December 1982)
In December 1982, US military forces intervened in Syria in retaliation for attacks on US aircraft flying over Lebanon.

106 France–Chad (August 1983)
On 13 August 1983, French military forces intervened in Chad to assist the government in quelling a Libyan-sponsored rebellion.

107 United States–Grenada (October 1983)
On 25 October 1983, US military forces intervened in Grenada following the overthrow of Prime Minister Maurice Bishop.

108 France–New Zealand (July 1985)
On 10 July 1985, French military forces intervened in New Zealand, sinking the Greenpeace ship *Rainbow Warrior* in Auckland harbor in order to prevent the ship from disrupting French nuclear tests in the South Pacific.

109 United States–Egypt (October 1985)
On 10 October 1985, US military forces intercepted an Egyptian airliner carrying the hijackers of the Italian cruise ship *Achille Lauro* following the murder of Leon Klinghoffer, a US citizen.

110 France–Chad (January 1986)
In January 1986, French military forces intervened in Chad to repel an invasion from Libya.

111 United States–Libya (March 1986)
On 25 March 1986, US military forces destroyed a Libyan missile base and sank two Libyan ships in retaliation for attacks on US aircraft flying over the Gulf of Sidra.

112 United States–Libya (April 1986)
On 14 April 1986, US military forces attacked Libya in retaliation for the terrorist bombing of a German disco in which US military personnel had been killed.

113 France–Togo (September 1986)
On 25 September 1986, French military forces intervened in Togo following a coup against President Gnanssingbe Eyadema.

114 France–Congo-Brazzaville (September 1987)
On 6 September 1987, French military forces intervened in Congo-Brazzaville to assist the government in capturing rebel leader Pierre Anga.

115 United States–Iran (October 1987)
On 19 October 1987, US military forces destroyed two Iranian oil platforms and three Iranian warships in retaliation for Iranian mines laid in the Persian Gulf.

116 United States–Honduras (March 1988)
On 16 March 1988, US military forces intervened in Honduras to repel an invasion from Nicaragua.

117 United States–Philippines (December 1989)
In December 1989, US military forces intervened in the Philippines to assist the government of Corazon Aquino in repelling a coup attempt.

118 United States–Panama (December 1989)
On 20 December 1989, US military forces intervened in Panama to capture General Manuel Noriega following the murder of a US marine in Panama.

119 France–Gabon (May 1990)
In May 1990, French military forces intervened in Gabon to rescue French hostages and to quell riots following the death of opposition leader Joseph Rendjambe.

120 United States–Liberia (August 1990)
On 6 August 1990, US military forces intervened in Liberia to evacuate US citizens and foreign nationals from Monrovia following a rebellion led by Charles Taylor.

121 United States–Saudi Arabia (August 1990)
On 8 August 1990, US military forces intervened in Saudi Arabia to prevent a possible invasion from Iraq.

122 United Kingdom–Bahrain (August 1990)
On 8 August 1990, British military forces intervened in Bahrain in response to the Iraqi invasion of Kuwait.

123 United Kingdom–Iraq (August 1990)
On 10 August 1990, British military forces imposed a naval blockade on Iraq following Iraq's invasion of Kuwait.

124 United States–Iraq (August 1990)
On 12 August 1990, US military forces imposed a naval blockade on Iraq following Iraq's invasion of Kuwait.

125 France–Comoros (August 1990)
In August 1990, French military forces intervened in the Comoros to quell the attempted overthrow of Said Mohammed Djohar.

126 France–Rwanda (October 1990)
In October 1990, French military forces intervened in Rwanda in response to an invasion by Rwanda Patriotic Front rebels from Uganda.

127 France–Chad (November 1990)
On 28 November 1990, French military forces intervened in Chad to protect French citizens in N'Djamena as rebels led by Idriss Débay advanced toward the capital.

128 United States –Somalia (January 1991)
In January 1991, US military forces intervened in Somalia to evacuate US citizens and foreign nationals following the overthrow of the government of Siad Barre.

129 United States–Iraq (January 1991)
On 16 January 1991, US and British military forces intervened in Iraq following Iraq's invasion of Kuwait.

130 United Kingdom–Iraq (January 1991)
On 16 January 1991, US and British military forces intervened in Iraq following Iraq's invasion of Kuwait (see above).

131 United States–Iraq (April 1991)
On 16 April 1991, the US, British, and French military forces intervened in Iraq to create a "safe haven" for Kurdish refugees following rebellion against the Iraqi government

132 United Kingdom–Iraq (April 1991)
On 16 April 1991, the US, British, and French military forces intervened in Iraq to create a "safe haven" for Kurdish refugees (see above).

133 France–Iraq (April 1991)
On 16 April 1991, the US, British, and French military forces intervened in Iraq to create a "safe haven" for Kurdish refugees (see above).

134 France–Djibouti (May 1991)
In May 1991, French military forces intervened in Djibouti to assist the government in disarming and deporting Ethiopian rebels.

135 France–Zaire (September 1991)
In September 1991, French military forces intervened in Zaire to restore order following a military mutiny.

136 France–Central African Republic (September 1991)
In September 1991, French military forces intervened in the Central African Republic to rescue French citizens and foreign nationals following unrest there.

137 United States–Haiti (October 1991)
In October 1991, US military forces intervened in Haiti to evacuate US citizens and foreign nationals following a coup against Jean-Bertrand Aristide.

138 France–Chad (December 1991)
In December 1991, French military forces intervened in Chad to assist the government against rebels invading from Senegal in support of former president Hissène Habré.

139 Russia–Moldova (May 1992)
In May 1992, Russian military forces intervened in Moldova to assist rebels in Transnistria.

140 United States–Sierra Leone (May 1992)
In May 1992, US military forces intervened in Sierra Leone to evacuate US citizens and foreign nationals following a military coup.

141 Russia–Tajikistan (June 1992)
In June 1992, Russian military forces intervened in Tajikistan to assist the government in quelling a separatist rebellion.

142 Russia–Armenia (June 1992)
In June 1992, Russian military forces intervened in Armenia to assist in military actions against Azerbaijan.

143 United States–Iraq (August 1992)
On 26 August 1992, US, British, and French military forces began surveillance operations in southern Iraq to ensure compliance with resolution 688 following Iraqi attacks against the Shia population in southern Iraq.

144 United Kingdom–Iraq (August 1992)
On 26 August 1992, US, British, and French military forces began surveillance operations in southern Iraq (see above).

145 France–Iraq (August 1992)
On 26 August 1992, US, British, and French military forces began surveillance operations in southern Iraq (see above).

146 United States–Liberia (October 1992)
In October 1992, US military forces intervened in Liberia to evacuate US citizens and foreign nationals from Monrovia following unrest there.

147 United States–Somalia (December 1992)
On 8 December 1992, US military forces intervened in Somalia to restore order and to safeguard the delivery of humanitarian aid.

148 France–Zaire (January 1993)
On 29 January 1993, French military forces intervened in Zaire to evacuate French citizens and foreign nationals following an attack on the French Embassy and the murder of the French ambassador during military rioting prompted by complaints over military pay.

149 United States–Iraq (January 1993)
On 17 January 1993, US military forces attacked a nuclear fabrication facility in Iraq in response to Iraq's refusal to cooperate with UNSCOM weapons inspectors.

150 France–Rwanda (February 1993)
On 9 February 1993, French military forces intervened in Rwanda following the resumption of fighting between government forces and FPR rebels.

151 United States–Bosnia-Herzegovina (April 1993)
On 12 April 1993, NATO forces began engaging Yugoslavian aircraft found to be violating a UN-imposed ban on military flights over Bosnia-Herzegovina.

152 United Kingdom–Bosnia-Herzegovina (April 1993)
On 12 April 1993, NATO forces began engaging Yugoslavian aircraft found to be violating a UN-imposed ban on military flights over Bosnia-Herzegovina. (see above).

153 France–Bosnia-Herzegovina (April 1993)
On 12 April 1993, NATO forces began engaging Yugoslavian aircraft found to be violating a UN-imposed ban on military flights over Bosnia-Herzegovina. (see above).

154 Russia–Georgia (June 1993)
In June 1993, Russian military forces intervened in Georgia to quell a rebellion in Abkhazia and South Ossetia.

155 United States–Iraq (June 1993)
On 26 June 1993, US military forces attacked the headquarters of the Iraqi Intelligence Service following an attempt to assassinate former President George H. W. Bush.

156 United States–Somalia (July 1993)
In July 1993, US military forces remaining in Somalia deployed as a "Quick Reaction Force" in support of UNOSOM II.

157 United States–Haiti (October 1993)
On 16 October 1993, US military forces imposed a naval blockade on Haiti following the overthrow of Jean-Bertrand Aristide.

158 United States–Bosnia-Herzegovina (March 1994)
On 13 March 1994, NATO forces attacked Serbian positions in Bosnia-Herzegovina after UNPROFOR forces had been prevented from entering the town of Maglaj in northern Bosnia. On 30 August, NATO forces resumed air strikes when Serbian forces continued to threaten Sarajevo. In May 1995, NATO forces bombed an arms depot in Bosnia-Herzegovina following the placement of Serbian artillery around Sarajevo.

159 United Kingdom–Bosnia-Herzegovina (March 1994)
On 13 March 1994, NATO forces attacked Serbian positions in Bosnia-Herzegovina, and again in August 1994 and in May 1995 (see above).

160 France–Bosnia-Herzegovina (March 1994)
On 13 March 1994, NATO forces attacked Serbian positions in Bosnia-Herzegovina, and again in August 1994 and in May 1995 (see above).

161 France–Cameroon (March 1994)
In March 1994, French military forces intervened in Cameroon following a border dispute with Nigeria.

162 France–Rwanda (April 1994)
In April 1994, French military forces intervened in Rwanda to evacuate French citizens and foreign nationals after fighting broke out between Hutus and Tutsis following the death of Rwandan President Juvénal Habyarimana.

163 France–Rwanda (June 1994)
On 23 June 1994, French military forces intervened in Rwanda to protect civilians and disarm Hutu militias.

164 United States–Haiti (September 1994)
On 19 September 1994, US military forces intervened in Haiti to restore President Jean-Bertrand Aristide to power.

165 United States–Bosnia-Herzegovina (December 1995)
On 15 December 1995, NATO forces intervened in Bosnia-Herzegovina to enforce a ceasefire agreement.

166 United Kingdom–Bosnia-Herzegovina (December 1995)
On 15 December 1995, NATO forces intervened in Bosnia-Herzegovina to enforce a ceasefire agreement (see above).

167 France–Bosnia-Herzegovina (December 1995)
On 15 December 1995, NATO forces intervened in Bosnia-Herzegovina to enforce a ceasefire agreement (see above).

168 United States–Liberia (April 1996)
On 9 April 1996, US military forces intervened in Liberia to evacuate US citizens and foreign nationals following the resumption of civil war.

169 France–Central African Republic (April 1996)
In May 1996, French military forces intervened in the Central African Republic to evacuate French citizens and foreign nationals following a military mutiny.

170 United States–Iraq (September 1996)
On 3 September 1996, US military forces attacked Iraqi surface-to-air missile sites in southern Iraq, extending the southern "no-fly" zone following Iraqi actions against the Kurdish population of Irbil in northern Iraq.

171 United States–Albania (March 1997)
On 14 March 1997, US military forces intervened in Albania to evacuate US citizens and foreign nationals from Tirana following unrest resulting from the collapse of a pyramid scheme.

172 United States–Sierra Leone (May 1997)
On 30 May 1997, US military forces intervened in Sierra Leone to evacuate US citizens and foreign nationals from Freetown following the overthrow of President Ahmed Tejan Kabbah.

173 France–Congo-Brazzaville (June 1997)
On 3 June 1997, French military forces intervened in Congo to evacuate French citizens and foreign nationals from Brazzaville following unrest there.

174 United States–Eritrea (June 1998)
In June 1998, US military forces intervened in Eritrea to evacuate US citizens and foreign nationals from Asmara following the outbreak of war with Ethiopia.

175 United States–Afghanistan (August 1998)
On 20 August 1998, US military forces attacked suspected terrorist training camps in Afghanistan in response to the bombing of US embassies in Nairobi and Dar es Salaam.

176 United States–Sudan (August 1998)
On 20 August 1998, US military forces attacked a pharmaceutical

plant in Sudan in response to the bombing of US embassies in Nairobi and Dar es Salaam.

177 United States–Iraq (December 1998)
On 16 December 1998, US and British military forces began bombing Iraq in response to Iraq's refusal to cooperate with UNSCOM inspectors.

178 United Kingdom–Iraq (December 1998)
On 16 December 1998, US and British military forces began bombing Iraq in response to Iraq's refusal to cooperate with UNSCOM inspectors (see above).

179 United States–Yugoslavia (March 1999)
On 24 March 1999, NATO forces began bombing Yugoslavia in response to President Slobodan Milosevic's refusal to accept the Rambouillet Agreement.

180 United Kingdom–Yugoslavia (March 1999)
On 24 March 1999, NATO forces began bombing Yugoslavia in response to Milosevic's refusal to accept the Rambouillet Agreement (see above).

181 France–Yugoslavia (March 1999)
On 24 March 1999, NATO forces began bombing Yugoslavia in response to Milosevic's refusal to accept the Rambouillet Agreement (see above).

182 United States–Yugoslavia (June 1999)
On 9 June 1999, NATO forces intervened in Yugoslavia following Yugoslavia's acceptance of a joint EU–Russian peace proposal.

183 United Kingdom–Yugoslavia (June 1999)
On 9 June 1999, NATO forces intervened in Yugoslavia following Yugoslavia's acceptance of a joint EU–Russian peace proposal (see above).

184 France–Yugoslavia (June 1999)
On 9 June 1999, NATO forces intervened in Yugoslavia following Yugoslavia's acceptance of a joint EU–Russian peace proposal (see above).

185 United Kingdom–Sierra Leone (May 2000)
On 7 May 2000, British military forces intervened in Sierra Leone to evacuate British citizens and foreign nationals from Freetown following the collapse of the Lome Peace Agreement.

186 United Kingdom–Sierra Leone (September 2000)
On 10 September 2000, British military forces intervened in Sierra Leone to destroy a rebel militia that had been holding British troops hostage.

187 United States–Iraq (February 2001)
On 16 February 2001, US and British military forces bombed air-defense targets in Iraq.

188 United Kingdom–Iraq (February 2001)
On 16 February 2001, United States and British military forces bombed air-defense targets in Iraq (see above).

189 United States–Afghanistan (October 2001)
On 7 October 2001, US military forces intervened in Afghanistan to assist the Northern Alliance in overthrowing the Taliban regime that had been harboring Osama bin Laden.

190 United Kingdom–Afghanistan (December 2001)
On 22 December 2001, British military forces intervened in Afghanistan following the overthrow of the Taliban government.

191 France–Ivory Coast (September 2002)
On 24 September 2002, French military forces intervened in Ivory Coast to evacuate French citizens and foreign nationals from Bouake following coup attempt against President Laurent Gbagbo.

192 United States–Yemen (November 2002)
On 3 November 2002, a secret US military drone fired a missile at a car carrying Qaed Salim Sinan al-Harethi and five other al-Qaeda members suspected in the bombing of a US warship.

193 United States–Philippines (February 2003)
In February 2003, US military forces intervened in the Philippines to assist the government against Abu Sayyaf guerrillas.

194 United States–Iraq (March 2003)
On 19 March 2003, US and British military forces intervened in Iraq in response to its refusal to cooperate with UNMOVIC weapons inspectors.

195 United Kingdom–Iraq (March 2003)
On 19 March 2003, US and British military forces intervened in Iraq in response to its refusal to cooperate with UNMOVIC weapons inspectors (see above).

196 United States–Liberia (August 2003)
On 14 August 2003, US military forces intervened in Liberia to secure the port of Freetown for humanitarian aid and serve as a rapid-reaction force in support of an international peacekeeping force.

NOTES

1 THE FUNCTIONING OF THE UN CHARTER AS A RESTRAINT ON MILITARY ACTION

1 Note, however, the frequency with which less powerful states also have undertaken arguably illegal uses of armed force. See Weisburd (1997).
2 Guzman (2002: 1846–7, 1868–9) presents a range of options for preventing defection, but he acknowledges that they are unlikely to be effective in multilateral settings because of collective-action problems.
3 This incremental view of international law is based on Boyle's (1985: 164–6) functional theory of law as both incremental and dynamic.
4 The only explicit power given to the Security Council to authorize enforcement action involves forces under direct UN control, in accordance with Article 43 of the Charter. In practice, however, the Security Council has exercised an implicit power of authorizing enforcement action by individual states. See Blokker (2000).
5 On prescriptions/proscriptions and the parameters that delimit them, see Shannon (2000: 295).

2 THE UN CHARTER AND LEGAL ARGUMENTATION

1 Although a social-science theory should be evaluated more on the basis of its empirical claims than on the basis of its assumptions, this assumption is consistent with post-revisionist Cold War historiography, including Leffler (1992), Wohlforth (1993), and Trachtenberg (1999), and is borne out in the empirical chapters that follow. On the role of assumptions in social-science theory, see Moe (1979: 216–17) and Mearsheimer (2001: 30). On the role of nuclear weapons in maintaining the status quo, see Jervis (1989: 29–35).
2 At present, the United Kingdom is the only permanent member of the UN Security Council that accepts the compulsory jurisdiction of the ICJ.
3 Note that some disagreements (particularly those regarding the term "armed aggression") arise from distinctions among the Chinese, French, Russian, English, and Spanish texts of the Charter, which under Article 111 "are all equally authentic."
4 The following analysis of legal arguments as accounts for perceived violations of international law draws extensively from Shannon's (2000: 293–305) work regarding international norms, although Shannon uses political psychology to explain state action as a result of the motivated biases of state leaders and does not consider arguments as signals nor the role of international law per se.
5 An affirmative defense is an assertion that, assuming the complaint to be true, constitutes a defense to it. See Garner (1999: 430).

6 This typology is based on Boyle's (1985: 108–12) typology of legal claims, although Boyle includes claims of reference in his typology of legal claims.
7 The United States offered no formal legal justification for its participation in the NATO air campaign against Yugoslavia. For a discussion of the US position, see Glennon (2001: 25–7).
8 The dataset used herein draws from Tillema and Van Wingen (1982), Webster (2003), Wyllie (1984), Van Wingen and Tillema (1980), Moose (1985), Schmid (1985), Chipman (1989), Somerville (1990), Rouvez (1994), Robinson (2001), Zuljan (2001), Bloomfield and Moulton (2000), Federation of American Scientists (2002b), and Peace Pledge Union (2002), as well as various news sources. Appendix A discusses case selection and methodology, while Appendix B provides detailed case-coding rules. Appendix C provides a brief overview of all 196 cases examined.
9 Major powers offered no arguments for their actions in 54 out of 196 cases (27.6 percent). Coding these cases as cases in which legal claims did not have priority over nonlegal claims, major powers offered arguments in which legal claims had priority over nonlegal claims in 106 out of 196 cases (54.1 percent).
10 Freedom House scores are available for July 1972 through November 2004. For coding used outside of this time span, see Appendix B.
11 It is assumed, for the purposes of this analysis, that the Cold War began immediately following World War II and ended at the beginning of 1990.
12 Nor does the end of the Cold War appear to have any effect. The coefficient on COLD_WAR is negative, but with confidence of only 44 percent.
13 In four cases (2.0 percent of the 196 cases), major powers offered only nonlegal arguments for their actions, and in 54 cases (27.6 percent of the 196 cases), major powers offered no arguments for their actions.

3 PERSUASION, LEGITIMATION, AND RESTRAINT

1 Defined in this way, legitimacy does not have the same significance that it does in much of the literature, which derives from Weber's (1968: 31–7) definition of legitimacy as a widespread belief that an order is obligatory or binding.
2 A retorsion is a lawful act by an aggrieved party against a wrongdoer, while a reprisal is an arguably illegal act by an aggrieved party against a wrongdoer. See Zoller (1984: 2–27, 35–43).
3 This typology draws upon Padelford (1948: 231–45).
4 Implicit authorization may also include instances when the Security Council discusses a resolution that gives explicit authorization or approval to an action, but that resolution fails because it is vetoed by another major power.
5 Keal (1983: 2, 10, 149) argues that such counter-arguments are more likely to be offered in the General Assembly than in the Security Council, because a major power "stands to gain political kudos by leading the protest in that forum." Recall from above that the major power using armed force is likely to misrepresent its particular understanding of law, also, because the actions it has taken might threaten the existing order if all states were to engage in them, but it perceives such actions to be insignificant in the particular case because of a tacit understanding with the other major powers that they occurred within an area in which it has preponderant interest.
6 This process is similar to the "rhetorical entrapment" and "shaming" processes outlined by Schimmelfennig (2001: 62–76). It involves "rhetorical action," which Schimmelfennig defines as "the strategic use of norm-based arguments." However, the processes outlined by Schimmelfennig pertain to collective out-

comes and are based on communal identity among states and a communal standard of legitimacy.

7 This discussion of strategies of denial and rhetorical evasion draws extensively from Shannon's (2000) work, although Shannon uses political psychology to explain state actions as a result of the motivated biases of state leaders and does not considers arguments as signals or the role of international law per se.

8 Not all communal obligation theorists concur. For example, Falk (1969: 67) explicitly rejects this implication, arguing that spheres of influence are part of a "special ordering principle" and have a communal basis because their "adherence corresponds with widely shared community expectations as to the character of reasonable behavior."

9 The probability of no response increases also if the actions taken occurred within a region in which a major power has preponderant interest. These 377 observations are not included in the cross-tabulation, because what are of interest here are the types of responses given, and the prudential restraint model has no implications for the probability of major powers offering counter-arguments in response to the actions of another major power. However, even if these observations were to be included in the cross-tabulation, the concave downward relationship observed in Table 3.2 would obtain.

10 States need not offer arguments and counter-arguments within the Security Council, although it provides a convenient forum in which to do so. See Chayes and Chayes (1995: 125).

4 THE IMPACT OF THE UN CHARTER ON US MILITARY INTERVENTION IN THE CARIBBEAN REGION, 1953–61

1 US primary source materials are collected in *Foreign Relations of the United States* (cited as *FRUS*) and the *Department of State Bulletin* (cited as *DSB*). Selected documents are reprinted in Kornbluh (1998). UN debates are summarized in the *United Nations Yearbook* (cited as *UNYB*), while UN documents are available from documents.un.org. Schlesinger Jr. (1965) and Berle and Jacobs (1973) provide useful first-hand accounts of US policy-making processes. Important secondary sources include Diederich (1978), Wyden (1979), Immerman (1982), Gleijeses (1995), Rabe (1996), and Schlesinger and Kinzer (1999).

2 Schlesinger and Kinzer (1999: 150–2) note that most of the weapons aboard the freighter were unsuited to Guatemala's defense needs and/or not functional, although US policy-makers were unaware of it at the time.

3 Consultations with OAS members continued, however. See Slater (1967: 122).

4 On Soviet intervention in Hungary, see Chapter 6.

5 Although Mann ardently opposed the invasion, he acquiesced because he "did not want to leave the impression that [he] would not support whatever the president decided to do." See Gleijeses (1995: 32).

6 According to Schlesinger Jr. (1965: 271), Stephenson had not been made aware that the operation would proceed. Note here Kennedy's instructions that "nothing said at the United Nations should be less than the truth, even if it could not be the full truth."

7 The assumption of the CIA, however, seems to have been that if the invasion were to fail, Kennedy would fall back to the original plan of flying in a provisional government to request military assistance from the United States. See Gleijeses (1995: 37–9).

5 THE IMPACT OF THE UN CHARTER ON ANGLO-FRENCH MILITARY INVERVENTION IN EGYPT, 1956

1 British primary source materials are collected in *British Documents on the End of Empire* (cited as *BDEE*) and *Documents on International Affairs* (cited as *DIA*), while French primary source materials are collected in *Documents Diplomatiques Français* (cited as *DDF*). Selected documents are reprinted in Marston (1988) and Gorst and Johnman (1997). UN debates are summarized in the *United Nations Yearbook* (cited as *UNYB*), while UN documents are available from documents.un.org. Eden (1960), Nutting (1967), and Lloyd (1978) provide first-hand accounts of the crisis from the British perspective, while Beaufre (1969) provides a first-hand account from the French perspective. Important secondary sources include Carlton (1989), Vaisse (1989), Kyle (1991), and Kelly and Gorst (2000).

2 First Sea Lord Mountbatten agreed with Monckton and considered resigning in protest because of his concern that other states would view the proposed intervention as an "aggressive war" and would withhold oil shipments from the United Kingdom and/or pursue closer ties to the Soviet Union. According to Mountbatten, the UN Charter system had been designed "precisely in order to prevent actions like the one we have now embarked on." See Kyle (1991: 215–16).

3 In addition to Egypt's refusal to allow Israeli navigation on the Suez Canal and in the Gulf of Aqaba, the Nasser government had organized *fedayeen* raids into Israeli territory from Gaza. According to Warner (1979: 234), Israeli Prime Minister David Ben-Gurion was initially reluctant to join in the operation, protesting that he was "not prepared to accept a division of functions whereby . . . Israel volunteered to mount the rostrum of shame so that Britain and France could lave their hands in the waters of purity."

4 Under the Tripartite Declaration of 1950, the United States, the United Kingdom, and France committed themselves to stabilizing the Middle East region and intervening with military force, if necessary, to prevent any change in the borders established under the Armistice of 1949.

5 Eden appears to have hidden the details of Israeli involvement from the members of the Cabinet, although no minutes from this meeting were kept. See Warner (1979: 238) and Kyle (1991: 301–4).

6 According to Nutting (1967: 116), Egyptian forces were engaged in combat between 75 and 125 miles east of the Suez Canal at the time the ultimatum was issued.

7 For a summary of states' responses to Anglo-French military intervention in Egypt, see Weisburd (1997: 32–3).

6 THE IMPACT OF THE UN CHARTER ON SOVIET MILITARY INTERVENTION IN HUNGARY, 1956

1 Soviet primary source materials, including handwritten notes recorded by CPSU General Secretary Vladimir Malin and Jan Svoboda, an assistant to KPČ First Secretary Antonín Novotný, are collected in the *Cold War International History Project Bulletin* (cited as *CWIHPB*). Selected documents are reprinted in Békés *et al.* (2002). UN debates are summarized in the *United Nations Yearbook* (cited as *UNYB*), while UN documents are available from documents.un.org. Although somewhat inaccurate, Khrushchev's first-hand account of the crisis is recorded in Talbot (1970) and in Schecter and Luchkov (1990). Important secondary sources include Granville (1995, 2004), Kramer (1996), and Kirov (1999).

2 Khrushchev noted at a meeting of Warsaw Pact states the following day that it was necessary in the given situation "to balance the need for strong measures" with "principles of mutual assistance" and "legal requests for assistance." See *CWIHPB 1995*, 5: 53–5.
3 As Kramer (1996: 368) notes, Soviet policy-makers may have been willing to accept the end of HWP dominance in Hungary, but they were unwilling to accept Hungary's withdrawal from the Warsaw Pact.
4 Nagy had taken refuge in the Yugoslav Embassy on 4 November. He remained there until 22 November, when he was abducted by KGB agents, having left the embassy with assurance of safe conduct from the Yugoslav government.

7 THE IMPACT OF THE UN CHARTER ON US–BRITISH MILITARY INTERVENTION IN IRAQ, 1990–98

1 US primary source materials are collected in the *Department of State Dispatch* (cited as *DSD*). Selected documents and speeches by both US and British policy-makers are reprinted in Federation of American Scientists (2002a). UN debates are summarized in the *United Nations Yearbook* (cited as *UNYB*), while UN documents are available from documents.un.org. Albright (2003), Baker (1995), Bush and Scowcroft (1998), Clinton (2004), Powell and Persico (1995), and Ritter (1999) provide first-hand accounts from the US perspective, while Major (1999), Munro (1996), and Thatcher (1993) provide first-hand accounts from the British perspective. Important secondary sources include Woodward (1991), Hiro (1992, 2001), Freedman and Karsh (1993), and Graham-Brown (1999).
2 On 3 August 1990, there were approximately 140,000 Iraqi troops in Kuwait, many of which were deployed in positions near the border with Saudi Arabia. According to Freedman and Karsh (1993: 86–8), US policy-makers were concerned about a possible Iraqi advance into Saudi Arabia. Hiro (1992: 120–2), however, disputes this assertion, arguing that US policy-makers intended to attack Iraq from the very beginning.
3 Note that on 13 November 1990, Iraq had requested that the IAEA make public the results of a recent inspection showing no evidence that Iraq had nuclear weapons or that it had diverted stores of highly-enriched uranium from its Osirak reactor. See Hiro (1992: 251–2).
4 Aircraft from Kuwait, Saudi Arabia, France (and later Canada) assisted in the air offensive. Egypt, Syria, Morocco, Pakistan, Bangladesh, Niger, and Senegal provided additional military forces for a possible ground offensive, while Turkey deployed ground forces along its border with Iraq and allowed coalition aircraft to use its airbases (as did Qatar). France provided ground troops also, but along with The Netherlands (which provided two frigates), it refused to attack targets outside of the Kuwait area of operations. See Hiro (1992: 311–21).
5 The legal position ultimately adopted by the United Kingdom is somewhat more complicated than this. As reported to the House of Commons by Defence Secretary Geoff Hoon on 26 February 2001, "we are entitled to patrol the no-fly zones to prevent a grave humanitarian crisis. That is the legal justification in international law. It does not rest on resolution 688, although that resolution supports the position we have adopted." See Hansard (2003).
6 This is not to say that humanitarian concerns were not present. However, as Graham-Brown (1999: 109, 120) notes, US policy-makers viewed the "no-fly" zones from the very beginning as an "important strategic tool" and, rather tellingly, justified them as necessary to ensure the safety of aircraft monitoring

compliance with Security Council Resolution 688 – without mentioning Iraqi ground forces.

7 Fighting had broken out between Kurdish Democratic Party (KDP) and Patriotic Union of Kurdistan (PUK) factions in northern Iraq, and KDP leader Mustafa Barzani requested the assistance of the Iraqi military on 20 August.

8 This operation was designated Operation "Desert Strike."

9 This development marked the end of Operation "Provide Comfort," although US and British planes continued to patrol the northern "no-fly" zone under the new designation Operation "Northern Watch."

10 The memorandum included a secret protocol between Iraqi Deputy Prime Minister Tariq Aziz and the UN Secretary-General Kofi Annan that "presidential sites" would be inspected only once. See Ritter (1999: 181).

11 Earlier statements by Secretary of State Albright that sanctions would not be lifted even "if Iraq complies with its obligations concerning weapons of mass destruction" certainly did nothing to enhance the persuasiveness of US legal claims. See Cockburn and Cockburn (1999: 43, 263).

8 THE IMPACT OF THE UN CHARTER ON US–BRITISH MILITARY INTERVENTION IN IRAQ, 1999–2003

1 The *Downing Street Memos* (cited as *DSM*), a set of internal British government documents leaked to the press in September 2004, are available from www.downingstreetmemo.com. Certain speeches and public statements by US and British policy-makers are available from Federation of American Scientists (2002a). UN documents are available from documents.un.org. Clarke (2004) and Suskind (2004) provide first-hand accounts from the US perspective, while Cook (2004) and Short (2005) provide first-hand accounts from the British perspective. Important secondary sources include Hiro (2001, 2004), Page (2002), Woodward (2002, 2004), Purdum (2003), Weisman (2003b), Wintour and Kettle (2003), Kampfner (2004), and Van Natta Jr. (2006).

2 Previously, Rumsfeld had argued against issuing a white paper laying out the evidence that the al-Qaeda organization was responsible for the September 11 terrorist attacks, because he believed that doing so would "set an awful precedent." According to Rumsfeld, national security decisions had to be made "on the best available evidence," which might fall "far short of courtroom proof," and issuing a white paper regarding the September 11 attacks would create an expectation of a higher evidentiary standard in future situations in which the use of armed force might be contemplated. See Woodward (2002: 135–6).

3 According to the report released on 24 September by the United Kingdom Foreign and Commonwealth Office (2002), "Saddam has continued to produce chemical and biological weapons . . . continues in his efforts to develop nuclear weapons, and . . . has been able to extend the range of his ballistic missile programme." The report also contained the now infamous claim that "[t]he Iraqi military are able to deploy these weapons within forty five minutes of a decision to do so." According to Lord Hutton (2004: 320), "10 Downing Street wanted the [report] to be worded to make as strong a case as possible in relation to the threat posed by Saddam Hussein's WMD, and . . . made written suggestions . . . as to changes in the wording of the draft," but also instructed that "nothing should be stated . . . with which the intelligence community were not entirely happy."

9 THE CONTINUED SALIANCE OF THE UN CHARTER SYSTEM

1 While it might be argued that the modern media help in making relevant facts known, nearly one out of four cases examined addressed questions of fact, suggesting that the impact of the modern media is limited. Moreover, many of these cases did not reach the Security Council, and their relevant facts remain ambiguous to this day. It seems unlikely, either, that technology is making such questions of fact less salient, given the difficulties of ascertaining which states have provided weapons or support to various armed groups or precisely when a use of armed force was undertaken in relation to other events claimed to have precipitated such use of armed force.

2 Using large-n analysis, Young (2003: 12) concludes that situations in which US policy-makers considered international law when formulating crisis strategies were more likely to result in compromise than those in which they did not.

3 According to Kiraly (1999: xi), Soviet military forces exerted "great effort" to overcome Hungarian rebels fighting in the streets of Budapest. Soviet casualties included 722 killed, 1251 wounded, and the loss of approximately 400 tanks.

4 Brainard and O'Hanlon's (2003) estimate, which does not include the United Kingdom, is based on a scenario in which the United States bears 50 percent of the military costs and 15 percent of the reconstruction costs. NB: Johnstone (2004: 835) also cites this study in support of his own, similar conclusions.

5 Byers (2002a: 403) suggests that US policy-makers did not rely on existing Security Council resolutions in justifying military action against Afghanistan because they feared that China and Russia would then be able to offer similar arguments for their own military actions, to the detriment of US interests.

REFERENCES

Abbott, K. W. and Snidal, D. (1998) "Why States Act through Formal International Organizations," *Journal of Conflict Resolution*, 42(1): 3–32.

—— (2000) "Hard and Soft Law in International Governance," *International Organization*, 54(3): 421–56.

—— (2002) "Values and Interests: International Legalization in the Fight against Corruption," *Journal of Legal Studies*, 31(1): 141–78.

Abbott, K. W., Keohane, R. O., Moravcsik, A., Slaughter, A.-M., and Snidal, D. (2000) "The Concept of Legalization," *International Organization*, 54(3): 401–19.

Aceves, W. J. (1997) "Institutionalist Theory and International Legal Scholarship," *American University Journal of International Law & Policy*, 12(2): 227–66.

Aita, J. (1992a) "Iraq Systematically Repressing Kurds, Shia, UN Told," *USIA News Report* (Washington, DC), 11 August.

—— (1992b) "Security Council To Review Iraq Human Rights Situation," *USIA News Report* (Washington, DC), 10 August.

Albright, M. (2003) *Madam Secretary*, New York: Miramax Books.

Alvarez, J. E. (2001) "Do Liberal States Behave Better? A Critique of Slaughter's Liberal Theory," *European Journal of International Law*, 12(2): 183–246.

—— (2003) "Hegemonic International Law Revisited," *American Journal of International Law*, 97(4): 873–88.

Andrews, B. (1975) "Social Rules and the State as a Social Actor," *World Politics*, 27(4): 521–40.

Arend, A. C. (1998) "Do Legal Rules Matter? International Law and International Politics," *Virginia Journal of International Law*, 38(2): 107–53.

Atkins, G. P. and Wilson, L. C. (1972) *The United States and the Trujillo Regime*, New Brunswick, NJ: Rutgers University Press.

Austin, J. (1832; reprint 2000) *The Province of Jurisprudence Determined*, Amherst, NY: Prometheus Books.

Axelrod, R. (1984) *The Evolution of Cooperation*, New York: Basic Books.

Baker, J. A. (1995) *The Politics of Diplomacy: Revolution, War & Peace, 1989–1992*, New York: G. P. Putnam's Sons.

Baldwin, T. and Wastell, D. (1998) "Cook Warns Blair over Backing for Iraq Raids," *Daily Telegraph* (London), 22 February.

Barringer, F. (2003) "Eclipsed by Events, UN Officials Wonder about the Past and Ponder the Future," *New York Times*, 18 March.

Beaufre, A. (1969) *The Suez Expedition, 1956*, London: Faber & Faber.
Beetham, D. (1991) *The Legitimation of Power*, Atlantic Highlands, NJ: Humanities Press International, Inc.
Békés, C., Byrne, M., and Rainer, J. M. (eds) (2002) *The 1956 Hungarian Revolution: A History in Documents*, Budapest: Central European Press.
Bentham, J. (1789; reprint 1843) "Principles of International Law," in J. Bowring (ed.) *The Works of Jeremy Bentham*, Edinburgh: W. Tait, 535–60.
Berecz, J. (1986) *1956 Counter-Revolution in Hungary: Words and Weapons*, Budapest: Akadémiai Kiadó.
Berle, B. B. and Jacobs, T. B. (eds) (1973) *Navigating the Rapids, 1918–1971: From the Papers of Adolf A. Berle*, New York: Harcourt Brace Jovanovich, Inc.
Bernstein, R. and Gordon, M. R. (2006) "Berlin File Says German's Spies Aided U.S. in Iraq," *New York Times*, 2 March.
Blokker, N. (2000) "Is the Authorization Authorized? Powers and Practice of the UN Security Council To Authorize the Use of Force by 'Coalitions of the Able and Willing,'" *European Journal of International Law*, 11(3): 541–68.
Bloomfield, L. P. and Moulton, A. (2000) *CASCON International Conflict Database*. Available online: web.mit.edu/cascon/caselist.html (accessed 20 June 2003).
Blum, W. (1995) *Killing Hope: U.S. Military and CIA Interventions since World War II*, Monroe, ME: Common Courage Press.
Bodansky, Y. (2005) *The Secret History of the Iraq War*, New York: Regan Books.
Bone, J. (1997) "Americans Fail to Win UN Consensus on Military Action," *The Times* (London), 12 November.
Bowett, D. (1958) *Self-Defence in International Law*, Manchester: Manchester University Press.
—— (1972) "Economic Coercion and Reprisals by States," *Virginia Journal of International Law*, 13(1): 1–12.
Bowie, R. R. (1974) *Suez, 1956*, Oxford: Oxford University Press.
Bowles, C. (1971) *Promises To Keep: My Years in Public Life, 1941–1969*, New York: Harper & Row.
Boyle, F. A. (1985) *World Politics and International Law*, Durham, NC: Duke University Press.
Brainard, L. and O'Hanlon, M. E. (2003) "The Heavy Price of America's Going It Alone," *Financial Times* (London), 6 August.
Broder, J. M. (1998) "Clinton Says Iraq Can Avert Attack by Giving in to UN," *New York Times*, 14 November.
Brownlie, I. (1963; reprint 1981) *International Law and the Use of Force by States*, Oxford: Clarendon Press.
—— (2003) *Principles of Public International Law*, Oxford: Oxford University Press.
Bull, H. (1995) *The Anarchical Society: A Study of Order in World Politics*, New York: Columbia University Press.
Bumiller, E. (2003) "Bush Goes Global To Lobby for Votes on UN Measure," *New York Times*, 26 February.
Burns, J. (2003) "Anti-War Group Beset by Strategy Arguments," *Financial Times* (London), 22 March.
Burns, R. (2006) "Report: Russia Gave Iraq Details about War," *New York Times*, 25 March.

Bush, G. H. W. and Scowcroft, B. (1998) *A World Transformed*, New York: Vintage Books.

Bush, G. W. (2002) *The National Security Strategy of the United States*, Washington, DC: White House. Available online: www.whitehouse.gov/nsc/nss.pdf.

Butcher, T. (1998) "Britain Sends Carrier to Gulf as Tension Rises," *Daily Telegraph* (London), 17 January.

Byers, M. (1999) *Custom, Power and the Power of Rules*, Cambridge: Cambridge University Press.

—— (2002a) "Terrorism, the Use of Force and International Law after 11 September," *International and Comparative Law Quarterly*, 51(2): 401–14.

—— (2002b) "The Shifting Foundations of International Law: A Decade of Forceful Measures against Iraq," *European Journal of International Law*, 13(1): 21–41.

Campbell, T. M. (1973) "Nationalism in America's UN Policy, 1944–1945," *International Organization*, 27(1): 25–44.

Carlton, D. (1989) *Britain and the Suez Crisis*, London: Basil Blackwell.

Caron, D. D. (1993) "The Legitimacy of the Collective Authority of the Security Council," *American Journal of International Law*, 87(4): 552–88.

Carr, E. H. (1946; reprint 1964) *The Twenty Years' Crisis, 1919–1939: An Introduction to the Study of International Relations*, New York: Harper & Row.

Chayes, A. and Chayes, A. H. (1995) *The New Sovereignty: Compliance with International Regulatory Agreements*, Cambridge, MA: Harvard University Press.

Checkel, J. T. (2001) "Why Comply? Social Learning and European Identity Change," *International Organization*, 55(3): 553–88.

Chimni, B. S. (1993) *International Law and World Order: A Critique of Contemporary Approaches*, London: Sage Publications.

Chipman, J. (1989) "French Military Power and Black Africa since 1960," *French Power in Africa*, London: Basil Blackwell, 114–67.

Christensen, T. J. and Snyder, J. (1990) "Chain Gangs and Passed Bucks: Predicting Alliance Patterns in Multipolarity," *International Organization*, 44(2): 137–68.

Clarke, R. A. (2004) *Against All Enemies: Inside America's War on Terror*, New York: Free Press.

Claude Jr., I. L. (1966) "Collective Legitimization as a Political Function of the United Nations," *International Organization*, 20: 367–79.

Clinton, B. (2004) *My Life*, New York: Alfred A. Knopf.

Cockburn, A. and Cockburn, P. (1999) *Out of the Ashes: The Resurrection of Saddam Hussein*, New Brunswick, NJ: HarperCollins.

Cohen, R. (1980) "Rules of the Game in International Politics," *International Studies Quarterly*, 24(1): 129–50.

Cook, R. (2004) *The Point of Departure: Diaries from the Front Bench*, London: Pocket Books.

Cortell, A. P. and Davis, J. W. (1996) "How Do International Institutions Matter: The Domestic Impact of International Rules and Norms," *International Studies Quarterly*, 40(4): 451–78.

Crawford, V. P. (1990) "Explicit Bargaining Outcomes," *American Economic Review*, 80(2): 213–19.

Crosbie, S. K. (1974) *A Tacit Alliance: France and Israel from Suez to the Six Day War*, Princeton, NJ: Princeton University Press.

D'Amato, A. (1982) "What 'Counts' as Law?" in N. G. Onuf (ed.) *Law-Making in the Global Community*, Durham, NC: Carolina Academic Press, 83–108.

Dao, J. and Shanker, T. (2003) "Powell Defends Information He Used To Justify Iraq War," *New York Times*, 31 May.

David, S. R. (1989) "Why the Third World Matters," *International Security*, 14(1): 50–85.

Davies, H. (1998a) "Clinton Urges Saddam To Heed UN Warning," *Daily Telegraph* (London), 4 March.

—— (1998b) "Call for Iraq Raid Wins Little Support," *Daily Telegraph* (London), 7 November.

Desch, M. C. (1989) "The Keys that Lock Up the World: Identifying America's Interests in the Periphery," *International Security*, 14(1): 86–121.

DeYoung, K. and Pincus, W. (2003) "U.S. Hedges on Finding Iraqi Weapons," *Washington Post*, 29 May.

Diederich, B. (1978) *Trujillo: The Death of the Goat*, Boston, MA: Little, Brown and Company.

Dinstein, Y. (1988) *War, Aggression and Self-Defense*, Cambridge: Grotius Publications Ltd.

Drozdiak, W. (1998) "Nations Find Fault with Air Strikes," *Washington Post*, 17 December.

Duelfer, C. (2004) *Comprehensive Report of the Special Advisor to the DCI on Iraq's WMD*, Langley, VA: CIA. Available online: www.cia.gov/cia/reports/iraq_wmd_2004/index.html (accessed 3 August 2006).

Dworkin, R. (1986) *Law's Empire*, Cambridge, MA: Harvard University Press.

Eden, A. (1960) *Full Circle*, Boston, MA: Riverside Press.

Falk, R. A. (1969) "The Interplay of Westphalia and Charter Conceptions of International Legal Order," in R. A. Falk and C. E. Black (eds) *The Future of the International Legal Order*, Princeton, NJ: Princeton University Press, 32–70.

—— (1995) "Appraising the UN at 50: The Looming Challenge," *Journal of International Affairs*, 48(2): 625–46.

Farer, T. J. (2002) "Beyond the Charter Frame: Unilateralism or Condominium?" *American Journal of International Law*, 96(2): 359–64.

—— (2003) "The Prospect for International Law and Order in the Wake of Iraq," *American Journal of International Law*, 97(3): 621–8.

Fawcett, J. (1982) *Law and Power in International Relations*, London: Faber and Faber, Ltd.

Fearon, J. D. (1995) "Rationalist Explanations for War," *International Organization*, 49(3): 379–414.

Federation of American Scientists (2002a) *FAS News*, Washington, DC: FAS. Available online: www.fas.org/news/ (accessed 21 October 2003).

—— (2002b) *United States Military Operations*, Washington, DC: FAS. Available online: www.fas.org/man/dod-101/ops/ (accessed 21 October 2003).

—— (2006) *Official Intelligence-Related Documents*, Washington, DC: FAS. Available online: www.fas.org/irp/offdocs/index.html (accessed 7 August 2006).

Ferencz, B. B. (1972) "Defining Aggression: Where It Stands and Where It's Going," *American Journal of International Law*, 66(3): 491–508.

—— (1995) "The United Nations Consensus Definition of Aggression: Sieve or Substance?" paper presented at the Washington Conference on Law and the World, Washington, DC, October.

Finch, G. A. (1957) "Post-Mortem on the Suez Debacle," *American Journal of International Law*, 51(2): 376–80.

Fisher, R. (1978) *Points of Choice: International Crises and the Role of Law*, Oxford: Oxford University Press.

Franck, T. M. (1984) "Of Gnats and Camels: Is There a Double Standard at the United Nations?" *American Journal of International Law*, 78(4): 811–33.

—— (1988) "Legitimacy in the International System," *American Journal of International Law*, 82(4): 705–59.

—— (1990) *The Power of Legitimacy among Nations*, Oxford: Oxford University Press.

—— (1999) "Break It, Don't Fake It," *Foreign Affairs*, 78(4): 116–18.

—— (2003) "What Happens Now? The United Nations after Iraq," *American Journal of International Law*, 97(3): 607–20.

Franck, T. M. and Weisband, E. (1971) *Word Politics: Verbal Strategy among the Superpowers*, New York: Oxford University Press.

Freedman, L. and Karsh, E. (1993) *The Gulf Conflict, 1990–1991: Diplomacy and War in the New World Order*, Princeton, NJ: Princeton University Press.

Freedom House (2006) *Survey of Freedom in the World, 1972–73 to 2003–04*, Washington, DC: Freedom House. Available online: www.freedomhouse.org/ (accessed 20 June 2006).

Gaddis, J. L. (1986) "The Long Peace: Elements of Stability in the Postwar International System," *International Security*, 10(4): 99–142.

Gall, N. (1963) "How the Agency Killed Trujillo," *The New Republic*, 13 April.

Garner, B. A. (ed.) (1999) *Black's Law Dictionary*, St. Paul, MN: West Group.

Gaujac, P. (2001) "France and the Crisis of Suez: an Appraisal, Forty Years On," in D. Tal (ed.) *The 1956 War: Collusion and Rivalry in the Middle East*, London: Frank Cass, 47–64.

Gellman, B. (2004) "Iraq's Arsenal was Only on Paper," *Washington Post*, 7 January.

George, A. L. and McKeown, T. J. (1985) "Case Studies and Theories of Organizational Decision Making," *Advances in Information Processing in Organizations*, 2: 21–58.

Gertz, B. (2001) "China Fortifying Iraq's Air-Defense System," *Washington Times*, 20 February.

Gibbons, R. (1992) *Game Theory for Applied Economists*, Princeton, NJ: Princeton University Press.

Gilpin, R. G. (1981) *War & Change in World Politics*, Cambridge: Cambridge University Press.

Ginsburgs, G. (1958) "A Case Study in the Soviet Use of International Law: Eastern Poland in 1939," *American Journal of International Law*, 52(1): 69–84.

Gleijeses, P. (1995) "Ships in the Night: The CIA, the White House and the Bay of Pigs," *Journal of Latin American Studies*, 27(1): 1–42.

Glennon, M. J. (2001) *Limits of Law, Prerogatives of Power: Interventionism after Kosovo*, New York: Palgrave, Inc.

GlobalSecurity.org (2003) *Iraq Special Weapons News*. Available online: www.globalsecurity.org/wmd/library/news/iraq/ (accessed 14 November 2003).

Golden, J. (1974) "Force and International Law," in F. S. Northedge (ed.) *The Use of Force in International Relations*, London: Faber and Faber, Ltd., 194–219.

Goldsmith, C. (2000) "In the Know? Sir Gladwyn Jebb: Ambassador to France," in S. Kelly and A. Gorst (eds) *Whitehall and the Suez Crisis*, London: Frank Cass, 79–97.

Goldsmith, J. L. and Posner, E. A. (2002) "Moral and Legal Rhetoric in International Relations: A Rational Choice Perspective," *Journal of Legal Studies*, 31(1–Part II): S115–S40.

—— (2005) *The Limits of International Law*, Oxford: Oxford University Press.

Goldstein, J., Kahler, M., Keohane, R. O., and Slaughter, A.-M. (2000) "Introduction: Legalization and World Politics," *International Organization*, 54(3): 385–99.

Gorst, A. and Johnman, L. (1997) *The Suez Crisis*, London: Routledge.

Graefrath, B. (1998) "International Crimes and Collective Security," in K. Wellens (ed.) *International Law: Theory and Practice*, The Hague: Martinus Nijhoff Publishers, 237–52.

Graham-Brown, S. (1999) *Sanctioning Saddam: The Politics of Intervention in Iraq*, London: I. B. Tauris Publishers.

Granville, J. (1995) *In the Line of Fire: The Soviet Crackdown on Hungary, 1956–1957*, Moscow: Young Russia.

—— (2004) *The First Domino: International Decision Making during the Hungarian Crisis of 1956*, College Station, TX: Texas A&M University Press.

Gray, C. (2000) *International Law and the Use of Force*, Oxford: Oxford University Press.

Grice, A. (2003) "Defiant Blair Says UN Has No Veto on War," *Independent* (London), 14 January.

Grotius, H. (1625; reprint 1901) *The Rights of War and Peace*, London: M. Walter Dunne.

Guzman, A. T. (2002) "A Compliance-Based Theory of International Law," *California Law Review*, 90(6): 1823–87.

Győrkei, J. and Horváth, M. (1999) "Additional Data on the History of the Soviet Military Occupation," in J. Győrkei and M. Horváth (eds) *Soviet Military Intervention in Hungary, 1956*, Budapest: Central European Press, 5–128.

Hansard (2003) *House of Commons Daily Debates*. Available online: www.publications.parliament.uk/pa/cm/cmhansrd.htm (accessed 21 November 2003).

Harnden, T. and Sparrow, A. (2002) "Blair Commits Britain to War," *Daily Telegraph* (London), 9 September.

Harnden, T., Broughton, P. D. and Aris, B. (2003) "France and Russia Will Vote No," *Daily Telegraph* (London), 11 March.

Hasenclever, A., Mayer, P. and Rittberger, V. (1997) *Theories of International Regimes*, Cambridge: Cambridge University Press.

Henkin, L. (1971) "The Reports of the Death of Article 2(4) are Greatly Exaggerated," *American Journal of International Law*, 65(3): 544–8.

—— (1979) *How Nations Behave: Law and Foreign Policy*, New York: Columbia University Press.

Higgins, R. (1970) "The Place of International Law in the Settlement of Disputes by the Security Council," *American Journal of International Law*, 64(1): 1–18.

Higgins, T. (1987) *The Perfect Failure: Kennedy, Eisenhower and the CIA at the Bay of Pigs*, New York: W. W. Norton & Company.

Hilaire, M. (1997) *International Law and the United States Military Intervention in the Western Hemisphere*, The Hague: Kluwer Academic Publishers.

Hilderbrand, R. C. (1990) *Dumbarton Oaks: The Origins of the UN and the Search for Post-War Security*, Chapel Hill, NC: University of North Carolina Press.

Hiro, D. (1992) *Desert Shield to Desert Storm: The Second Gulf War*, New York: Routledge.

—— (2001) *Neighbors, Not Friends: Iraq and Iran after the Gulf Wars*, New York: Routledge.

—— (2004) *Secrets and Lies: Operation 'Iraqi Freedom' and After*, New York: Nation Books.

Hirschman, A. O. (1980) *National Power and the Structure of Foreign Trade*, Berkeley, CA: University of California Press.

Hoagland, J. (1999) "The Iraq Mess," *Washington Post*, 6 August.

Hobbes, T. (1650; reprint 1999) *The Elements of Law Natural and Politic*, Oxford: Oxford University Press.

—— (1651; reprint 1994) *Leviathan; or, the Matter, Forme, and Power of a Commonwealth Ecclesiasticall and Civil*, Indianapolis, IN: Hackett Publishing Company, Inc.

Hoffmann, S. (1961) "International Systems and International Law," *World Politics*, 14(1): 205–37.

—— (1968) "International Law and the Control of Force," in K. W. Deutsch and S. Hoffmann (eds) *The Relevance of International Law*, Cambridge, MA: Schenkman Publishing Company, 21–46.

Hollis, R. (2006) "The United Kingdom: Fateful Decision, Divided Nation," in R. Fawn and R. Hinnebusch (eds) *The Iraq War: Causes and Consequences*, Boulder, CO: Lynne Reinner, 37–47.

Hoopes, T. and Brinkley, D. (1997) *FDR and the Creation of the UN*, New Haven, CT: Yale University Press.

Hoyt, E. C. (1985) *Law & Force in American Foreign Policy*, Lanham, MD: University Press of America.

Huntington, S. P. (1999) "The Lonely Superpower," *Foreign Affairs*, 78(2): 35–49.

Hurd, I. (2000) *Legitimacy, Authority, and Power at the UN Security Council*, Ph.D. dissertation, New Haven, CT: Yale University.

Hutton, B. (2004) *Report of the Inquiry into the Circumstances Surrounding the Death of Dr. David Kelly C.M.G.*, London: The Stationary Office. Available online: www.the-hutton-inquiry.org.uk (accessed 9 December 2005).

Hyde, A. (1983) "The Concept of Legitimation in the Sociology of Law," *Wisconsin Law Review*, 1983(2): 379–426.

Ikenberry, G. J. (2001) *After Victory: Institutions, Strategic Restraint, and the Rebuilding of Order after Major Wars*, Princeton, NJ: Princeton University Press.

Immerman, R. H. (1982) *The CIA in Guatemala: The Foreign Policy of Intervention*, Austin, TX: University of Texas Press.

International Atomic Energy Agency (1995) *UNSCOM/IAEA Note for the File–22 August 1995*, Vienna: IAEA. Available online: www.casi.org.uk.info/unscom 950822.pdf (accessed 12 March 2004).

Jackson, J. H. and Sykes, A. O. (1997) "Questions and Comparisons," in J. H.

Jackson and A. O. Sykes (eds) *Implementing the Uruguay Round*, Oxford: Oxford University Press.

Jacobson, H. K. and Weiss, E. B. (2001) "Strengthening Compliance with International Environmental Accords," in P. F. Diehl (ed.) *The Politics of Global Governance*, 2nd ed. Boulder, CO: Lynne Reinner Press, 406–35.

Jervis, R. (1970) *The Logic of Images in International Relations*, New York: Columbia University Press.

—— (1976) *Perception and Misperception in International Politics*, Princeton, NJ: Princeton University Press.

—— (1989) *The Meaning of the Nuclear Revolution: Statecraft and the Prospect of Armageddon*, Ithaca, NY: Cornell University Press.

Johnman, L. (2000) "Playing the Role of a Cassandra: Sir Gerald Fitzmaurice, Senior Legal Advisor to the Foreign Office," in S. Kelly and A. Gorst (eds) *Whitehall and the Suez Crisis*, London: Frank Cass, 46–63.

Johnson, E. (2000) "The Diplomats' Diplomat: Sir Pierson Dixon, Ambassador to the United Nations," in S. Kelly and A. Gorst (eds) *Whitehall and the Suez Crisis*, London: Frank Cass, 179–97.

Johnston, A. I. (2001) "Treating International Institutions as Social Environments," *International Studies Quarterly*, 45: 487–515.

Johnstone, I. (1991) "Treaty Interpretation: The Authority of Interpretive Communities," *Michigan Journal of International Law*, 12(2): 371–419.

—— (2003a) "The Role of the UN Secretary-General: The Power of Persuasion Based on Law," *Global Governance*, 9(4): 441–58.

—— (2003b) "Security Council Deliberations: The Power of the Better Argument," *European Journal of International Law*, 14(3): 437–80.

—— (2004) "US–UN Relations after Iraq: The End of the World (Order) as We Know It?" *European Journal of International Law*, 15(4): 813–38.

Kampfner, J. (2004) *Blair's Wars*, New York: Free Press.

Keal, P. (1983) *Unspoken Rules and Superpower Dominance*, New York: St. Martin's Press.

Keck, M. E. and Sikkink, K. (1998) *Activists beyond Borders: Advocacy Networks in International Politics*, Ithaca, NY: Cornell University Press.

Keesing's (1990) "Gulf Crisis – Iraq's Justification of Invasion," *Keesing's Record of World Events*. Available online: keesings.gvpi.net/ (accessed 7 November 2003).

Kelly, S. and Gorst, A. (eds) (2000) *Whitehall and the Suez Crisis*, London: Frank Cass.

Kennan, G. F. (1951) *American Diplomacy, 1900–1950*, Chicago: University of Chicago Press.

Keohane, R. O. (1986) "Reciprocity in International Relations," *International Organization*, 40(1): 1–27.

Kessler, G. (2004) "France Was Ready To Send Troops to Iraq, Book Says," *Washington Post*, 6 October.

King, G., Keohane, R. O., and Verba, S. (1994) *Designing Social Inquiry: Scientific Inference in Qualitative Research*, Princeton, NJ: Princeton University Press.

Kiraly, B. (1999) "Preface," in J. Győrkei and M. Horváth (eds) *Soviet Military Intervention in Hungary, 1956*, Budapest: Central European Press.

Kirov, A. M. (1999) "Soviet Military Intervention in Hungary, 1956," in J.

Győrkei and M. Horváth (eds) *Soviet Military Intervention in Hungary, 1956*, Budapest: Central European Press, 129–208.

Koh, H. H. (1997) "Why Do Nations Obey International Law?" *Yale Law Journal*, 106(8): 2599–659.

Kohen, M. G. (2003) "The Use of Force by the United States after the End of the Cold War, and Its Impact on International Law," in M. Byers and G. Nolte (eds) *United States Hegemony and the Foundations of International Law*, Cambridge: Cambridge University Press, 197–231.

Kornbluh, P. (ed.) (1998) *Bay of Pigs Declassified: The Secret CIA Report on the Invasion of Cuba,* New York: The New Press.

Koskenniemi, M. (1989) *From Apology to Utopia: The Structure of International Legal Argument*, Helsinki: Lakimiesliiton Kustannus.

Kramer, M. (1996) "New Evidence on Soviet Decision-Making and the 1956 Polish and Hungarian Crises," *Cold War International History Project Bulletin*, 8/9: 358–84.

Krasner, S. D. (1982) "Structural Causes and Regime Consequences: Regimes as Intervening Variables," *International Organization*, 36(2): 185–205.

—— (1999) *Sovereignty: Organized Hypocrisy*, Princeton, NJ: Princeton University Press.

Kratochwil, F. V. (1989) *Rules, Norms, and Decisions: On the Conditions of Practical and Legal Reasoning in International Relations and Domestic Affairs*, Cambridge: Cambridge University Press.

Kreps, D. and Wilson, R. B. (1982) "Reputation and Imperfect Information," *Journal of Economic Theory*, 27(2): 253–79.

Kritsiotis, D. (1998) "Reappraising Policy Objections to Humanitarian Intervention," *Michigan Journal of International Law*, 19(4): 1005–50.

Ku, C. and Diehl, P. F. (2003) "International Law as Operating and Normative Systems: An Overview," in C. Ku and P. F. Diehl (eds) *International Law: Classic and Contemporary Readings*, 2nd ed. Boulder, CO: Lynne Rienner Publishers, 1–19.

Kyle, K. (1989) "Britain and the [Suez] Crisis, 1955–1956," in W. R. Louis and R. Owen (eds) *Suez, 1956: The Crisis and Its Consequences*, Oxford: Clarendon Press, 103–30.

—— (1991) *Suez*, New York: St. Martin's Press, Inc.

LaGuardia, A. (1997) "Albright Fails To Win Arab Backing for Strikes on Iraq," *Daily Telegraph* (London), 17 November.

—— (2003a) "Blair Restrained Bush from Attacking Iraq after September 11," *Daily Telegraph* (London), 21 March.

—— (2003b) "Warning Signs Missed by Blair and Bush," *Daily Telegraph* (London), 18 March.

LaGuardia, A. and Harnden, T. (2001) "Britain and US Ready To Raid Iraq Again," *Daily Telegraph* (London), 19 February.

LaGuardia, A. and Jones, G. (2002) "Saddam Dossier Rejected as Lies," *Daily Telegraph* (London), 19 December.

Leffler, M. P. (1992) *A Preponderance of Power: National Security, the Truman Administration, and the Cold War*, Stanford, CA: Stanford University Press.

Lipson, C. (1984) "International Cooperation in Security and Economic Affairs," *World Politics*, 37: 1–23.

Lloyd, S. (1978) *Suez, 1956: A Personal Account*, London: Johnathan Cape.

Lobel, J. and Ratner, M. (1999) "Bypassing the Security Council: Ambiguous Authorizations To Use Force, Cease-Fires and the Iraqi Inspection Regime," *American Journal of International Law*, 93(1): 124–54.

Lockwood, C. (1996) "We Cannot Support You, France Tells US," *Daily Telegraph* (London), 6 September.

—— (1997) "Iraq Continues Arms Sites Ban," *Daily Telegraph* (London), 5 November.

—— (1998) "UN Snubs Britain over Iraq," *Daily Telegraph* (London), 13 February.

Lockwood, C. and Nundy, J. (1996) "World Reaction: What did Saddam Do Wrong? Asks France," *Daily Telegraph* (London), 4 September.

Lucas, W. S. (ed.) (1996) *Britain and Suez: The Lion's Last Roar*, Manchester: Manchester University Press.

Major, J. (1999) *John Major: The Autobiography*, London: HarperCollins.

Marston, G. (1988) "Armed Intervention in the 1956 Suez Canal Crisis: The Legal Advice Tendered to the British Government," *International and Comparative Law Quarterly*, 37(4): 773–817.

McCoubrey, H. and White, N. D. (1992) *International Law and Armed Conflict*, Aldershot, UK: Dartmouth.

McDougal, M. S. (1960) "Some Basic Theoretical Concepts about International Law: A Policy-Oriented Framework of Inquiry," *Journal of Conflict Resolution*, 4(3): 337–54.

Mearsheimer, J. J. (1994/95) "The False Promise of International Institutions," *International Security*, 19(3): 5–49.

—— (2001) *The Tragedy of Great Power Politics*, New York: W. W. Norton.

Mitzen, J. (2001) *Toward a Visible Hand: The International Public Sphere in Theory and Practice*, Ph.D. dissertation, Chicago: University of Chicago.

—— (2005) "Reading Habermas in Anarchy: Multilateral Diplomacy and Global Public Spheres," *American Political Science Review*, 99(3): 401–17.

Moe, T. M. (1979) "On the Scientific Status of Rational Models," *American Journal of Political Science*, 23(1): 215–43.

Moose, G. E. (1985) "French Military Policy in Africa," in W. J. Foltz and H. S. Bienen (eds) *Arms and the African*, New Haven, CT: Yale University Press.

Moravcsik, A. (1997) "Taking Preferences Seriously: A Liberal Theory of International Politics," *International Organization*, 51(4): 513–53.

Morgenthau, H. J. (1940) "Positivism, Functionalism, and International Law," *American Journal of International Law*, 34(2): 260–84.

Morgenthau, H. J. and Thompson, K. W. (1993) *Politics among Nations: The Struggle for Power and Peace*, Boston: McGraw-Hill.

Morrow, J. D. (1994) "Modeling the Forms of International Cooperation: Distribution versus Information," *International Organization*, 48(3): 387–423.

—— (2000) "Alliances: Why Write Them Down?" *Annual Review of Political Science*, 3: 63–83.

Mueller, J. (2000) "Public Opinion as a Constraint on U.S. Foreign Policy: Assessing the Perceived Value of American and Foreign Lives," paper presented at the International Studies Association, Los Angeles, CA, 14–18 March.

Munro, A. (1996) *An Embassy at War: Politics and Diplomacy behind the Gulf War*, London: Brassey's.

Murphy, S. D. (1999a) "Current Practice of the United States Relating to International Law: Air Strikes against Serbia," *American Journal of International Law*, 93(3): 628–35.

—— (1999b) "Current Practice of the United States Relating to International Law: Humanitarian Intervention in Kosovo," *American Journal of International Law*, 93(1): 167–70.

Myers, S. L. (1997) "Clinton Is Sending Second Carrier to Gulf," *New York Times*, 15 November.

Nadelmann, E. A. (1990) "Global Prohibition Regimes: The Evolution of Norms in International Society," *International Organization*, 44(4): 479–526.

Nutting, A. (1967) *No End of a Lesson: The Story of Suez*, London: Constable.

O'Connell, D. P. (1975) *The Influence of Law on Sea Power*, Manchester: Manchester University Press.

Office of the British Prime Minister (2003) *Prime Minister's Speeches*. Available online: www.number-10.gov.uk/output/Page5.asp (accessed 21 November 2003).

Olson, M. (1971) *The Logic of Collective Action: Public Goods and the Theory of Groups*, Cambridge, MA: Harvard University Press.

Oye, K. A. (1985) "Explaining Cooperation under Anarchy: Hypotheses and Strategies," *World Politics*, 38(1): 1–24.

Pace, E. (1990) "U.N. Calls on Navies To Block Iraq's Trade; Resolution Permits Use of Force, U.S. Says," *New York Times*, 26 August.

Padelford, N. J. (1948) "The Use of the Veto," *International Organization*, 2(2): 227–46.

Paecht, A. (1999) *Kosovo as a Precedent: Towards a Reform of the Security Council?*, Brussels: North Atlantic Assembly.

Page, S. (2002) "Iraq Course Set from Tight White House Circle," *USA Today*, 11 September.

Pagedas, C. A. (1995) "Continuity and Change: The United States, Great Britain and Military Intervention in the Cold War," in A. M. Dorman and T. G. Otte (eds) *Military Intervention: From Gunboat Diplomacy to Humanitarian Intervention*, Aldershot, UK: Dartmouth, 53–79.

Paletz, D. L. (1994) "Just Desserts?" in W. L. Bennett and D. L. Paletz (eds) *Taken by Storm: The Media, Public Opinion, and US Foreign Policy in the Gulf War*, Chicago: University of Chicago, 277–92.

Pape, R. A. (1997) "Why Economic Sanctions Do Not Work," *International Security*, 22(2): 90–136.

—— (2005) "Soft Balancing against the United States," *International Security*, 30(1): 7–45.

Payne, R. A. (2001) "Persuasion, Frames and Norm Construction," *European Journal of International Relations*, 71(1): 37–61.

Peace Pledge Union (2002) *Major Wars and Armed Conflicts since 1945*, London: PPU. Available online: www.ppu.org.uk/war/index.html (accessed 14 November 2002).

Powell, C. L. and Persico, J. E. (1995) *My American Journey*, New York: Random House, Inc.

Preston, J. and Purdum, T. S. (2002) "UN Inspectors Can Return Unconditionally, Iraq Says," *New York Times*, 17 September.

Price, R. (1998) "Reversing the Gun Sights: Transnational Civil Society Targets Land Mines," *International Organization*, 52(3): 613–44.
Purdum, T. S. (2003) *A Time of Our Choosing: America's War in Iraq*, New York: Times Books.
Rabe, S. G. (1996) "The Caribbean Triangle: Betancourt, Castro, and Trujillo and U.S. Foreign Policy, 1958–1963," *Diplomatic History*, 20(1): 55–78.
Rabin, M. (1990) "Communication between Rational Agents," *Journal of Economic Theory*, 51: 144–70.
Rainer, J. M. (1993) "1956, The Other Side of the Story: Five Documents from the Yeltsin File," *Hungarian Quarterly*, 34(129).
Ramsbothan, O. and Woodhouse, T. (1996) *Humanitarian Intervention in Contemporary Conflict: A Reconceptualization*, Cambridge: Polity Press.
Reisman, W. M. (1984) "Coercion and Self-Determination: Construing Charter Article 2(4)," *American Journal of International Law*, 78(3): 642–5.
—— (1991) "Allocating Competences To Use Coercion in the Post-Cold War World: Practices, Conditions, and Prospects," in L. F. Damrosch and D. J. Scheffer (eds) *Law and Force in the New International Order*, Boulder, CO: Westview Press, 26–47.
Reiter, D. and Stam, A. C. (2002) *Democracies at War*, Princeton, NJ: Princeton University Press.
Rennie, D. (2003) "Nervous Arab Allies 'Secretly Backed American War Effort,'" *Daily Telegraph* (London), 28 April.
Risse, T. (2000) "'Let's Argue!': Communicative Action in World Politics," *International Organization*, 54(1): 1–39.
Ritter, S. (1999) *Endgame: Solving the Iraq Problem Once and for All*, New York: Simon & Schuster.
Roberts, A. (1999) "NATO's 'Humanitarian War' Over Kosovo," *Survival*, 41(3): 102–23.
Robinson, J. (2001) *Britain's Small Wars: The History of British Military Conflicts since 1945*. Available online: www.britains-smallwars.com/ (accessed 20 June 2003).
Robinson, J. A. (1999) "Dynamic Contractual Enforcement: A Model of Strikes," *International Economic Review*, 40(1): 209–30.
Rouvez, A. (1994) *Disconsolate Empires: French, British and Belgian Military Involvement in Post-Colonial and Sub-Saharan Africa*, Lanham, MD: University Press of America.
Rubin, J. P. (2000) "Countdown to a Very Personal War," *Financial Times* (London), 29 September.
Russell, R. B. (1958) *A History of the United Nations Charter: The Role of the United States, 1940–1945*, Washington, DC: The Brookings Institution.
Russett, B. M. (1974) "International Behavior Research: Case Studies and Cumulation," *Power and Community in World Politics*, San Francisco: Freeman, 13–30.
Ryan, S. (2000) *The United Nations in International Politics*, New York: St. Martin's Press.
Sanger, D. E. (2003) "Canvassing the Votes To Gain Legitimacy," *New York Times*, 13 March.
Sanger, D. E. and Myers, S. L. (2001) "Bush Faults China on Its Aid to Iraq for Radar System," *New York Times*, 23 February.

Sanger, D. E. and Preston, J. (2002) "Iraq Arms Report Has Big Omissions, US Officials Say," *New York Times*, 13 December.

Schachter, O. (1964) "The Quasi-Judicial Role of the Security Council and the General Assembly," *American Journal of International Law*, 58(4): 960–5.

—— (1977) "The Invisible College of International Lawyers," *Northwestern University Law Review*, 72(2): 217–26.

—— (1983) "The Nature and Process of Legal Development in International Society," in R. Macdonald and D. M. Johnston (eds) *The Structure and Process of Legal Development in International Society*, Dordrecht: Martinus Nijhoff Publishers.

—— (1984a) "Self-Help in International Law," *Journal of International Affairs*, 37: 231–46.

—— (1984b) "The Legality of Pro-Democratic Invasion," *American Journal of International Law*, 78(3): 645–50.

—— (1984c) "The Right of States To Use Armed Force," *Michigan Law Review*, 82(5–6): 1620–46.

—— (1986) "In Defense of International Rules on the Use of Force," *University of Chicago Law Review*, 53(1): 113–46.

—— (1991) *International Law in Theory and Practice*, Boston, MA: Martinus Nijhoff Publishers.

Schauer, F. (1987) "Precedent," *Stanford Law Review*, 39(3): 571–605.

Schecter, J. L. and Luchkov, V. V. (eds) (1990) *Khrushchev Remembers: The Glasnost Tapes*, Boston, MA: Little, Brown and Company.

Schimmelfennig, F. (2001) "The Community Trap: Liberal Norms, Rhetorical Action, and the Eastern Enlargement of the European Union," *International Organization*, 55(1): 47–80.

Schlesinger Jr., A. M. (1965) *A Thousand Days: John F. Kennedy in the White House*, Boston, MA: Houghton Mifflin Company.

Schlesinger, S. (2003) *Act of Creation: The Founding of the United Nations*, Boulder, CO: Westview Press.

Schlesinger, S. and Kinzer, S. (1999) *Bitter Fruit: The Story of the American Coup in Guatemala*, Cambridge, MA: Harvard University Press.

Schmid, A. P. (1985) *Soviet Military Interventions since 1945*, New Brunswick, NJ: Transaction Books.

Schwarzenberger, G. (1939) "The Rule of Law and the Disintegration of the International Society," *American Journal of International Law*, 33(1): 56–77.

—— (1941) *Power Politics: An Introduction to the Study of International Relations and Post-War Planning*, London: Jonathan Cape.

—— (1955) "The Fundamental Principles of International Law," *Recueil Des Cours*, 87(1): 191–385.

Schwebel, S. M. (1972) "Aggression, Intervention and Self-Defense in Modern International Law," *Recueil Des Cours*, 136(2): 411–95.

Schweller, R. L. (1996) "Neorealism's Status-Quo Bias: What Security Dilemma?" *Security Studies*, 5(3): 90–121.

Scott, M. B. and Lyman, S. M. (1968) "Accounts," *American Sociological Review*, 33(1): 46–62.

Scott, S. V. (1994) "International Law as Ideology: Theorizing the Relationship between International Law and International Politics," *European Journal of International Law*, 5(3): 313–24.

Shannon, V. P. (2000) "Norms Are What States Make of Them: The Political Psychology of Norm Violation," *International Studies Quarterly*, 44: 293–316.

Shawcross, W. (2004) *Allies: The US, Britain, Europe, and the War in Iraq*, New York: Public Affairs.

Sheikh, A. (1974) *International Law and National Behavior: A Behavioral Interpretation of Contemporary International Law and Politics*, New York: John Wiley & Sons.

Sherwell, P. (1997) "Saddam Turns Defeat into Victory as UN Goes Back in," *Daily Telegraph* (London), 23 November.

Short, C. (2005) *An Honourable Deception? New Labour, Iraq, and the Misuse of Power*, London: Gardner's Books.

Silber, L. (1998) "UN Deeply Divided Over Use of Force," *Financial Times* (London), 6 February.

Simmons, B. A. (2000) "The Legalization of International Monetary Affairs," *International Organization*, 54(3): 573–602.

Slater, J. (1967) *The OAS and United States Foreign Policy*, Columbus, OH: Ohio State University Press.

Slaughter, A.-M. (1995) "International Law in a World of Liberal States," *European Journal of International Law*, 6(4): 503–38.

Somerville, K. (1990) *Foreign Military Intervention in Africa*, New York: St. Martin's Press, Inc.

Spence, M. (1973) "Job Market Signaling," *Quarterly Journal of Economics*, 87(3): 355–74.

Spinoza, B. (1670; reprint 1951) "A Theologico-Political Treatise," in F. Cordasco (ed.) *The Chief Works of Benedict de Spinoza*, New York: Dover Publications, Inc., 13–278.

—— (1677; reprint 1951) "A Political Treatise," in F. Cordasco (ed.) *The Chief Works of Benedict de Spinoza*, New York: Dover Publications, Inc., 287–387.

Stein, T. L. (1985) "The Approach of the Different Drummer: The Principle of the Persistent Objector in International Law," *Harvard International Law Journal*, 26(2): 457–82.

Stevenson, R. W. (2003) "France and China Rebuff Bush on Support for Early Iraq War," *New York Times*, 8 February.

Stone, J. (1958) *Aggression and World Order: A Critique of United Nations Theories of Aggression*, Berkeley, CA: University of California Press.

Stromseth, J. E. (2003) "Law and Force after Iraq: A Transitional Moment," *American Journal of International Law*, 97(3): 628–42.

Sugden, R. (1989) "Spontaneous Order," *Journal of Economic Perspectives*, 3(4): 85–97.

Suskind, R. (2004) *The Price of Loyalty: George W. Bush, the White House, and the Education of Paul O'Neill*, New York: Simon & Schuster.

Talbot, S. (ed.) (1970) *Khrushchev Remembers*, Boston, MA: Little, Brown and Company.

Thatcher, M. (1993) *The Downing Street Years*, New York: HarperCollins.

Thompson, A. (2001) *Channeling Power: International Organizations and the Politics of Coercion*, Ph.D. dissertation, Chicago: University of Chicago.

Tillema, H. K. and Van Wingen, J. R. (1982) "Law and Power in Military Intervention: Major States after World War II," *International Studies Quarterly*, 26(2): 220–50.

Trachtenberg, M. (1999) *A Constructed Peace: The Making of the European Settlement, 1945–1963*, Princeton, NJ: Princeton University Press.

Tyler, P. E. (2004) "Britain Drops Charges in Leak of US Memo," *New York Times*, 26 February.

United Kingdom Central Office of Information (1993) *Britain and the Gulf Crisis*, London: COI.

United Kingdom Foreign and Commonwealth Office (2002) *Iraq's Weapons of Mass Destruction: The Assessment of the British Government*, London: FCO. Available online: www.fco.gov.uk/Files/kfile/iraqdossier.pdf (accessed 25 September 2002).

United States Central Intelligence Agency (n.d.) *Prewar Status of Iraq's Weapons of Mass Destruction*, Langley, VA: CIA. Available online: www.fas.org/irp/gulf/cia/index (accessed 29 February 2004).

Vaisse, M. (1989) "France and the Suez Crisis," in W. R. Louis and R. Owen (eds) *Suez, 1956: The Crisis and Its Consequences*, Oxford: Clarendon Press, 131–43.

Van Evera, S. (1997) *Guide to Methods for Students of Political Science*, Ithaca, NY: Cornell University Press.

—— (1999) *Causes of War: Power and the Roots of Conflict*, Ithaca, NY: Cornell University Press.

Van Natta Jr., D. (2006) "Bush Was Set on Path to War, British Memo Says," *New York Times*, 27 March.

Van Wingen, J. and Tillema, H. K. (1980) "British Military Intervention after World War II: Militance in a Second-Rank Power," *Journal of Peace Research*, 17(4): 291–303.

Vattel, E. d. (1758; reprint 1863) *Law of Nations; or, Principles of the Law of Nature, Applied to the Conduct and Affairs of Nations and Sovereigns*, Philadelphia: T & J W Johnson.

Vertzberger, Y. Y. I. (1994) "The International Milieu and Foreign Military Intervention: When and How Much Does the Milieu Matter?" *Journal of Strategic Studies*, 17(3): 139–79.

Voeten, E. (2002) "Resisting the Lonely Superpower: Responses of States in the United Nations to U.S. Dominance," *Journal of Politics*, 66(3): 729–54.

—— (2005) "The Political Origins of the UN Security Council's Ability To Legitimize the Use of Force," *International Organization*, 59(2): 527–57.

Waldock, C. H. M. (1952) "The Regulation of the Use of Force by Individual States in International Law," *Recueil Des Cours*, 81(2): 451–517.

Warbrick, C. (1991) "Current Developments in International Law: Invasion of Kuwait by Iraq – Part I," *International and Comparative Law Quarterly*, 40(2): 482–92.

Warner, G. (1979) "'Collusion' and the Suez Crisis of 1956," *International Affairs*, 55(2): 226–39.

Watson, A. (1992) *The Evolution of International Society: A Comparative Historical Analysis*, London: Routledge.

Watts, A. (2000) "The Importance of International Law," in M. Byers (ed.) *The*

Role of Law in International Politics: Essays in International Relations and International Law, Oxford: Oxford University Press, 5–16.

Weber, M. (1968) *Economy and Society: An Outline of Interpretive Sociology*, Berkeley, CA: University of California Press.

Webster, J. (2003) *The Simonides Complete Warzone Listing, 1900–1999*. Available online: www.simonides.org/users/bibliotheca (accessed 20 June 2003).

Weil, P. (1983) "Towards Relative Normativity in International Law?" *American Journal of International Law*, 77(3): 413–42.

Weinberger, S. (2003) "Institutional Signaling and the Origins of the Cold War," *Security Studies*, 12(4): 80–115.

Weisburd, A. M. (1997) *Use of Force: The Practice of States, 1945–1991*, State College, PA: Pennsylvania State University Press.

Weisman, S. R. (2003a) "Powell Says More Inspectors in Iraq Are 'Not the Answer,'" *New York Times*, 15 February.

—— (2003b) "A Long, Winding Road to a Diplomatic Dead End," *New York Times*, 17 March.

Weisman, S. R. and Barringer, F. (2003) "Urgent Diplomacy Fails to Gain US Nine Votes in the UN," *New York Times*, 10 March.

Weller, M. (1999/2000) "The U.S., Iraq and the Use of Force in a Unipolar World," *Survival*, 41(4): 81–100.

Weston, B. H. (1991) "Security Council Resolution 678 and Persian Gulf Decision Making: Precarious Legitimacy," *American Journal of International Law*, 85(3): 516–35.

Wheeler-Bennett, J. and Nicholls, A. (1972) *The Semblance of Peace: The Political Settlement after the Second World War*, London: Macmillan.

White House (2003) *Presidential News and Speeches*. Available online: www.whitehouse.gov/news/ (accessed 21 November 2003).

Willard, A. R. (1988) "Incidents: An Essay in Method," in W. M. Reisman and A. R. Willard (eds) *International Incidents: The Law that Counts in World Politics*, Princeton, NJ: Princeton University Press, 25–39.

Williams, I. (2006) "The Role of the United Nations," in R. Fawn and R. Hinnebusch (eds) *The Iraq War: Causes and Consequences*, Boulder, CO: Lynne Reinner, 257–68.

Williamson, O. (1985) *The Economic Institutions of Capitalism: Firms, Markets, Relational Contracting*, New York: The Free Press.

Winrow, G. (2006) "Turkey: Recalcitrant Ally," in R. Fawn and R. Hinnebusch (eds) *The Iraq War: Causes and Consequences*, Boulder, CO: Lynne Reinner, 197–208.

Wintour, P. and Kettle, M. (2003) "Blair's Road to War," *Guardian* (London), 26 April.

Wohlforth, W. C. (1993) *The Elusive Balance: Power and Perceptions during the Cold War*, Ithaca, NY: Cornell University Press.

Wolfrum, R. (1994) "Article 1," in B. Simma (ed.) *The Charter of the United Nations: A Commentary*, Oxford: Oxford University Press, 49–56.

Woodward, B. (1991) *The Commanders*, New York: Simon & Schuster.

—— (2002) *Bush at War*, New York: Simon & Schuster.

—— (2004) *Plan of Attack*, New York: Simon & Schuster.

Wurmser, D. (1999) *Tyranny's Ally: America's Failure To Defeat Saddam Hussein*, Washington, DC: The AEI Press.

Wyden, P. (1979) *Bay of Pigs: The Untold Story*, New York: Simon & Schuster.

Wyllie, J. H. (1984) *The Influence of British Arms: An Analysis of British Military Intervention since 1956*, London: George Allen & Unwin.

Young, K. (2003) "International Law in Crisis Decision Processes: Effects on the Dynamics and Outcomes of U.S. Foreign-Policy Crises," paper presented at the Annual Meeting of the International Studies Association, Portland, OR, February.

Young, O. R. (1982) "Regime Dynamics: The Rise and Fall of International Regimes," *International Organization*, 36(2): 277–97.

Zoller, E. (1984) *Peacetime Unilateral Remedies: An Analysis of Countermeasures*, Dobbs Ferry, NY: Transnational Publishers, Inc.

Zuljan, R. (2001) *Wars of the World: Armed Conflict Event Database*. Available online: www.onwar.com/aced/index.htm (accessed 14 November 2002).

INDEX

www.ingramcontent.com/pod-product-compliance
Ingram Content Group UK Ltd.
Pitfield, Milton Keynes, MK11 3LW, UK
UKHW011004180926
475701UK00004B/555
* 9 7 8 0 4 1 5 4 9 5 1 5 8 *